REVELATIONS OF
A TV DIRECTOR

REVELATIONS OF A TV DIRECTOR

ROYSTON MAYOH

Scratching Shed Publishing Ltd

Ashford
SAFE HANDS · QUICK FEET · STRONG IDEAS

This book is dedicated to my family.
My wife Sarah, *above*, who has given me a wonderful
second 'life' that is so evident within its pages.
Our sons and their wives, Joshua and Rachel;
Noah, Yasmin and our grandson Otto; Adam and Lana.
And finally our daughter Beth (1974-2022), *below*,
who tragically died before it was published.

Camera operator Royston Mayoh on the set of Coronation Street – *while on loan from ABC to Granada in the early 1960s – prior to becoming a television producer/director. Note the roller caption machine in the background.*

Contents

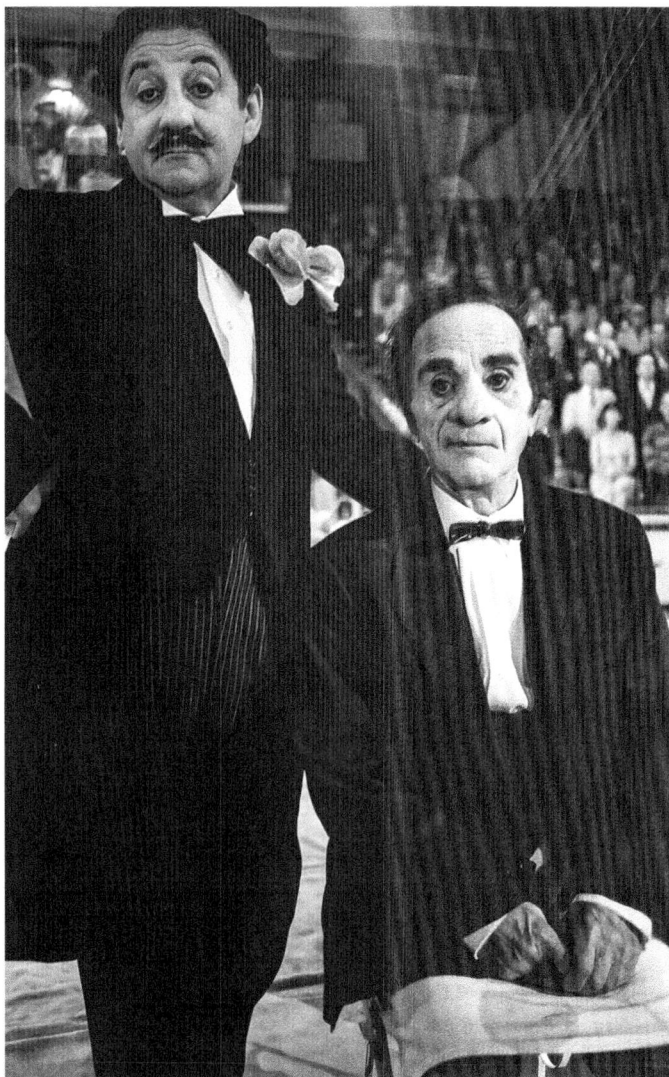

Freddie Davies, left, pictured with George Carl on the set of Peter Chelsom's 1995 film Funny Bones. *George will return in chapter four...*

Foreword

* Freddie Davies *

IN the realm of entertainment, few professions capture the collective imagination quite like that of a top television director and producer. These individuals possess an uncanny ability to create worlds, captivate audiences and shape the cultural landscape. They are the unsung heroes behind our favourite TV shows, responsible for translating scripts into visual masterpieces and orchestrating the magic that unfolds on our screens.

In this, his remarkable memoir, Royston Mayoh embarks on just such a captivating journey to the very pinnacle of success. With unparalleled access and a wealth of insider knowledge, we are given an exclusive glimpse into the intricacies of television production. He takes us back to the shows we all grew up with, most of which produced and directed by Royston himself.

We witness the rise of a true visionary, a talent who from humble beginnings became a trainee director in the early 1960s before overcoming many obstacles in achieving greatness in a profession he loved. We are privy to the trials and tribulations faced by Royston and the sacrifices he made during the relentless pursuit of excellence that propelled him to the top.

As we delve deeper into his stories, we are taken to a fascinating behind-the-scenes world wherein creativity and business acumen collide. We gain invaluable insights into the challenges and delicate balance between artistic vision and commerciality. The author's experiences, anecdotes and wisdom shed light on the industry's inner workings, unravelling the mysteries behind the creation of beloved programmes and the dynamics of working with a team of talented professionals.

But this book is not merely a celebration of success; it is an exploration of the human spirit. It delves into the personal struggles, the moments of doubt and uncertainty, and the perseverance required to overcome setbacks. We witness the emotional toll that comes with the relentless pursuit of perfection and the sacrifices made in the name of art.

Through it all, the author's passion for his craft shines through, inspiring us to think big and reach for the stars. His journey serves as testament to the power of dedication, hard work, and unwavering belief in oneself. It reminds us that no dream is too hard to achieve and that the path to greatness is often paved with setbacks.

This book is not only a treasure trove of industry insights, it is a source of inspiration for aspiring television directors and producers, as well as anyone with a passion for storytelling and the workings of the entertainment industry. It is a reminder that attaining great heights is not limited to a select few, but is rather a possibility for all of us who dare to believe and are willing to put in the work.

So, dear reader, prepare to be enthralled, educated and inspired by the indomitable spirit of Mr Royston Mayoh, television director and producer, a man who rose to the top. May his story ignite your own creative spark and empower you to pursue *your* dreams, no matter how audacious they may seem.

Freddie Davies
September 2023

Roy pictured with entertainers Mike and Bernie Winters during production of the popular ABC TV show Big Night Out *in the early-1960s.*

A rare picture of Royston operating a 16mm ARRI film camera, circa 1970.

Introduction

SO, right off the top, the first question has to be '...What's this book all about..?' In short it's about me! And now you should be asking 'Who are you?' followed by '...Why would I want to read a book about a happily married man enjoying all that life can offer, including a fee-paying hobby as an actor..?'

Those of you who are serious actors will immediately spot my choice of the word 'hobby' as a definite no-no! So in an attempt to justify that, my proper job (before I retired) was that of a television producer/director, and in the modern television industry there isn't much demand for those of us who are 60-plus. An opportunity arose that shone a new light at the end of a dark tunnel. So before having to retire from life itself I followed this light and took up the challenge of becoming a new actor by attending an acting course.

I experienced, first-hand, that acting is a full-on, full-time, totally time consuming and thoroughly emotionally draining occupation riddled with rejections, self-doubt and disappointments. What other nice things can I say about acting except that I love it and wish I'd discovered this way of life so much earlier in my career. This revelation is never more true than in those brief moments waiting in the wings for a signal from someone informing me – 'You're on!'

The process is always the same and involves learning my dialogue from a script. Sounds easy enough, but in reality it's a hard slog. It's not just all those unfamiliar 'words', but also the countless tortuous mental battles necessary to embed them into my subconscious and thereby generate an involuntary physical reflex.

The only reason for doing this is the thought of regurgitating these words (with automatic physical actions) – or as it is properly known '...delivering them...' – in the company of other actors who have undoubtedly gone through a similar private experience. The performance itself is always full of joy (provided my verbal contributions are properly embedded), offering moments that can't be experienced or duplicated anywhere else in life.

It was in one of those off-stage moments waiting in the wings, that my mind recently began to wander. Instead of relaxing while I was waiting to perform (as many actors quite rightly recommend) my mind travelled back to what I was doing in a similar situation in my old job, way back when.

In those days, my mind would have been permanently occupied, thinking ahead to ensure that all the scenes and jobs scheduled for that day would be completed and not compromised by unnecessary hurrying. I would have been applying a complex 'pace' code from start to finish.

My mind would also have been full of the detail of the job at hand and where it fitted into the overall, finished production. These would be concerns about creating a decision list (shot list) embracing shot size, shot type and camera movements; equipment needed; potential lighting problems; potential sound problems; potential personnel problems; potential issues in post-production; inherent difficulties with scriptwriters, executive producers, commissioning editors or even the agents who were representing the artists on the set that day.

I would also have been concerned about the budget, duration and pace of the scene, plus continuity. Any decent TV or film shoot would have had a continuity specialist as part of its crew. Sometimes they were so engaged in looking at the physical props they failed to spot a change in the delivery of a line by an actor who thought they were just 'feeding' a 'never-to-be-used' line for somebody else.

Other ongoing problems would be about the vagaries of the actors themselves, who sometimes failed to deliver the 'brilliance' they'd produced in their audition or outside rehearsal. The entire list of concerns, as described above, would have been superimposed one on top of another, making what can only be described as a 'brain fart' of frightening proportions. So?

I hope you will agree that waiting to deliver a line or two was in no way comparable to the pressure the director would have been silently experiencing at that very same moment and, for that matter, every moment in his or her long day.

As an actor it's in these brief waiting times when you just know it's no use going over the lines again, simply because you've learnt them the hard way. Now, the simple reality is: 'If you don't know 'em now... you're never going to!'

Those 'waiting moments' were a perfect opportunity to answer the question: 'Why would anyone want to read a book about me?'

Imagine the scene.

Ten to twenty people are comprehensively ignoring you and busily getting on with their own highly specialised jobs, a situation that occurs in any television and film production the world over. The only difference between a TV and film production would be in the number of people actively engaged in doing that. It was during one of these moments of apparent 'invisibility' that my mind began to gravitate toward some of the more unusual moments that led to this bizarre and most current form of pleasurable torture.

In short, the question 'would anyone want to read a book about me?' brought into focus the many odd moments I have experienced while working in the industry and was all the motivation I required.

Well, that and the increasing number of people who were telling me: 'You should write a book!'

I began to make notes, hundreds of notes, during many blank moments and realised that if I didn't create some form of mental structure for these thoughts to rattle round in they would begin to interfere with the job in hand – acting!

The most workable mental 'construct' I settled on was to imagine that these meanderings were research and development fodder for some nebulous publication to be written so far in the future that Twitter had become curiously old-fashioned and regarded as passé!

I had no strong intention of actually completing it, but the flood of random thoughts grew so strong that I began to think they might be of interest to someone. On the whole my life has been full of good fortune but, of course, there have also been moments which never should have happened and moments I should have made more of.

I've had numerous false starts in the telling of this tale and written enough drafts to fill a dozen or more industrial skips. However, being encouraged to persevere by my best friend (who is also my wife) I persisted and developed a determination to finish it.

The entire process has had the added advantage of preventing me from noticing my retirement!

I do hope you enjoy the read.

REVELATIONS
of a TV Director

By ROYSTON MAYOH

1.
The Luckiest Man on the Planet

IF you are one of my 2,000 'friends' (according to social media) you may recognise this chapter's title as the strapline on my Facebook (Meta) page. The figure can't be right, however, because I only send out 250 Christmas cards. Still, there is no point attempting to argue with the anonymity of a well-crafted algorithm.

I believe the mere fact of being alive and smiling is enough reason to celebrate, choosing the tag because I genuinely believe it to be true. And the older I get and start to look back over my eighty-one years on this planet, I find I believe it more and more.

Being Royston Mayoh is an odd experience. Anyone viewing telly from the late 1960s to the early 1980s might recognise the name as it often appeared alongside the words 'Produced and Directed by' on hundreds of popular light entertainment programmes.

It was also liberally used by a star of the 1960s and '70s, Hughie Green, on his show, *Opportunity Knocks*. Hughie regularly, and very effectively, employed it for editorial reasons. Expressions such as

'Now friends, I think we have a picture of that, don't we Royston..?' put my name in people's living rooms, which just might account for a large chunk of those 1,800 Facebook pals.

Everything good that has ever happened to me throughout my showbusiness career has come as a result of a lucky accident or, if you prefer, serendipity. From the start, there was never a time when I was aware of having a plan. Never once did I think: 'If I do this, I'll get that'. Somehow things just happened, some good, some bad. But whatever they were, they were never controlled, pre-planned or manufactured by myself in order to move on or up.

Chance meetings or being in the right place at the right time, even bumping up against a stranger, caused those crossroads in my life that sent me off in different directions to how I'd been happily moving along. And what was true in my career, was also true in my private life. It is an extraordinary thing to realise, suddenly, that your success has not simply come about through sheer hard graft. There have been occasions (not many) when young people starting out have asked me for my secret. It would have seemed rude to answer 'luck', but that would have been far more accurate than waffling on.

Take the time, in 1990, when I was lecturing at Stonehills, an alternative college in Gateshead, or to use its preferred title the North Eastern Media and Technical Educational College (NEMTEC). I had just been fired from the north east's then-ITV network Tyne Tees, 'filling in' before I found a more profitable pastime.

The students were a diverse bunch who all seemed to be from financially stable families; this was after all a private college with quite substantial course fees. They were very keen and interested in learning and therefore a delight to teach.

I had only recently met Sarah, the lady who was to become my best friend, lover and wife (as she is to this day). Sarah was a very popular lecturer in the art of journalism and documentary-making (a 'worthy' profession), while I was proficient in the art of directing TV entertainment shows, widely – and unfairly, I feel – looked down on as 'lowest common denominator' stuff. As a result, Sarah and I made a good double act and I know that our classes really benefitted from our shared knowledge and friendly banter.

Sadly, we had decided early on that NEMTEC had no real future because it was not affiliated to any British university or college and therefore unable to deliver an industry-recognised qualification at the end of the student contract, so a certificate meant diddly squat. The days were busy and enjoyable, but promised no real future for the lecturers either (all of whom were industry professionals who for all manner of reasons were temporarily out of work).

One day, Johnny Overton, a superb audio engineer (one time Head of Sound at Tyne Tees, now retired and hating every minute of it), came into the common room and said, 'Roy, a phone call for you at reception.' When I arrived and picked up the receiver (these were pre-mobile days) a gruff cockney voice at the other end said: 'Hello, old mate! Are you free for lunch in Monte Carlo on Tuesday?'

In any circumstance, the question could be described as bizarre, but I recognised the voice immediately. Rocky Oldham was one of the most charismatic, honest and trustworthy TV producers I knew so I thought for about three seconds and replied: 'Yes of course, old fruit.' Nor did I require details, absolutely sure it would involve chunky, well-paid, meaningful and noteworthy work. This was Rocky. 'How d'you fancy lunch in Monte Carlo?' Not a question you expect to be asked in an abandoned Pentecostal Church in Gateshead.

Days later, I flew from Newcastle down to London and met the man himself, naturally eager to know what the job entailed. He had a wicked enigmatic smile on his weather-beaten face and revealed nothing, except that I was simply to create some 'smiles' and would learn more once we got there!

From Heathrow we flew to Rome before boarding a helicopter to Monaco. Rocky hailed a cab and, in his usual authoritative cockney and not so usual fractured French, gave the driver a destination while promising me the best lunch in the Principality.

Having driven past some of the most luxurious and beautiful architecture imaginable, we soon pulled up outside what seemed to be a very plain building. 'Wait 'til you see what they serve!' Rocky said, as he paid for the ride. And he was right! This hidden gem served the best fish 'n' chips in Monte Carlo. While we ate, my friend explained the conundrum he had been given.

Entertainment conglomerate Time Warner were to make a short film promoting a forthcoming FIFA World Cup concert in Rome that July. Apparently, they had ploughed through thousands of feet of film footage looking for usable shots of Plácido Domingo, José Carreras or Luciano Pavarotti smiling and had failed to find anything suitable. The Time Warner executives had asked Rocky to help, the only person they knew who might have the remotest chance of obtaining something. His brief (should he accept it) was to gather together some shots of these famous singers going about normal activities with cheerful grins on their faces.

In a week's time, these three giants of the music world would be doing a full rehearsal. And why were we in Monte Carlo? This was where it would happen... in a special private concert for His Serene Highness Rainier III, Sovereign Prince of Monaco, and his entire family. Any rumour that the 'Four Tenors' (Carreras, Domingo, Pavarotti AND their conductor, Zubin Mehta), were doing this for a tax-free sum of $10million each in Monte Carlo and then a concert in Rome free of charge, would have been scurrilous to say the least!

Time Warner had made it clear that Pavarotti would refuse point-blank to be snapped so much as holding a football never mind kicking one, so Rocky was not to waste his time or, more importantly, anger the great man by suggesting anything football related.

Only one week after our fish 'n' chips lunch we were on our way back to the Principality for the actual shoot, only this time, before boarding the flight, I purchased a full-sized plastic football at WH Smith's in the airport. 'You're not really thinking of taking that cheap, tacky ball into the first class cabin to Nice are you..?' scowled Rocky.

'I am,' I assured my friend, and not only was this ball going with us to Nice, but I'd also be taking it on the chopper to Monte Carlo. Our crew had divided opinions as to whether I was crackers. They all knew Rocky and I had made a crazy bet about getting the great Pavarotti to kick it but were convinced I was bluffing and that it would quickly blow over. Realising we were serious and the game was afoot, and very likely to remain afoot, their loyalties were split between Rocky (who paid them) and myself (the director who was about to make them work for their money).

On the one hand, Rocky had been involved with the Pavarotti circus on many occasions. He knew what caused this superstar and his considerable entourage to tick. On the other, I was known for award shows and music specials.

This silly bet did not detract from the reality of our brief, which was simply to get a musical montage of Plácido Domingo, José Carreras, Luciano Pavarotti and, if possible, Mehta all smiling. Time Warner added that they also wanted a new soundtrack of the three tenors performing 'Libiamo' from Verdi's *La traviata* (affectionately known as 'The Brindisi'). The record company were hoping this well known drinking song would do as well as 'Nessun Dorma' (the aria from Puccini's *Turandot*) had for Pavarotti. Rocky and I itched to see what these three great male singers would do about the long female chorus that traditionally features in the middle of the opera.

The tenors reached Monte Carlo by different means; Carreras by boat, Domingo land and Pavarotti, very late at night, by helicopter. Surely, the thought of the lovely lolly they'd be making would put a smile on their faces, we thought, opting to hijack the trio on film as they arrived. The shots we took were okay, but standard stuff, no smiling. We were in the presence of 'The Three Grumpy Old Men'!

Once the crew saw how this extraordinary superstar machine worked, how singers were cosseted and surrounded by heavy-duty minders, they knew Rocky had won his bet. I had lost. After all, not only would we have to make them smile, but I also had to persuade Pavarotti to kick my football.

Anyone who knew anything about the guy was aware of his love of soccer, his passionate support for Juventus and early years as a striker for Modena FC. They wanted to see him with a football, but his management, agent, wife, best friend and anyone of importance had put a blanket ban on any such request. There I was, in my five-star hotel room, staring at the biggest television set in the world, so big it made my WH Smith's purchase look like a cricket ball. But the thing kept shouting at me: 'Don't give up! Don't let Rocky win! Get Pavarotti to kick me!' The only problem was how?

By now it was evident that to ask Pavarotti directly would be a total waste of time and energy, so I had to devise a plot. Suddenly it came to me. Pavarotti was soon due to check into the venue for his rehearsal. And that venue also happened to be my hotel.

We had permission to film him getting out of the car and entering reception, so I had my cameras in position and ready to roll (one outside the hotel, a second in the foyer). Not one member of the crew (certainly not Rocky!) had any idea of my plot, I was keeping it very much to myself. It went like this:

> No man with a love for the game could simply walk past
> a football without kicking it!

Even if the great Tenor fell over the thing, I would still have valuable footage, possibly of interest to news channels. But no way would he simply waddle on by. But for this to work my timing must be perfect.

The distorted words 'Pavarotti-Pavarotti' squeaked out of the walkie-talkies and there it was, the limo, approaching in the distance and heading straight for us. 'Now!' I thought.

Having leapt forward through the swing doors with my beloved prop (I hate football), I placed the thing dead centre of the welcome mat outside. 'Turn over' I yelled at the crew. 'Okay!' I thought, job done. 'Let's see what happens.' I turned to watch the potential award-winning action take place.

To my absolute horror – and Rocky's delight – the concierge had seen what I was up to. He ran out of the hotel, retrieved the ball and brought it back into the foyer. I was furious and stared at him with a level of hatred usually reserved for murderers. He had lost me my big chance. The car door opened and out stepped – a nonentity.

Our runner, totally misinterpreting my crestfallen look, rushed in: 'Sorry, guv! I thought it was him; it's certainly his limo,' and my face again lit up. A second chance perhaps? I could have kissed him. Storming over to the concierge, elegant in his medieval costume and powdered wig and therefore looking quite ridiculous with a football clutched to his chest, I put my face up close and said, with venom: 'If you touch my ball again I will shove it up your arse.' It mattered not that he spoke little or no English. Body language, together with my unambiguous array of gestures, left no doubt as to my meaning.

This French flunky was not going to blow it. Our runner was told to delay any announcement of the arrival of the opera star until he was certain it was Pavarotti. We waited ages, in fact a rumour started that he wasn't coming at all. But then, just as everyone was thinking about going for a beer, the sound of 'Pavarotti-Pavarotti ... it really *is* Pavarotti' fizzed out of the walkie-talkies like a fanfare.

Here was my moment! A glance at the concierge (whose defeated shrug said 'I promise not to touch it'), a whimper to the crew 'turn over, fellas...' and there I was, determined to get it right this time.

Every car has a blind spot when its occupants can't see the hotel entrance for the briefest of moments. That was my chance to get the football in place, before anyone could do a thing about it.

It's all in the timing!

Shaking like a leaf I watch for the right moment. Then, in a flash, I am out of the revolving doors and the ball is centered on the mat. As the car pulls up, I'm back in the foyer. Pavarotti gets out, sees the football, smiles and kicks the bloody thing. Success – and then some!

A member of his entourage, seeing that Pavarotti is pleased, kicks it back! Sheer joy. Not only do we have a smile for the chaps at Time Warner, but we also have a shot of him kicking a football.

Pavarotti enters the hotel holding the ball. 'Whose is this?' he glares. 'Mine,' I proudly say. The great man throws it to me, gestures to his chin and with a big broad smile says: 'Snap!' Johnny Overton (sound) and Graham Brown (camera) roar with laughter, noting the only similarity between me and the great man is the beard. I really don't care what this 30 stone operatic tenor says to me now because we've captured it on film. Rocky owes me £100 and life is beautiful.

Naturally, I never took the £100. Rocky's expression of disbelief was, and remains, reward enough. And as far as smiles are concerned it was a case of 'one down, three to go.'

Next day, we were back in the hotel for a shoot, the Four Tenors (including conductor Mehta) clad in full dress suits while posing for a battery of cameras lining up for promotional World Cup shots, when Pavarotti spots me in the crowd. 'Where's my football?' he asks in a hushed authoritative tone, the sort of sound and expression he had perfected to get anybody to do anything at any time anywhere.

I run (an action never usually seen by the crew) upstairs, grab the football (I still hate football) and in the solitude of my hotel room kiss the damn thing. Returning, I throw it into a circle comprising Plácido Domingo, José Carreras, Luciano Pavarotti and Zubin Mehta. Plácido heads to Carreras. Carreras passes to Mehta. Mehta dribbles for a bit and passes to Pavarotti, who is tackled by Domingo. Domingo to José. José back to Plácido. Plácido to Luciano! We are now treated to Pavarotti doing back-heel dribbles, followed by six or seven minutes of the most bizarre match ever staged.

For a while, it was on YouTube for all to see until Ron Howard's feature-length documentary *Pavarotti* used a dozen or so key shots from our film (notably the football kicking shots) and Time Warner took our 4:00 promo off the video channel 'for copyright reasons'. I'm just pleased I still have a copy of the original to look at whenever I want to think of magic times spent with wonderful Rocky Oldham.

Anyway, Time Warner got their smiles, an impromptu football match edited to Puccini's 'Brindisi' as performed by the Three Tenors and accompanied by the Monte Carlo Symphony Orchestra, plus a complete multi-camera video of the concert itself. Rocky and I got our pay cheques and to this day the very sound of the name Pavarotti thrills me almost as much as his voice.

PS: Question. What did these three great tenors do about the female chorus in the middle of the 'Brindisi'?

Answer: They tossed for it!

PPS: The beautiful Rocky Oldham passed away on 29th April 2019, but I will never forget his laughter, his talent, his friendship or the fact that he died without coughing up my £100!

MUCH earlier in my career I was privileged to be the Programme Director on many episodes of *This Is Your Life*. This series of weekly half-hour biographical entertainment shows was a major success for ITV, as presented by Eamonn Andrews.

Traditionally it was transmitted live every Wednesday at 7.00pm, in its heyday enjoying ratings of around 19 million a week to make it one of the top three shows on all channels, an institution no less.

Before each series started we made a few pre-recorded shows to hold back in case something happened to prevent the live one from taking place. Every week one such recording would run parallel to the live show so programme controllers could cut to it at any time and still finish our slot at 7.30, which was regarded as the beginning of weekday peak time (and that usually meant *Coronation Street*).

The immediacy and necessary changes in pace and genre from one show to another always produced bucket-loads of adrenaline and problems that demanded immediate solutions.

From a famous sportswoman one week to a Shakespearean actor the next; international chef to opera singer to jockey to member of Parliament ... and on and on through bandleaders, aristocracy, authors, adventurers, circus clowns, masterminds, impressionists, ex-convicts ... no two weeks were the same.

As one of its two directors I was privileged to come into contact with some of the most extraordinary and charismatic people of the era. From 1973 to 1979, I was involved in directing 177 episodes starting with star of TV magic, David Nixon, and ending with Miss Bluebell, whose show we shot live from the 'Folies Bergère' in Paris. Along the way, we featured Peter Ustinov, Christopher Lee, Ray Milland, Beryl Reid, Wilfred Hyde-White, Stéphane Grappelli, Earl Mountbatten, Jule Styne and, well, 169 other equally successful and famous people. During each half-hour tribute, Eamonn 'surprised and celebrated' each featured 'subject' with people important to their past. More often than not, many of these 'surprises' were famous themselves, flown in from all four corners of the earth.

An average number of surprise guests per episode would be in the region of 30 to 40. It was a fast moving show, the more surprises the better. So it would be fair to say that being involved at the sharp end of *This Is Your Life* saw me party with 7,000-plus celebrities.

I say 'party' as the show celebrated well known lives. It wasn't a documentary or exposé or even a diary. It was blatant festivity from beginning to end, positivity personified.

Once an episode came off-air, its entire cast and production team moved from studio to sizeable secure room where it was played back to the 'subject' and his or her contributors and friends. This preview was shown on what was in those days the only giant TV screen available – a 27-incher!

There have been two books about *This Is Your Life,* one written by producer Malcolm Morris, the other by producer Jack Crawshaw. I recommend both to know more about this amazing programme.

As one of its directors I witnessed wondrous moments I'll never forget. While embarking on this book, it did occur to me that I probably had enough notes to write solely about my times with *This Is Your Life*, but instead will share a few unique moments I hope you will enjoy.

This Is Your Life was a show like no other. Despite its documentary style, it was consigned to the Light Entertainment Department but more than any other such show of that era ran the risk of failure and legal action every week of transmission. This meant office discipline, involving code-words and secrecy, was more like a department of MI5 and we occupants of that office felt like some underground sect.

Delving into lives required sensitivity and discretion. As I say, *This Is Your Life* was a celebration, never an exposé. Our aim wasn't to be controversial. Delicate, personal and very private details did come to light during the research phase sometimes, which is why the office ran on such secure lines. Following transmission all notes and background research were shredded.

Of course, viewers were kept unaware of these real hazards while being entertained by manufactured and controlled drama within the body of the programme. This, in itself, made *This Is Your Life* unique.

Usually a series would be 26 programmes. The entire production crew (about 16 people) were involved in all stages of preparation and research. One team (including two researchers) would look at the feasibility (aka FEEZA) of a programme some six weeks ahead of time. However, they were also responsible for the show then in production while assisting other teams in the hunt for new 'subjects'. Due to the complexity of this teamwork that all our teams' individual 'ducks' were facing the same way was of paramount importance.

This meant that three teams of two researchers could leapfrog through an entire series. We two directors did likewise, one doing the opening sequence (known as the pick-up) while the other was responsible for the live studio, or location, shoot. Hence, an entire production team consisting of one producer, two directors, two PAs, six Researchers, two writers, one programme co-ordinator and a secretary. These 15 plus host Eamonn Andrews were all trusted with occasionally delicate but always confidential information gleaned from the close family and friends of our victim.

During a period of about 30 weeks each year this relatively small group was charged with keeping the names of upcoming stars and their tales an absolute secret from everyone outside this immediate 16. Not surprisingly this was done with great pride by every member of the team on every series. We all took it upon ourselves not to be the one responsible for stopping or ruining a show. To the best of my knowledge there was never a single leak, which is a tribute to the trust and caring Thames TV earned from staff and freelancers.

In 1955, Eamonn had been the first subject of this then brand new show to arrive from the USA. It had already been an enormous hit in the States, so the BBC had decided to try it out here. The first presenter was also the programme's creator, Ralph Edwards.

A deceptively simple format always began with the host in an unfamiliar situation from which he confronted a very unsuspecting public figure by appearing out of the blue and surprising them with a Big Red Book and the words 'Tonight [name], this is your life...'

For the next 30 minutes this person would be further surprised by people and events that had enjoyed significance on their road to becoming a celebrity. The final line of every show came when the host presented the 'script' (contained within the Big Red Book held by the host from the start) to the subject, while repeating '[name], this is your life...' just as he had done at the start.

At the close of the first episode, the programme's creator and host Ralph Edwards turned to Eamonn Andrews, (a very popular sports commentator back then) and uttered: 'Eamonn Andrews, this is your life... and should you wish to accept it your own series will start next week.' Nobody involved in or watching that historic television moment could possibly have guessed that *This Is Your Life* would stay at the top of the UK TV ratings for the next 48 years!

Sadly, Dubliner Eamonn passed away from heart failure, aged 64, in 1987 and before long the Big Red Book was handed to another national broadcasting icon, Michael Aspel. He continued to host the show until 2003, when the Big Red Book was finally put to rest itself. My days as programme director on *This Is Your Life* were wondrous days and I still look back with amazement at what surprises were in store for us all each and every week.

Eamonn hadn't just hosted the show, he was somewhat ironically its heart. He had a set of non-negotiable principles and like many of the established professionals occupying our television screens in the 1960s and '70s, knew that to surrender to short-termism for the sake of a newspaper headline was surefire suicide in the long run. Born in 1922, an Irish junior middleweight boxing champion in his youth, Eamonn knew exactly what made the programme tick and what it took to make it a guaranteed ratings success every week of every series. He passed down his wisdom and strict canon of principles and mandatory regulations (initially acquired, no doubt, from the Ralph Edwards 'Bible') to every producer, researcher, writer and director. Custodian of the programme, his word was final. Eamonn respected the roles of everyone, but with the proviso that the fixed nucleus of underlying principles of this unique format were strictly adhered to.

And, oh such secrecy! During a potential programme's research and development stages, its subject would be allocated a code name to which only Eamonn, the producer, lead researcher and director were privy. This enabled open forward planning on a huge white-board at one end of the production office, next to a pointing Lord Kitchener cartoon and slogan 'Careless Words Cost Lives', a parody of the World War One poster declaring 'Your Country Needs You'.

To any passer-by or ambitious journalist (of whom there were many) this highly-detailed whiteboard was complete gibberish and to ensure secrecy, the methodology of creating our code words never followed the same path. It was impossible to extract the identity of the 'subject' from it because no logic whatsoever was attached. For example the code word for Muhammad Ali in 1978 may have been 'egg-timer' (or not – you will never know!).

Wednesday at 7.00pm meant that *This Is Your Life* went out on a night traditionally considered the best for evening viewership (hence the similarly popular variety show *Wednesday At Eight*). The first 30 seconds of pre-title action were crucial to its success. If we didn't grab the viewers then, our production team knew, the rest of the show would suffer, or even fail, ratings-wise. This surprise sequence was always the invention of a tight-knit group specifically involved with that episode and a sheer joy to be part of because the idea was not only to surprise the subject, but also the viewer with scenarios that were unusual, riddled with danger and entertaining.

What enjoyment we had in dreaming up and then making such scenarios happen. Not one was a straightforward 'pick-up'. None of us would have allowed it! Nor was the drama only on-screen.

On 10th November 1976, we were about to surprise the British Explorer (and founder of the Scientific Exploration Society) Colonel John Blashford-Snell CBE. We'd discovered that the Colonel was the guest on BBC Radio 2's popular celebrity programme *Desert Island Discs*, whose presenter and founder was Roy Plomley.

Snell's contribution was to be recorded in a small radio studio in Portland Place, around 200 yards from Broadcasting House, the BBC's iconic HQ. We knew that when Plomley was off-air he'd make the short trip across the road to meet up with BBC executives in the main building. One of our researchers, meanwhile, had observed a small traffic island just outside. The creative juices began to flow and a script idea soon emerged that had a play on the word 'island'.

Eamonn, in disguise (he loved being in disguise), would make his opening remarks from outside the famous frontage in Portland Place. Crossing to the traffic island he would then lean on the orange Belisha beacon and say something like: '...our special guest tonight has been to some of the remotest islands on the planet and has had many surprises, but this is one island that will hopefully provide the biggest surprise of all...' A camera on top of a building directly opposite would then pick up Plomley and the Colonel as they left the small studio to make their way along the pavement and onto the traffic island where – 'Whoopee!' – they'd be confronted by Eamonn Andrews who, after some explanation, would deliver his famous words: '...because tonight, Colonel John Blashford-Snell, this is your life...' And that, in turn, would lead to opening titles mixing to a live Thames TV Euston Studio a couple of miles away on the corner of Tottenham Court Road. Nothing could be simpler, planned to the second. 'Pick-up' successfully completed, another first class edition of *This Is Your Life* was surely on its way. However...

We had not factored in the lifestyle and mind of Colonel John Blashford-Snell CBE, or the drama that took place in the solitude of his own complex head. The full story did not come out until during hospitality (following transmission), when the Colonel turned the usually unflappable Eamonn Andrews a paler shade of white.

Colonel John Blashford-Snell CBE was an important military figure who, naturally, had a personal driver (whom, alas, we had not factored in). Unbeknownst to us, the *Desert Island Discs* producer knowing what was about to happen confided in the Colonel's driver and asked him to re-position himself outside the main building as this was where the 'surprise' would occur. The driver did explain that this could be a mistake, but the radio man knew better.

Having recorded *Desert Island Discs*, Plomley and the Colonel made their studio exit. Whereupon the Colonel could not see his car, as expected, triggering a series of major alerts in his security conscious mind. Undeterred, he stealthily continued to walk along the pavement when, out of the corner of his eye, he saw a suspicious movement and what looked to be a rifle, high up on a nearby roof.

Preparing himself mentally for a personal 'situation', he was then suddenly confronted by an Irish voice from a man appearing from nowhere and obviously in disguise. The Colonel later told Eamonn that he nearly shot him before, thankfully, recognising his distinctive brogue just in time! On the recording, you can just see the Colonel start to undo his jacket in readiness to... well, the mind boggles. This was an era when IRA terrorism was very much a threat.

Not one member of the *This Is Your Life* team (including Eamonn himself) had figured that his disembodied voice might be associated with a paramilitary threat. What's that quote about familiarity being 'a magician that is cruel to beauty...'?

There was another memorable occasion a couple of years later, on Wednesday 13th March 1978 to be precise, when we were about to embark on an edition of *This Is Your Life* featuring comedy actor Terry Scott, star of *Carry On* films and the sitcom *Terry and June*.

We discovered he was due at a book signing in a department store in Leatherhead and established that the journey, by limo, from the back entrance of this store to Thames TV on London's Euston Road would take 45 minutes. So, to guarantee we could safely get on the air at 7.00 pm, we'd have to complete the pick-up in Surrey no later than 6.15pm, leaving 45 minutes for the subject and Eamonn (plus producer) to reach the studio some 17 or so miles away. No problem!

A constant dilemma re devising unpredictable and entertaining pick-ups was the fact that Eamonn himself was more recognisable to the general public than the majority of stars we featured. This meant our first priority was getting our host to the pick-up unseen.

The PR company organising Terry Scott's book event established the positioning of the table, chairs and queue of people waiting for his autograph and, most importantly for us, the direction of Terry Scott's eyeline while cheerfully signing their purchases.

The crew and Eamonn would all arrive unobserved via the Goods Inward back entrance. However, one problem remained. Eamonn would have a good two-minute walk through crowds of shoppers before reaching the table that contained Terry Scott and his books.

It was essential too that no one should recognise Eamonn before the moment he confronted the target on every pick-up. Ideas about how this might be achieved were discussed by the *This Is Your Life* team, the beard and overcoat suggestion always first to be elbowed.

Eventually it was suggested that we could hide Eamonn and the Big Red Book inside a rack of clothing that could be pushed through the crowd to shouts of 'mind your backs' and 'coming through' and so on. No matter how big a throng this ended up being, it was a device that could get Eamonn and his Big Red Book inches from Terry. We even mused that he may be slightly irritated and confused by this intrusion, which made the whole idea even more appealing. So, idea bought and sold ... next item!

Now we had to fabricate a trolley full of clothes so Eamonn could sit (and breathe) inside the trolley and climb out with dignity while brandishing the iconic red tome and a microphone. After some totally unworkable ideas, I'm afraid I suggested it should be filled with as many clothes (on hangers) as it could hold, spray the entirety with glue and, once solidified, take a hedge-trimmer to cut out the innards of this solid lump of clothing to make a space, with seat, for Eamonn's invisible trip through the store.

Bonkers ideas like this were always met by a chorus of 'It'll never work...' by an ever-present army of sceptics but applauded by prop-makers who pray for such opportunities to succeed. The device was brilliantly manufactured in the Thames TV property department in Teddington, signed off by me and delivered (covered in cardboard) to the Leatherhead superstore 'Goods Inward' with large notices (Do Not Touch – Fragile) emblazoned on this crucial bit of equipment.

The day came. Eamonn secretly entered the back door, tried the trolley on for size and expressed delight at its dimensions, albeit grumbling a bit with his iconic twisted half-smile about the smell of burnt glue. The camera crew was in position, already filming Terry Scott as he busily signed books. He didn't question their presence as this was quite a regular occurrence at such events.

Dressed in brown overalls, producer Jack Crawshaw and I pushed the trolley along, shouting out 'mind your backs', 'thank yous' and 'coming throughs' as planned, while crowds of shoppers moved and reacted as we had hoped. Terry, thankfully, did throw a few dirty looks at these two noisy workmen pushing a trolleyful of clothes to within inches of his signing. He may well have been thinking about having a quiet word with these disruptive fellows but, before he had the opportunity, out leapt Eamonn! The crowd went wild, Eamonn uttered those famous words 'Sorry to interrupt you, but tonight, Terry Scott, this is your life...' and that was that. Job done!

After reactions and apologies to the waiting crowd, thrilled to see Eamonn and a live *This Is Your Life* in action, but less than thrilled not to get their book signed, we now had to negotiate a drive back to the studios with the producer and myself in one car, the film on the back of a motor cycle, and Eamonn on his own ploughing through his forthcoming script at the rear of the motorcade.

Our programme manager, together with Terry Scott and his agent, went ahead in the lead limousine. Their car left minutes before the main motorcade in order to get Terry Scott into make-up, rig him with a radio mic and assure him that he was in for a real treat, without any nasty or embarrassing surprises (this assurance was always given after the pick-up and prior to the show as 99.9 per cent of celebrities chosen as 'subjects' were concerned about their public image. We would reassure them that their agent and/or manager had approved what was about to happen.)

On our way to Euston, however, fog set in. Our driver Harry said he'd try to pick up speed to meet a schedule timed on a clear day. Soon, we were pulled over by a police car. Naturally we stopped and tried to explain our urgency, stressing our significant part of the *This Is Your Life* programme due to be aired live in a matter of minutes.

The policeman gave us a very old-fashioned stare as if to say 'Pull the other one' before, suddenly, his snarl changed to disbelief and then to a smile of sheer amazement when out of the mist emerged a very real Eamonn Andrews holding the Big Red Book. Eamonn's driver had seen our car pulled over, so instead of overtaking us and continuing their journey Eamonn had said: 'Pull up behind, I think they may need some help.' Eamonn was right about that!

PS: Weeks after this Terry Scott show I was summoned to a senior manager's office in Teddington and severely reprimanded for not noticing that the wrong rack of clothes had been sprayed with glue and cut to smithereens to accommodate a rather large Eamonn Andrews. I was horrified to discover that the rack we used was full of specially designed costumes for the forthcoming drama *Edward & Mrs Simpson,* starring Edward Fox and Cynthia Harris.

By sheer chance, this rack of clothing had been waiting in a cul-de-sac between Studios one and two and mistaken by the prop men as the *This Is Your Life* job. After all, one lot of old clothes looks very much like another when you're in a hurry to get the job done! Later, I was informed that the considerable cost of the costumes was redeemed following a claim for 'Damaged In Transit'.

Few moments of sheer silliness, meanwhile, can beat the words spoken by our most conservative host (note the small 'c') just before surprising footballer Denis Law in February 1975: 'Hello! This is Eamonn Andrews speaking to you from inside an Easter Egg...' No way could any viewer have possibly associated those words with Law, which of course was the object of the entire exercise. The pick-up was usually live and never failed to generate a few more grey hairs.

As outlined earlier, JICTAR (Joint Industry Committee for Television Audience Research) could usually tell within ten seconds of the opening titles whether the show would retain its massive natural audience or shed a few who decided that this week's subject wasn't their cup of tea. If ratings did dive (rare), an immediate post-mortem would identify where the team had gone wrong. You will note that both success and failure were always seen as a team effort.

While one director took on all the heavy duty organisation of this vital two-minute audience grabber, the other was shooting tributes from people who couldn't be there. Oftimes we used this device to convince the subject of an unfortunate absence, only to spring a physical appearance just before the end, a guaranteed tear-jerker!

DURING the summer of 1978, it was decided that I should spend three weeks in the USA to shoot inserts for a batch of high-profile shows we planned to make and transmit over the Christmas period. So together with ace researcher Debbie Gaunt and writer/researcher Maurice Leonard, I flew to Burbank, Hollywood, to film tributes from a shopping of list of American superstars.

I say 'shopping list'. It was more of a wishlist as nothing had been confirmed, just pencilled 'possible'. It was up to Debbie and Maurice to sort availability and locations once we arrived on the West Coast.

The targets as drawn up by the *This Is Your Life* team contained potential contributors who had expressed a desire to take part, but were unable to travel to the UK. They included names like Anthony Quinn, Tom Jones, the entire family and friends of Muhammad Ali and Kirk Douglas. Our producer, Jack Crawshaw, wrote me a note saying he would like Douglas, star of *Spartacus* and *The Heroes of Telemark*, to enter riding a horse, jump off, do his 30-second tribute to camera, jump back on the horse and ride off into the sunset. Yeah, right! Or as Maurice Leonard put it: 'Piece of piss, dear boy!'

One shoot had been arranged for precisely 07.30 in Paramount

Studio H. We were reliably informed that John Wayne would make himself exclusively available to us (the UK crew) for the sole purpose of doing a one-minute tribute to his friend and co-star in the highly-acclaimed Otto Preminger war film of 1965, *In Harm's Way*. Our shopping-list for tributes read like a VVIP list at the *Vanity Fair* post-Oscar bash and the 'John Wayne job' was first cab off the rank.

Having landed in LA around midnight (their time) we were just about to get our heads down for some proper sleep when a bright-eyed and bushy-tailed Maurice informed us he'd just spoken with John Wayne's management who had demanded we 'turn-over' (start) no later than 08.30am. So we all took a deep breath, unloaded our 16mm filming equipment and, having washed and had a change of socks, agreed to arrive at 07.00 '*avinad*' (a technical expression meaning 'having had' breakfast, tea, coffee, buns or whatever people needed to get their hearts going at that time in a morning).

The reason for choosing seven o'clock was to make double sure that our crew had set up and tested the equipment and technical levels well in advance of the 08.30 deadline. We had no idea what to expect from a man who was more of a Supernova than a real person.

Maurice and I figured that once the crew had finished whingeing about working so early – any start before nine they usually referred to as 'twat o'clock' – we'd be set up, warmed up, lined up, lit up and sound-checked with no further technical tweaking required when Wayne arrived on set. From the studio facilities manager (organised by John Wayne's son/manager) we pre-ordered a stand-alone make-up mirror, moveable make-up table and make-up chair, specifying that the latter must be of a type Wayne would be happy to sit in. Our first job (at 06.46) was to locate such. And as Maurice and I walked towards the vast black studio there it was, almost blocking our way ... a trolley bearing the printed sign 'John Wayne/UK Filming – Do Not Touch'. At which we both instinctively squealed like a pair of five-year-old girls and gave each other a high five.

We pulled the trolley into the dark studio (normally a Hollywood expression for a studio not in use, but in this case actually meaning there were no lights on) and within minutes our electrician found a mains plug. We quickly set up the table, chair and make-up mirror, all of which positioned in a pool of light surrounded by a gorgeous velvet blackness. By 07:29, though, there was no sign of John Wayne. At 07:45 there was no sign of John Wayne. At 08:00 there was no sign of John Wayne. But then, at precisely 08:30, John Wayne, *the* John Wayne, suddenly materialised from a distant darkened corner in all his spotlit magnificence. In he walked towards the film crew, exactly like John Wayne. In fact, as we later agreed, it was probably the best impression of a John Wayne walk any of us had ever seen.

He then asked me what I would like him to do. I told him I'd like him to sit in the chair and, against the backdrop of our make-up props, deliver his tribute to Patricia Neal straight into the camera. He asked for a cue to speak – he got one. Then he made his tribute sincerely, faultlessly and brilliantly. He asked if 'we' were happy. Happy? We were over the moon!

After declaring a wrap, John Wayne invited Maurice and I into his RV for drinks. And there we remained for three phenomenal and captivating hours, chatting with this true icon who knew the history of *This Is Your Life* with its American host, Ralph Edwards.

When the RV door eventually opened our theatrical set-up had disappeared, to be replaced by small groups of people, about 50 or so positioned around the periphery of this enormous studio. It was now their turn to be astounded, as we'd been some hours earlier, at the sudden appearance of John Wayne. The applause was deafening. Maurice and I were given a lesson in what it was like, each and every day, to be a global superstar. Each group came from a different part of the world and had won some John Wayne-related quiz or event whose first prize was to meet or have a photo taken with The Duke. Every 'snap' taken received 100 per cent enthusiasm, smiles and energy from a living legend. It was a fantastic scene that acted as a 1,000-volt motivator at the outset of our amazing trip.

Next morning, Maurice gleefully announced that at 4:00pm (an unusually civil time for anything of value to happen in our business) we were off to film another huge star, Anthony Quinn, on Sunset Boulevard in the Beverly Hills Hotel.

Maurice had completed all the permissions necessary for filming there and I decided that this late start was a perfect opportunity to get some GVs of Los Angeles for potential future use under any establishing script that Tom Brennan and Roy Bottomley (the Programme Associates and sometime writers of *This Is Your Life*) might write into one of the scripts leading up to one of our clips. At which our 'aged' cameraman, Pete Hughes, thought it a good idea to seat himself and his 16mm camera on the luggage rack of our hire car, the better to catch our journey from downtown Los Angeles to the famous hotel. Such a cumbersome way of getting GVs (general views), of course, pre-dated the now ubiquitous drones.

To describe Pete as 'aged' is entirely accurate, not rude. He acted 'aged' and never ceased to stun and amuse us with anecdotes of his youth as a film cameraman in the Korean War. The night before our encounter with John Wayne, we'd been eating in Trader Vic's, back then a brand new American diner-type tiki bar chain. It had been a late one and we were all exhausted. Pete seemed unusually quiet, sad and emotional. 'Alright, Pete?' I ventured. He took a deep breath. 'Yeah,' he said. 'I just looked at my watch and suddenly thought of my wife.' We were moved by this romantic admission, until he broke the magic wand in half. 'She will be getting up for a pee about now.'

But back to his GVs. We'd rigged the camera on a 'moy' mount on the rack, secured it with bungee hooks, ropes and a couple of mountaineering carabiners. Peter climbed up and secured himself to the lot. Soon we were on a roundabout near Grauman's Chinese Theatre, home to the sidewalk full of famous hand and footprints. I asked our driver to take one more revolution to ensure Pete had a good shot of this Hollywood landmark. At which the guy took a sudden swerve to accommodate my request and, from the car roof, we heard the one word: 'Fuuuuuuck'!

At the very first opportunity, we pulled over to check if Pete was still up there. And if so, was he okay? The poor bloke was white as a sheet and, helped by a few more expletives, queried our sanity. In an attempt at empathy, I asked how he'd kept his position behind the camera. He replied: 'By the suction of my arse, dear boy!' After establishing that he had by now got enough footage, we helped our grumpy camera operator down and went to meet Anthony Quinn.

Having been overjoyed at how John Wayne had greeted us Brits, we were looking forward to meeting the star of *Zorba the Greek*, *Lawrence of Arabia* and *The Guns of Navarone*. Wayne had become an anglophile after having had such a good time shooting *Brannigan*, nevertheless the only film he ever made in the UK. So there was no reason to expect anything less from our next contributor.

Less, however, is what we got – a lot less. He treated our most pleasant and respectful Maurice like a lackey, pointing out he was a busy man with better things to do. He refused to use the setting we'd chosen, demanding that we film his piece-to-camera in a small and dimly lit alcove in the hotel grounds, a setting that could have been anywhere in the world, but not the beautiful Beverly Hills Hotel.

Quinn did a rambling three minutes to camera that we 'bought', thanked him for and wrapped. Such was his unpleasant manner, Mo and I decided London could have the problem of editing his three minutes down to a transmittable one. After asking His Grumpiness to sign a release form, we swiftly moved on to more pleasant pursuits.

Our next assignment was Tom Jones for a shoot that would this time be in Las Vegas. We agreed to go that very afternoon and, having checked out of our hotel, hit Route 66. On arrival we were to make contact with Mark Jones, Tom's young son, as organised by the singer's manager in London, Gordon Mills.

When we met, Mark pointed out that Tom had an extremely demanding on-stage performance to deliver. Afterwards, he would need a good hour's rest before thinking about anything else. The first opportunity we'd get to film his one-minute to camera would come no earlier than 2:00am. This meant Maurice, the crew and I had time to kill... and it isn't hard to find something to fill it with in Vegas.

Mr Jones, though, turned out to be the complete opposite of Mr Quinn. Shattered after a two-hour show, he was nevertheless keen to make a proper job of his tribute to Muhammad Ali. By the time we'd got his contribution in the can it was 04:00am! Not that you'd have noticed outside. It's strange to walk out into the street at such an hour and meet hustle and bustle you' would expect to see at midday. There are no clocks in Las Vegas.

After playing every table, or so it felt, before breakfast, we then decided to get some sleep and think about our next appointment in

Nogales, Arizona, which is right on the border with New Mexico. However, four hours into our kip Maurice was banging on our doors with news of another 'job' we had to 'sort' first here in Vegas!

Mo had received a telex from Jack Crawshaw, our producer in London, who after a good night's sleep himself was totally unaware of our new nocturnal way of life. Jack had received a message from the agency representing the legendary Joe Louis, another candidate for 'world's greatest boxer'. He held the World Championship for an incredible 12 years, from 1937 until his retirement in 1949. He had heard about our tribute to Ali, his hero, and demanded to take part.

Jack was also told that the 'Brown Bomber' (as he was dubbed) had suffered a stroke, no longer in the greatest of health. Before leaving, we should visit his mansion. What could be more showbiz?

Maurice now had the address, so we set off to what when we got there looked like a pretty ordinary bungalow in the circular bit of a cul-de-sac. Maurice double checked – this was the place – and took the plunge, walking up the garden path and ringing the bell. A very smart nurse answered and a quick thumbs-up from Maurice told us we were in business. We started unpacking our tackle from the car.

While we were doing so, a handyman told us that this house, all the medical equipment and staff had been donated and paid for by Frank Sinatra. I'm sure he didn't want this publicised at the time, but given how both men have since passed away I feel I'm not breaching confidentiality in revealing that side of Ol' Blue Eyes.

Anyway, I joined Maurice inside a house more hospital intensive care unit than home and now met a second nurse, without doubt the dominant 'matron'. She took Maurice and I into a small office, where she explained that Mr Louis, on top of all his other ailments, had recently had a stroke. Nevertheless, he remained determined to send a tribute and had dictated what he wanted to say over a couple of days to his carers. This matron took notes and had turned them into a 'short' statement that she gave to Maurice who, almost without looking, agreed to its use.

We both felt that being in the presence of this venerated icon of sport was enough in itself. For many, the Brown Bomber was more legendary than Ali. How amazing that this exalted luminary now regarded Muhammad Ali as the champ. Matron ushered us into a room whose display cabinet was full of cups and trophies of every shape. And there, in pride of place, were the Golden Gloves! I found myself rather flippantly saying: 'Well, Mo, we will be okay for cut-aways.' The atmosphere soon changed, though, when this superstar's wheelchair entered the room.

'Please don't tire Mr Louis out," the matron now chipped in, authoritatively. 'He has only just had medication.' Mo and I noticed the Brown Bomber's eyes move from her to us, a look that said 'Take no notice.' We smiled at Joe and he smiled knowingly back.

Matron also informed us that Mr Louis tended to dribble after speaking. Did we want her to keep this in check with a box of tissues? Judging by the obvious effort he had gone to, dressing and shaving, we suspected our star wanted to pay tribute without any hint of his medical circumstances. So we positioned the camera in front of the display cabinet in such a way that he was surrounded by his prizes.

Increasingly, though, it became apparent that we needed to get Joe's contribution filmed fairly swiftly. Matron collared me and said quietly: 'You'll have to do it one line at a time as he can't remember much for long.' I asked if I could crouch between Joe's legs, enabling me quickly to ensure he was dribble free. To my utter amazement, his hand turned over on his lap and he managed a thumbs up. I had to swallow my emotions as I fed world-renowned Joe Louis his lines (as typed up by matron). As each line was delivered, I'd reach up with a tissue coupled with a 'well done' or 'do you want to do it again' or 'he's gonna love that!' We formed a beautiful relationship and I was sorry when it was all over. The afternoon ended far too soon.

En route to Arizona we took a detour, via the Harrah's Hotel in Lake Tahoe, to capture a one-minute tribute from American crooner Johnny Mathis. After that and breaks in Phoenix and Tucson, we reached Nogales, where *The Villain*, starring Kirk Douglas, Ann-Margret and Arnold Schwarzenegger, was being filmed. We had an appointment with Kirk and had been warned he took no prisoners.

We set up our 16mm Arriflex camera, mounted on a battered Manfrotto tripod with half a kit of Colortran lighting, right in the middle of three, yes three, Transatlantic camera cranes (I swear one was an iconic Chapman Hercules) plus a bank of massive 10k Brute lighting and crew of what seemed like hundreds. It was, at the least, a humiliating experience – we were on the set of a Hollywood movie.

Naturally, before erecting our kit we were interrogated by several seriously oversized security staff genuinely shocked by our small number. They'd been briefed to expect some VIPs from Britain's top TV show to interview their star (and boss). And here we were, four travel-weary unimpressive chaps with one small bag of tackle. Upon explaining it was all we needed we were ushered to a pre-determined area, out of danger of accidentally landing ourselves a bit-part.

Shortly afterwards, we were confronted by a tiny chap in a black cowboy outfit who looked a bit like Kirk Douglas. He spoke... it was Kirk Douglas! 'What do you want?' he asked no-one in particular. 'We are here to film your one-minute-tribute to Patricia Neal, Mr Douglas,' I replied. There was a long pause. The legend spoke again. 'What do you want?' I repeated my request, paraphrasing it slightly. And, for a third time, he spat the words: 'What do you want?' This time directly at me.

I glanced at Maurice, who had a 'you're not going to put up with that shit, are you?' expression on his face. So I took a large breath. 'Well, if I'm honest,' I said, 'oh, and I'm the Director, by the way ... if I'm honest, I'd like you to ride over that incline, leap off your horse, walk up to camera, say whatever it is you wish to say as your tribute to Patricia Neal, and when you've said it leap back onto your horse and ride off through that small stream into the distance...'

I fully expected Mr Douglas to blow a gasket and depart. Instead he said: 'How much have you got in cash?' Maurice came to my rescue. '$200,' he said with pride. 'Thats okay. I'll send a wrangler over. Pay him the $200 and tell him what you told me. He'll set it up and when he is happy he'll come and get me... okay?'

At which, the great Kirk Douglas left as quickly as he had arrived. Over the next half-hour our wrangler organised fake grass, a mini trampoline, a bale of hay and a bucket of water. Having placed and tested those, he produced a beautiful black stallion clad in the sort of livery only a genuine 'Hollywood Baddie' would ride.

Having ignored us throughout all this, the wrangler now said:

'You're going to need to do this in three pieces. The first part will be the gallop up and dismount. Then you have to stop, so I can tether the horse. I suggest you mic Mr Douglas up then. The second part will be his dismount again, plus whatever dialogue you've agreed. Then you need to stop again, so I can rig the trampoline and grass 'hide'. You can also remove his mic at this point. The third and final part will be Mr Douglas jumping back onto the horse (using the mini-trampoline) and riding off to our stables, in that direction. Is that okay?'

'Okay? It's bloody wonderful!' I heard myself say, through tears of joy. And so it was.

It happened like clockwork. The piece to camera lasted well over a minute, but who cared? This was Kirk Douglas; solid gold. As with John Wayne, we were being given a masterclass in what international movie stardom is about. Nothing but complete virtuosity and *savoir-faire* from start to finish. Kirk rode off into the sunset and we never saw him again, Maurice didn't even have chance to ask him to sign a release form. We were overjoyed at his piece and started thinking about the possibility of a BAFTA. It was in any case a good enough reason to travel back to Tucson for a bit more quality bar-time there.

The following day we received a telex (no such thing as emails then – how we managed is a mystery, but we did). It instructed our PA Miriam and me to return immediately. She discovered that the swiftest route back to the UK was via Concorde.

As a ticket holder for a Concorde flight, it felt strange to walk straight past passengers queuing for the First Class Boeing 747s while going into a lounge that outdid anything else in the airport. It was an exceptional journey from start to finish, but the inside of the plane itself was remarkably small and take-off very worrying. It was like being tipped backwards while slapped with a hammer. I'll never forget looking out of the window. Looking up, all was black. But look down and all was blue. And the curvature of Earth... it's a planet!

At one point the captain announced: 'We're travelling at Mach 2, which is faster than a rifle bullet and twice the speed of sound [1,354 mph].' Following this revelation, the stewards offered everyone a glass of Dom Pérignon, although Miriam prefered a nice cup of tea.

We arrived at Heathrow, just three hours and ten minutes after leaving New York. It therefore seemed silly to phone the office and wait another hour for the official Thames TV car to collect us, so I grabbed a black cab for the relatively short trip to Teddington.

One week later, I received a severe reprimand from the Thames travel department for wasting company money like that. Not a word, to this day, about the expense of two tickets on Concorde, which in those days cost a small fortune! A black cab, however, was pure hedonism.

Naturally, we were eager to discover what everyone in the *This Is Your Life* office thought of our Kirk Douglas masterpiece. Maurice and I were inconsolable when we discovered that, as Kirk had gone over a minute, the boys (Roy Bottomley and Tom Brennan) had decided his words were more important than all that 'horsey stuff'. They hadn't even bothered to look at (or use) the gallop up to camera or leap back on the horse and ride off into the sunset.

Nobody, not even Jack Crawshaw, the producer, had seen our masterpiece. And nobody ever will because every bit of that binned film had been incinerated unseen and unconsidered by anyone other than our small crew and Kirk Douglas himself.

Forty-five years after the event, that still hurts!

The late great Mike Yarwood, 1941-2023.

The team behind Tyne Tees' music-based children's show Razzmatazz *from June 1981 to January 1987: presenter Alastair Pirrie; researchers Posy Harvey, Ken Scoffield and Ed Skelding; producer/director Royston Mayoh.*

2.
How Long Have You Been a Dwarf?

DISAPPOINTMENT. I've experienced very little of it during my lifetime, so on the rare occasion it did come along it cut like a knife, leaving me more confused than angry.

It's true to say disappointment comes when we expect something better. So live your life being amused by and often amazed at what life throws at you and the feeling will be rare. The flip side of that, of course, is that it has a far more debilitating effect when it does occur.

I never properly learned how to deal with disappointment, as from the moment I took control of my fate it was never an option. Eventually, though, it happened and I wasn't well enough prepared to bat it off as 'just one of those things'. Not surprisingly, it hurt!

I find it difficult to recall my childhood years in terms other than utility, a pointless existence. I was never disappointed then because I was the living embodiment of disappointment itself.

I'll return to this theme soon, but first we must digress slightly.

I imagine most people can recall a person or event that was to influence the direction of the rest of their life. More often than not, these significant moments would have happened at the beginning of an already chosen career path, providing a leg-up to the next level. Well, my own significant moment was not provided by an individual or event, but rather a building.

A rumour buzzed around the sixth form at Burnage Grammar School, Manchester, of a fantastic opportunity to earn £1 a day on a Saturday and Sunday working in Didsbury (a suburban village adjacent to Burnage). To make this even more intriguing, it was said that all you'd have to do was queue outside a particular fish 'n' chip shop at 5.00pm every Friday. You should identify yourself as being eligible for the job by clutching a pair of white plimsolls and stay in line until the stroke of 6.00pm, at which point a van would arrive, a man would get out and he would randomly choose six boys. They would then climb in the back, be driven one mile, and begin earning a quid a day over the coming weekend.

At the time I accepted this story at face value. It wasn't until many years later that some worldly-wise sceptic explained the underlying dangers inherent in such an unlikely scenario, especially involving young boys. I remember being both horrified and thankful that my naïvety had prevented me from questioning the 'opportunity'.

Anyway, I did queue outside that chippy on quite a few occasions; it was something exciting to do. Nor was I disappointed at not being chosen as I hadn't expected to be picked in the first place. Until...

One Friday, I was there as usual, clutching my pumps (nowadays they'd be trainers), the van arrived and wouldn't you know it, he pointed at me. It was the moment my life began! I'd been officially chosen as a fish 'n' chip boy. In more modern times this job was known as 'call boy' and then, much later, 'runner'.

Even now, 60-odd years later, I still gulp when I think about the anticipation of being bundled into that windowless van. The journey lasted less than five minutes, over before it began, half a mile up the road. Having got there, we were escorted into what I knew to be the Capitol cinema, whose doors had been closed to the Didsbury public for ages. The last film I'd seen there was *King Solomon's Mines*.

We lucky six entered the building, blatantly no longer a picture house, and were led up a long flight of stairs to what had originally been the circle, before being told to sit in a row and wait. Looking around, my first impression was that the place had been converted into a factory for making caravans. In a large area below us were ten or more in various stages of construction. Some had roofs yet to be fitted, some had their backs missing and some, very oddly, were fully-furnished with cushions and curtains, but had no sides to them. The strangest thing, however, was the enormous height between these caravans and the ceiling while, above us, huge lights blazed down. I remember thinking far too many, as they produced considerable heat. Perhaps they were destined for some foreign land with a climate much hotter than Manchester's?

My musings were soon interrupted by a man with a wooden leg, who introduced himself as Mr Lindsey. He'd appeared from nowhere and was suddenly in full flow, talking with a theatrical flourish, arms flailing as he began to orate. 'What you're seeing is the construction of an *Armchair Theatre* episode called "A Temporary Town", he revealed. 'It is to be transmitted in two weeks.'

Armchairs? Theatres? Temporary towns? Transmitted? What was this curious fellow banging on about?

Eventually I learned and it fired me up with an excitement that has stayed with me since. I didn't completey understand what I was looking at or what it all meant, but did know I was in love with it to the extent that I never wanted to leave or wake up!

This love affair never faded, even on those rare occasions during the next 50-plus years when the business dealt me severe blows. My profound love of the business stopped such disappointments being as painful as I am sure they deserved to be. That said, there were a couple of occasions when the hurt was such that I'll never forget it. Just writing that made me realise how lucky I am to have had so few. Each were, to say the least, chunky and well worth documenting as perfect examples of the sort of disappointments that are not just inconvenient but transformative. They could each be summed up in one word. The first is 'Thatcher', and the second 'Bollywood'.

I shall begin with 'Thatcher' because that one happened first.

ON 2 November 1982, Channel 4 was launched with a flourish, as a free-to-air British public-service TV network. My story though does not begin there; first we must go back to 1979 when I was employed by ATV at the behest of their Head of Entertainment, Jon Scofield, in Borehamwood, one of the most exciting periods of my life.

This particular morning I left my Hampstead flat for the short drive to their Elstree Studios and was met by my PA, Delores Shine. Everyone knew Delores at ATV, she was a real character whose word only a fool would attempt to argue with. She told me coffee would be delivered to an edit suite, where I was urgently required due to our schedule being brought forward after a cancellation elsewhere.

Better yet, given the change we could now get the whole project (a variety show, *Bernie Clifton On Stage*) done and dusted in a day. I asked Delores to tell the switchboard not to put any calls through to us there and said I wouldn't be available until tomorrow.

Our edit was brilliantly successful and we finished at 6:00pm, a good four hours earlier than estimated. Feeling extremely pleased with myself, I headed for the Elstree bar to celebrate with whoever may be at that most famous watering hole.

The route from the edit suite involved walking through the main reception area, whereupon I was greeted by a receptionist in full panic mode. Worried she had done wrong by not disturbing me, she said a Mr Clutterbuck had been trying to get hold of me urgently all afternoon. I knew the name immediately and phoned him from a pay-phone (no mobiles in those days). The chap in question was my bank manager and he asked me to get there quickly, he'd be waiting. He didn't reveal the problem. Having driven like a lunatic, I was then greeted with a drink as he began to explain all.

Weeks earlier, I had been asked to leave my home and five-year-old daughter by a distraught wife who, on her high horse, accused me of being unfaithful and threatened divorce proceedings. This was at a time when everyone I knew (including her) had dalliances if not full-blown affairs. I figured it would blow over given a spell apart. However, I had not been ready for Mr Clutterbuck's story.

He'd been desperately trying to contact me because that morning my wife had arrived at his office demanding that the contents of our joint-account be transferred immediately to a new account in her name only. Our bank manager tried to explain that such a dramatic transaction would be grossly unfair to her husband who'd had a long association with the place and Mr Clutterbuck personally. She said it was a perfectly legal request and if he refused to comply she would call the police, leaving Mr Clutterbuck with no option but to allow my wife to clean me out in one stroke.

Our account was particularly healthy at that point due to the highly productive period I'd been having. And her target included my 'tax account', which had always kept me one step ahead of the tax man. Mr Clutterbuck was upset about it and needed to explain he'd done everything possible to stop it from happening in my absence. It seemed so unfair, especially as it involved a lot of money.

The reality of divorce was hard to stomach; anyone who has been through the process knows it's a nightmare for everyone concerned. My solicitor warned there could be a 50/50 split with a possibility of an ongoing percentage of my income going to my ex-wife for 'the security, safety and well-being of our one child [Beth, aged 5].' He did not warn me of the possibility of total financial oblivion.

Such personal uncertainty was not having a great effect on my creativity and productivity at work. Constant preoccupation with marital matters spoiled my imagination during the preparation and rehearsals for shows ATV had graciously employed me to produce.

It must be remembered that all major TV companies demanded nothing but the best from their producer/directors. Should they suspect or receive evidence of a producer or director not delivering what they were paying for, as agreed in the contract, at least one clause in it (somewhere near the end) gave them the perfect opportunity not only to dispense with one's services, but also pretty much to guarantee similar future work would not be forthcoming.

It's true. There's no business like showbusiness!

On the one hand, I was trying to keep 'eyes and teeth' and give the impression that my mind was 100 per cent on the job. On the other, I was fretting about losing my daughter, my Rickmansworth home, my wife, my future income and my bank account (including my 'tax account'), quite the brain freeze.

In the middle of all this mayhem, a TV executive called Andrea Wonfor visited me in my office and asked if I would be interested in joining her at Tyne Tees TV in Newcastle. She had just become its programme controller and wanted me: '...to bring some "network" mindset to the station.' Andrea felt that the north east company had become too regional in its thinking and lost any ambition outside the area it served. She was swift to add that she couldn't afford to pay the sort of money my agent was demanding at that time. I was quick to tell Andrea that the agent worked for me, not the other way round (I paid a commission for her services). What sort of money was she considering? This was 1980. I knew the cost of living was far less on Tyneside than in London. I also knew that Newcastle was a great city with great people and a great nightlife! I'd already worked at Tyne Tees in 1968. during the time of the moon landing, which we watched on a portable telly in a fishing dock in North Shields.

In those days, I had been responsible for *The World of Monty Modlyn*, T*he Stuart Henry Speakeasy*, *Walk Right In* and *The Wally Whyton Style*. We'll come to those remarkable shows later in the book but for now I just want to deal with the hidden disappointment I walked into by accepting Andrea's offer.

This Tyne Tees opportunity took me nearly 300 miles away from London and Rickmansworth in particular. A much reduced income would scupper my ex-wife's reliance on the good money I'd been getting from commercials or music videos. And the job sounded relatively easy. I had worked with Geordies before and knew of their incredible capabilities. It sounded like a win-win situation and, being the lucky person I am, the timing seemed perfect.

So, in 1981, I began a new life as a divorcee there and to call it a happy time would be an understatement. It was glorious. We made good programmes and enjoyed watching the BBC and ITV 'borrow' some of the new technical innovations and visual effects we regularly introduced at Tyne Tees. Under Andrea's leadership, the channel went from being a solely regional programme maker to making the likes of *Supergran*, *Highway*, *Razzmatazz* and three or four other titles for the national ITV network. Furthermore, when Channel 4 kicked off a year later, Andrea got them to commission *The Tube*, the controversial tea-time live music show hosted by Jools Holland and Paula Yates that proved hugely popular with Britain's youth over five series, from November 1982 to April 1987.

My move to Tyne Tees was successful in so many ways. I was able to put Rickmansworth – and all it represented – to one side and concentrate on the job over six terrific years. Before then, I'd been a relatively young (well, 40) producer/director with a string of highly-rated Light Entertainment credits to my name, with the emphasis on 'Light'. Barry Cryer, a comedy legend for whom I had the highest respect before his death in January 2022, but didn't work with nearly often enough, once joked that Light Entertainment meant 'shows for the hard of thinking'. In truth, they require a certain skill to make and take a lot of work and time to get right, as shown by the number of naff ones every week on all channels (which, before Channel 4, meant just BBC1, BBC2 and ITV). At least my name was associated with some very successful ones and I had a decent reputation within the television industry at large.

I felt reasonably confident about my abilities, therefore, and was fully aware of my inabilities – an awareness that one of my mentors, the producer and director Milo Lewis, insisted I must always keep an eye on. Milo, who died in 1988, knew what he was talking about, having had a hand down the years in such popular series at *Bootsie and Snudge*, *Coronation Street* and *Thank Your Lucky Stars*. And, as already mentioned, the name Royston Mayoh was also now familiar to complete strangers, due to Hughie Green mentioning it so often on ITV's hugely influential talent show, *Opportunity Knocks*.

So life was pretty good at Tyne Tees – until 23 January 1987...

Weeks earlier, Channel 4 had asked us to supply its first ever Hogmanay show, to be broadcast on New Year's Eve 1986. They weren't looking for the traditional kilt and bagpipe offering however. In keeping with their independent remit, they required something entirely different and had charged Tyne Tees under our now-famous programme controller Andrea Wonfor – widely considered among the best of *all* regional controllers – with the task of inventing it.

Immediately, we went to work on formulating a programme that would be unique to C4 and nothing like any NYE celebration seen before on British television. Andrea called a meeting with her heads of department ... Peter McCue of Current Affairs, Heather Ging of Regional Programming and myself of Light Entertainment. Since I was also a programme director, Andrea wanted me both to produce and direct it, with the other heads becoming executive producers. Malcolm Gerrie, the producer of *The Tube*, was to be programme associate because Andrea wanted to use the influence associated with Jools Holland as a base for the show's music. She did not want an exact version of *The Tube*, but something very Channel 4.

We set to work devising a running order that might give the programme its own identity. And when someone rightly pointed out that the type of viewer C4 normally attracted would actually be out celebrating at midnight, not watching TV, it was agreed there would be little point in a show aimed specifically at that demographic. At the initial round table meeting all sorts of ideas were thrown around.

The one that generated most interest was the notion that Jools was home alone, watching telly in his spacious lounge. Suddenly the walls of his flat would collapse to reveal various bands and other guests – an idea that soon morphed into Jools himself being caught sitting on the loo. The show would be a sort of fantasy and its title eluded everyone until Jools's friend, Rowland Rivron, came up with the crazy idea of calling it *Come Dancing with Jools Holland*, guests wearing numbers on their back like ballroom dancers of yesteryear.

Despite the aversion to Hogmanay tradition, I had a notion that we should indeed feature a fully-kilted bagpiper walking around the battlements of a Scottish castle. Not too inventive you may think, but the Piper would be Rusty Goffe, one of the original Oompa Loompas from the 1971 film musical *Willy Wonka & the Chocolate Factory*, starring Gene Wilder.

Rusty was a great friend of mine. Aged 74 as I write, he still is. He plays 47 instruments and I knew one was bound to be bagpipes. Just over three feet tall, in full tartan regalia, he would traverse a 6ft by 6ft battlement rigged on a trolley that four stage-hands could pull onstage as appropriate. Naturally, he'd be playing that traditional New Years' song 'When Irish Eyes Are Smiling.' Everyone seemed pleased with that, so it became item 147 on the running order.

Our current affairs man Peter McCue then managed to persuade MP for Durham and ex-Home Secretary Leon Brittan to commit to an appearance. After some lengthy correspondence and negotiations regarding Brittan's fee and position in the running order, Peter had to verify in writing a commitment that Liverpool's ultra left-winger, Derek Hatton, would be on before Brittan and not be given a second more 'air time'. The contract also committed us to pay the Tory big-hitter a considerable fee and welcome his wife and daughter to both the live transmission and end-of-show party. All-in-all then, a long and arduous effort to get him there. We both thought he would be a worthy addition to proceedings. Oh, how wrong we were.

The rehearsals were full of anomalies, partly because C4 insisted on having a number of 'executive producers' check each item for suitability on what was still a relatively new channel. They disrupted the flow of schedules drawn up to coincide with various arrival times and external commitments of the sixty or so celebrities, bands and performers booked to fill a 90-minute slot. As producer/director, I oversaw these run-throughs technically and editorially through the control gallery. From time to time, we were visited by producers, agents, celebrities and other interested parties wishing to see how the production was looking and sounding, or who wished to change something that was about to become part of the programme.

One such visitation was from a well known BBC producer who had recently been acquired by C4 as a 'comedy adviser'. His name was Paul Jackson (who, incidentally, became Director of Comedy and Entertainment for ITV some nineteen years later, in 2006).

This particular intrusion came while we rehearsed a comedy trio who called themselves 'Who Dares Wins' (a promotional device for their forthcoming new series of that name on Channel 4), made up of Rory McGrath, Jimmy Mulville and Philip Pope. Their comedy was new, edgy and very Channel 4. One of their songs ended with an expression containing the word 'fuck'!

I remarked to the floor manager that if we were going to rerun this song could he ask them to leave that last line out, as the studio contained children who had come along to see their pop heroes, (other bands also taking part). As for the actual show, I was content that the word would be transmitted well after midnight so, in terms of regulations, well after the watershed. So, okay for transmission but not okay for three o'clock in the afternoon with an 'open' studio.

Moments after giving this instruction to Christine Llewellyn-Reeve, my floor manager, the door of my control gallery shot open and in walked a C4 posse of commissioning editors headed by Paul Jackson. He reprimanded me, saying 'This isn't the "David Fucking Nixon Show"... that song stays in. Am I quite clear?' His rudeness and authoritative attitude were confirmed and endorsed by the other members of the posse, including Mike Bolland, the most senior commissioning editor at Channel 4. After Jackson's 'directive', they all left as abruptly as they'd arrived.

Not used to seeing me take things sitting down, the entire gallery looked at me in disbelief. They all knew that I never intended to remove the song, I just asked that the 'language' be kept down during rehearsals in the very 'open' and casual studio environment. The incident had been so dramatic and unexpected we were all in shock. There was no point in doing anything other than shaking your head and moving on with this very tight rehearsal schedule. The matter was never mentioned again.

Staggered non-sequential rehearsals were completed, with a few holes left for the bits of magic any live performance would produce, having hopefully set the right environment and mood for magic to happen. Eventually, also as in any rehearsal schedule, there were long meal and studio breaks for such lighting adjustments and other technical amendments as had been exposed. Next up: dress rehearsal.

There is an urban myth (still quoted as fact) that if a dress-run is a disaster the 'performance' itself will be faultless, with the converse also applying. This worried us as ours ran to time and was faultless, which meant... something none of us wanted to think about.

And then, at 23:30pm, we were On The Air.

The opening scene, in which Jools now sat alone in his lounge imagining performances coming out of his walls, worked perfectly. His attempt at getting away from these images by locking himself in the loo, followed by all four walls of the loo collapsing to reveal a studio in full musical flow, also hit the spot. The Tyne Tees crew were working at their most dedicated level of expertise! Each item made for more atmosphere and magic than any of us had hoped for. The subsequent 105 minutes flew by and suddenly we were Off The Air.

The final tableaux had contained our entertainers and celebrities centre stage – including Roland Rivron, Ruby Wax, Paul Carrack, Uri Geller, Julia Hills, Noddy Holder, Gilson Lavis, Nick Lowe, Rik Mayall, Darryl Pandy, Nigel Planer, Chris Rea, Jonathan Ross, Mandy Smith and many many more. One was the American actor, singer and drag queen, Divine, who turned to Rusty Goffe alongside and asked him the most outstanding question of all time: 'How long have you been a dwarf?' For once, Rusty had no answer!

As we all came down from this high-powered 90 minutes of new television the phones started to ring with compliments by the score. Even Channel 4's director of programmes, Jeremy Isaacs, called Andrea to say it was the best C4 programme so far and had fitted the remit perfectly. The party lasted throughout the night, finishing with breakfast in one of Newcastle's finest Italian restaurants for those still breathing after such a wonderful New Year's treat.

So why, therefore, did this particular programme turn out to be so memorable and yet such a huge disappointment ?

I had been working for a while with a dislocated disc in my lower spine. I could still operate, but only while standing up. Thankfully, my job didn't require me to sit down at all and the amount of mental concentration over-rode the pain. Now the show was over I could get it fixed via a laminectomy at Newcastle Nuffield Hospital. The world was a beautiful place for the first 23 days of 1987.

Then, on January 23, Maggie Marfitt-Smith, a much respected senior member of the Tyne Tees administration who, at this point, reported directly to managing director David Reay, called me at home to ask if I could pop in to see David at 2.00pm that afternoon. Of course I agreed and this is where my first taste of disappointment in the industry I had grown to love came in. I walked into his office using two sticks, the sciatic pain caused by the slipped disc more acute than ever, and to my amazement saw our MD surrounded by an army of people I barely knew. He began talking like a robot while reading from a piece of paper, his statement going like this:-

'...being in breach of the 1984 Obscenities Act and bringing the company Tyne Tees into disrepute, I have no alternative other than to summarily dismiss you; ask you to return all company property, and now be escorted off the premises after picking up only your personal effects from your office...'

This was the very last thing I'd expected and quite bizarre given all the compliments and details of record viewing figures that had emerged since the transmission 23 days ago.

I'd known David since 1968, when I worked with him during his beginnings as a videotape operator. Some years later, I was directing a Hughie Green series, *The Sky's The Limit,* and because these shows were put together like a huge jigsaw puzzle, needed a central point to store tapes and make the final edit. I chose Tyne Tees and asked that David be my dedicated VTR Editor. We did two series of 13, and the show was a success. I often asked David to come over to the pub (Rose & Crown) for an end of day drink. He refused, explaining he was doing night school. During series four he volunteered to come for a drink and explained that now he'd finished night school and gained his degree he was free to join us.

Some months later, I noticed an advert in *The Guardian* for a technical supervisor at the Welsh station HTV. I showed it to David at the start of our next *Sky's The Limit* edit session, explaining that his degree would mean more at a new company than at Tyne Tees, and that he had all the requirements listed for this prestigious job. He hadn't even seen it advertised. He applied, got the job and some years after that, the position of MD for Tyne Tees was announced. I suggested he should apply. Perhaps you begin to see why I include this in a chapter entitled 'How long have you been a dwarf?'

That is by no means the end of this epic story or the reason for my tremendous sense of disappointment following dismissal from a job I loved. Some months later my fellow dismissee, Peter McCue, got a lead on how and why this had all occurred. In a nutshell, he discovered that Sir Ralph Carr Ellison   landowner, businessman, administrator, royal representative born into the landed gentry, Tyne Tees TV chairman and Lord Lieutenant of Tyne and Wear – had received a frantic phone call from Prime Minister Margaret Thatcher demanding that heads should roll to stop this regional television station from constantly flouting IBA regulations about language and watersheds. Peter learned all this by taking a gamble on employing a very well-known lawyer, so well connected he could mingle with the great and good and get to hear why the PM had made it.

The interesting point about this is that neither the BBC or ITV (in fact all broadcasters) are allowed to take a brief from any political leader or representative. UK broadcasters are all publishers and regulated in such a way that they are disallowed from becoming the mouthpiece of any Government of the day, but must self-balance any statement made by any politician.

As Peter McCue had been head of current affairs, he felt very strongly about a Prime Minister causing the dismissal of two senior programme-makers for what appeared to be very flimsy reasons. Peter smelt a rat and was determined to find out why Thatcher had become so hands-on in what should have been solely regulatory business if there had been any breach at all – which, as far as Peter and I were concerned, there had not. He shocked me one day by telling me this posh lawyer cost £14,000 a day. In 1986, that was an awful lot of money. But when he told me what this lawyer had discovered at the bar of the prestigious RAC Club, I immediately understood why £14,000 was a bargain.

I was also shocked that my union the ACTT (Association of Cinema and Television Technicians) had indicated how, in the event the dismissals were upheld, they would be willing to bear the legal costs. Later, the ACTT was swallowed up by BECTU (the more generic Broadcasting, Entertainment, Communication and Theatre Union) who I still support to this day. I will never forget how they supported me during this terrifying time.

Apparently, Margaret Thatcher received notice that her ex-Home Secretary, Brittan, had been making a fool of himself on a New Year's Eve TV show transmitted from Newcastle-upon-Tyne. Naturally she invited Mr Brittan into her office for an explanation. Mr Brittan was happy to tell the PM that as a local MP for Cleveland and Whitby, he had received an invitation to talk about government successes during the outgoing year of 1986. He explained how he saw this appearance on Tyne Tees, in his constituency, as good publicity for both the Party and Government. He, too, was horrified that during the programme, a comedian told viewers that he could tell what a person drank simply by looking at their face. A barman, for example, was told he was a 'beer in a bottle' type. The comic had picked out a few other people from the audience at random. One was a 'sherry in the afternoon' type, another 'warm white wine with friends'. To Mr Brittan's 'sheer embarrassment', the camera had settled on him, when the comedian told the audience and viewers at home that here was a 'brandy at his club, red wine at home and pink gin when out with his friends...' sort of a guy.

Well, the so-called 'Iron Lady' hit the roof at this, and discovered that it was the same company who, months before, had transmitted terrible language in the afternoon between a Bugs Bunny cartoon and the birthdays. Hence the phone call to Sir Ralph, asking for the programme-making team to be punished. Sir Ralph phoned David Reay and this was what led to the January 23 firing day.

The story, as told by Mr Brittan, suggested that the 'drinks by face' routine performed by the *Who Dares Wins* trio was ad-libbed (as it needed to look). And there was no way of proving that rosy-faced Leon had agreed to take part in it, especially to a PM whose mind was made up that this regional TV company should be punished.

But what about the swearing after Bugs Bunny? How did that come about? Well, Peter also unearthed how *The Tube*'s production crew (nothing to do with either Peter or myself) had decided to play a trick on Jools, its star presenter. One floor manager had run to the green room and asked him to come to the studio immediately as the network wanted a live promotion for the following day's show, Jools was happy to oblige. He was told they only wanted 15 seconds of chat and he was to start by saying 'Thanks Helen,' because that was the name of the person in London who'd be throwing him a link. The studio was put on a one minute alert, everyone in their place. Thirty seconds studio ... then ten, nine, eight etc ... and finally, a silent visual cue for Jools to look into the camera and begin.

'Thank you, Helen. Yes, tomorrow night I will be joined by the excellent Paula Yates and together we will introduce the wonderful music by the father of South African jazz, Hugh Masekela.' The floor manager indicates that Jools had ten seconds left. Jools, not used to riffing without notes, takes an unnoticed gulp: 'And not just that, we've got a great film from New Orleans featuring that legend from the 1950s, surely the biggest name in rock 'n' roll, Fats Domino!'

Jools glances at the floor manager for signs of there now being only a second or two from off-air. However, the floor manager is still showing the stretching sign, meaning 'keep talking'. So Jools goes into some complete gibberish about their time in New Orleans and meeting Fats that goes on for two more minutes, by which time he is a sweating, nervous wreck and the studio bursts into laughter.

It had all been a joke. There was no live network promotion spot. This was the crew having a 'jolly jest' at Jools's expense. However, because Jools is Jools, he laughed with the crowd and that was that.

Now wind the clock forward about six months and everyone has forgotten the wheeze, except Jools! So when they ask him to perform another live promotion spot... yes, you've guessed it! He waits for the countdown and cue and delivers the now immortal lines: 'Don't be a square, watch *The Tube* at 6:30 tomorrow night on Channel 4. Be there or be ungroovy fuckers,' throws two fingers at the camera and walks off. This time there is no laughter from the crew, just a stunned silence. A moment of broadcast history.

The phones started ringing and didn't stop for days. *The Tube* got enormous ratings as Jools attempted a public apology for his gaff, which of course it wasn't, but the truth is far less newsworthy.

Margaret Thatcher, meanwhile, had remembered this breach of the broadcasting code and, coupled with how the very same station had abused the privilege of having her ex-Home Secretary in their studios, felt motivated to vent her spleen at the Tyne Tees chairman, who felt duty bound to set the dismissal process into action.

That would be the end of the story had a member of Tyne Tees's technical staff, a videotape engineer called Robin Sinton, not phoned me up weeks after the sacking and said: 'Hi, Roy! You will probably tell me to shove this up my arse after all that's gone on, but I've just found a copy of the dress-run of that New Year's Eve show; it's a bit of a mess 'cos it's got burnt-in time-of-day code all over the bottom third of the frame. I was about to bin it, but thought you may like to bin it yourself.'

I could not believe my ears. Would this tape, by any chance, contain the shots (indelibly marked with the exact time of day they had happened) of Leon Brittan rehearsing the sketch he insisted had been a complete surprise to him? Robin came to my flat. We watched the tape together and there it was – in full colour too! I'm sure Robin had never been kissed full on the lips by a bearded man before, but on this day he most certainly was.

What happened next moved very fast. I rang Peter with the news. Peter rang his lawyer. The Lawyer called a judge. The Judge ordered a meeting in his chambers. Peter, already in London, organised a NUMATIC video playback machine and monitor to be delivered to the rooms and then went straight to King's Cross to wait for me, clutching the tape as if they were the Crown Jewels. The Judge ruled, there and then, that there was no case to answer and Geoffrey Howe (who had initially told our lawyer about the meetings between Thatcher and Brittan at number ten) was ordered to pass this new development on to the Prime Minister.

There was no apology. Peter McCue and I remained sacked. There was no way we could go back to the City Road studios as any thought of working there again was unviable. However, we did get a mumbled apology from David Reay who, it seemed very reluctantly, handed over a healthy cheque that, looking back on it today, ought to have been worth five times the amount. However, although this was the biggest disappointment in my career thus far, I viewed it – and the cheque – as the beginning of a new chapter in my life and had no idea what a brilliant chapter that would turn out to be.

But as for that other 'Bollywood' disappointment in my career, let's go not to India, but to Sun City in South Africa.

BY now, I'd re-established myself as a useful director and had worked all over the globe, but this particular episode had its origins in the newly-constructed Millennium Dome in Greenwich.

My friend, Andy Ward, was now working for media production company Endemol as a producer. He phoned one day to invite me to direct a new format for the Indian market with a working title of *The Bollywood Awards*. Having had a wonderful time in New Delhi and Bombay (as it used to be called, before becoming Mumbai), I naturally jumped at such a fantastic opportunity.

The client was an entertainment agency called Wizcraft and Andy had set up a meeting at Endemol, so we could formally receive the brief and begin planning what would be an enormous and most worthwhile undertaking. We gathered in the boardroom around a massive table, there must have been twenty or thirty of us. Andy also invited our favourite lighting director, sound director, floor manager, production manager and other key people we loved working with.

The Wizcraft contingent was surprisingly small and still hadn't formulated an established way of working in the Indian TV market, so I chaired the meeting and began by inviting them to share their vision for this forthcoming event. They were silent. We assumed we had a language problem, but soon realised they had little or no idea about the detail and assumed (there's that 'mother of all fuck-ups' word again) that we at Endemol would be supplying all that.

So we began by trying to prise out some idea of what awards they had in mind. Their minds stayed blank, so we suggested a few that all successful award shows include, such as a roll call of people who'd been essential to their industry but died in the last twelve months. This was swiftly agreed to. We asked how many commercial breaks had been agreed with their broadcasters. But again, very little info was forthcoming. The meeting was moving to a quick conclusion with an agreement that we should meet again in a month when we, Endemol, would propose a complete running order with ad breaks, awards, celebrity award-givers, guest performances ... in fact, a full working document to be amended at will. We also invited Wizcraft to chip in with requirements of their own if and when they had any.

Originating awards shows from square one with no precedent or history was not entirely new to Andy. He'd been involved in the birth of many such shows around the world, not least the Channel V Music Awards which Andy had produced and I had directed in India during previous years. Wizcraft had supplied its scenic riggers and painters. With late great Mick Klajinski in charge of infrastructure, security and just about everything except condoms (although he'd have done that too if asked), Andy had built a formidable outside broadcast team of overseas specialists. I was thrilled to be included in that complex package and had learnt never to be surprised at the problems that occurred from time to time.

For instance, in Delhi one day, Andy had found himself besuited in the 44°C heat attending a court hearing; the Indian Pole Vaulting Team suing him for having the audacity to build the corner of our stage at the very spot where the pole vaulters began their run. The fact that this area was not marked out in the middle of the vast Indira Gandhi stadium meant it took only a matter of minutes to resolve. Still, it cost Andy a full day and Mick a couple of sleepless nights considering the prospect of having to move the entire stage area eleven feet just to soothe athletes who could, I'm sure, have shifted just a few yards to the right!

During another Indian event, I was in the middle of directing cameras on the American band No Doubt, being sure to give each member of the band equal air-time and not fall into the trap of just featuring their lead singer, Gwen Stefani. It would have been an easy mistake to make as the rest of them stood relatively motionless. The shoot was going well and I had been able to add interest to the static ones by creating visual effects on a plush Grass Valley vision mixing unit when, suddenly, we heard a muffled voice on our intercom. It was the voice of a terror-stricken camera operator positioned at the furthest point from the stage, feeding us a super-wide shot. In as few words as he could muster, he was telling us that a policeman was holding a gun to his head and demanding he turn the sound down on the four hundred speakers situated around the stadium!

Our sound supervisor turned a few down at the back to prevent us losing a camera operator and this, together with a brown-paper envelope stuffed with rupees delivered by Andy himself seemed to do the trick. Andy had agreed the levels with the police beforehand but hadn't built in the possibility that there might be a change of shift during the actual performance.

Such curve balls were thrown at us regularly which, in all honesty, was a major part of the appeal of making shows in strange places.

The first International Indian Film Awards (IIFA) at the venue nowadays known simply as The Dome were another such occasion.

Circus people have a belief that if a dead bird is spotted on the ground near to where they are about to pitch their tent, the *Toba* (a term used to describe the specific area used and the business created in that area) will be unsuccessful. Well, there was no dead bird at the Dome on the morning that rehearsals were due to start. Instead there was a white-faced Andy Ward asking me to join him for a coffee on the other side of the Thames. Andy explained that Wizcraft had reneged on cash payment to cover services already incurred and unless they delivered it to Andy in this very café then rehearsals could not commence. Nor could they start without the director (me), which is why he had hijacked me at the entrance.

In the end, the money was unceremoniously delivered in a plastic bag, but the entire experience should have warned me then and there that this was the equivalent to a deceased parrot in a big top! The IIFA production was a relative success, but we all learnt a lot about what was possible and lacking in this brand new production.

A year later, the second event was in Johannesburg where, before long, we were heavily into rehearsals. At one point I had to stop the entire proceedings to explain to a disobliging choreographer that we had sixty-four items on the running order to rehearse, not just his three-minute dance number! I was only in my fifties at the time, but one South African newspaper described me as 'an elderly British film director' who had publicly 'told off' one of their local heroes.

The rehearsal process is complex. Each technician will take notes applicable to their specific observations made during trials. For this to happen efficiently over a wide range of specialities, each item is given a running order number that stays with it from the beginning of rehearsals to end of performance, so everyone involved can refer to item 132 instead of 'You know, the bit where the lady walks out...'

If items are added, they are numbered with 'a' or 'b'. When things are dropped, the number is deleted, without affecting all the others before or after the one ditched. Each technician has their particular shorthand when making notes, so a lot of space is left next to the action on the camera script in which to make them. There is unity in the way the show is broken down into sections, a system that is now almost universal in both film and television.

At the end of three or four days, it's not surprising that every camera script will look a complete mess to anyone other than the person who is using it. It may have rubbings out, which can mean something important to the technician. It can also have badly drawn diagrams and strange markings – indecipherable to all but their creator. One such scribble accompanied a scripted link by presenter Kabir Bedi, a well known Indian actor born in Pakistan with a career spanning India, the USA and Italy, with timings to allow for a major piece of equipment to be 'set' in readiness for the performance of a French acrobatic dance act. This was a form of trapeze that had to be anchored at four specific points around their equipment. During rehearsals we had decided upon and marked these anchorage sights and the act had tested the gear for sturdiness and safety.

We practised our stage crew bringing it out, unfurling the 'stays' and securing the anchors in a certain order to ensure the correct tension was achieved before the acrobats began their performance. We'd timed this as 30 secs (maximum), so a script was written and added to the teleprompter for presenter Kabir to perform. This too was rehearsed to ensure the words (as performed at the pace he normally spoke) would amount to at least 30 seconds. Let's say this was item 149 in the running order.

So, the complex rehearsals went exceptionally well. The lighting was superb, as indeed was the glamorous set in the middle of Sun City. A celebrity audience started to arrive and it was apparent that the first show from the Dome a year earlier had been so well received by the global Indian audience that this 2001 version was going to be even bigger and better in every way. It would be recorded for later transmission in the UK, too, possibly also destined for China.

Between dress rehearsal and transmission we had a two-hour break during which, after about 90 minutes, a technician stopped me on my way out of the gents. 'What's this all about, Guv?' he said, handing me a pristine hot-off-the-printer camera script that had been placed on his mixing desk, 'is someone taking the piss or what?' I quickly scanned through it and immediately spotted that all the numbers had been changed; now running uninterrupted from one to two hundred. And every 'a' and 'b' was replaced by new numbers. This was not just useless, but dangerous. I quickly gathered my PA, Andy and a few trusted friends to go around all the departments and collect every last one. It turned out that some 'helpful' members of Wizcraft, believing the technicians would like and appreciate tidy and freshly-typed and renumbered scripts, had revamped them.

Along with finding these new abominations we now also had to retrieve the originals from various containers and dustbins about the place. Thankfully they'd been too bulky to rip up, so those we did find were still in one piece. After about 20 minutes of searching the question remained: 'Had we managed to locate them all?'

Now, however, it was time to start the mental limber-up required before embarking upon 105 minutes of high-intensity concentration that employment on such complex shows demands. But this time, instead of adopting my usual pre-show motivational banter through our communication base in the control room, I was desperately checking that everyone was in possession of and reading their own script. And that meant everyone, from departmental heads to the numerous runners working to ensure a smooth production.

Naturally there were a few technicians we couldn't connect with at this precise moment, but all staff involved had been warned that these newly-numbered scripts must be ignored in favour of the ones marked up, rubbed out and defaced over three days of rehearsal.

At last we were in the final few minutes of countdown before the red 'ON-AIR' light was switched on. I was beginning to settle down from the sheer panic that had set in when the control room door was thrown open and there, red-faced and furious, was an 'associate producer' who yelled: 'How dare you embarrass me like this, after all the work I've done to make sense of all the changes that you've made since we started rehearsals!'

I can no longer remember if I was too bemused by this complete lack of knowledge of how a programme goes to air or whether I was so gobsmacked at the attempt by this person to blame me! I do recall taking a deep breath in order to summon up every diplomatic bone in my body, before replying at the top of my voice: 'Why don't you fuck off out of my sight?' Instead of the usual silence such profanity from a director over talk-back would typically receive, I can still hear the muted applause from every direction and speaker. The associate producer duly disappeared and I didn't see him again until we were on the flight back to London.

With personally marked-up scripts, we were soon on the air with everything running better than smoothly. Each item of creativity had that magic-something only those who've experienced working in a live situation can appreciate. There is no going back. Until we came to running order number 149, Kabir Bedi in the middle of a link written both to impart editorial information and allow for the completion of safe rigging.

One job a multi-camera TV director soon learns to do is scan the dozen or so monitors in a control room constantly. These monitors all surround one larger ON-AIR monitor.*

Out of the corner of one eye, on a screen feeding a shot from camera (not scripted to be used for a while), I spotted a silent but animated argument taking place around a key 'anchor point' which should have already been secured and completed. Turning my attention to this, I realised Kabir was nearing the end of his link and gently said to the floor manager 'Can you stretch Kabir? We are not ready for the next item.' But to my horror, Kabir didn't notice his gesture, a gesture that every presenter in every country on every programme (including Jools Holland) knows about and dreads. So on Kabir ploughed into his written script from the teleprompter to introduce: 'Ths spectacular acrobatic dance act from France...'

Naturally, the audience applauded and, naturally, I shouted the order 'Hold-Up'! Usually there is nothing extraordinary about this, except I was fully aware that we were transmitting live to somewhere in the region of 40 million viewers around Asia.

---

* *Years later a new Channel 4 commissioning editor complimented me, saying: 'Oh, Royston! I think you're so clever being able to watch all those televisions at the same time!' I felt unable to respond.*

And their screens had suddenly gone black.

Now here's the thing – and it's a question for every lecturer and media student in the world to consider: 'Would it have been better for business, ratings and notoriety to continue with the programme, knowing there was a perfect chance that 40 million viewers would be treated to the sight, live on air, of a French acrobatic act falling to their doom or, if not death, specific life-changing injuries?'

Or 'Was it better to stop and ensure that the rigging was 100 per cent safe before re-starting the awards show?'

The showman in me was not sufficiently developed to chance the route of continuance and possibility of global front page headlines, which is why I opted for the stop option. And that was a decision which cost me my job as the future TV director of choice for IIFA, a product in which I had invested so much time and care.

Was I upset by a turn of events that led Wizcraft to take what they had learnt from Endemol to a new production company? Damn right I was! Especially as not one person ever acknowledged the notoriety that would have become attached to their name had I allowed the potential horror story to continue, Would I take the same decision today? Damn right I would!

ONE moment of disappointment, shortly after my most enjoyable spell directing *The Kenny Everett Video Cassette* for Thames in 1981, hurt more than any other. It didn't change my career path, just made me realise what a shitty business I was enjoying.

Everyone at the company was thrilled to see it nominated for a BAFTA award; winning it would be a real bonus. As you'll read in a future chapter, we didn't, but that wasn't what temporarily destroyed me. It was a chance remark made by someone who had no idea of its weight and personal significance, made in passing at the Thames TV Riverside Bar during lunch a few days after the ceremony.

A member of the Light Entertainment casting department threw into the conversation this interesting snippet: '...of course it was a real pity Roy didn't win, because Philip [Jones] had said that if Roy *had* won the BAFTA he'd have been invited to produce and direct the new Mike Yarwood series.' Mike, a massive star at the time, was even bigger news right then because Philip, Head of Entertainment for Thames, had just lured him from the BBC. So I hadn't just missed winning a covetous BAFTA, I'd lost the opportunity to make a huge and potentially well-paid 1982 brand new Thames TV series.

It was, and still feels like, a devastating blow.

In fact, writing this book has suddenly become far more difficult and emotional. I was about to launch into the detail of why I was so disappointed at losing the chance of working with Mike after a gap of twenty years when, in August 2023, I was asked by the production company, Monster Films, to contribute to a documentary they were making for Channel 5 about a man who, though he had been retired for years, remained one of Britain's best known impressionists.

This request meant I had to put my pen down, forget that post-BAFTA disappointment and start recalling all the good things – and there were many – about our early days working together.

Channel 5, of course, wished to tell the story of a major celebrity, but my only experience of Mike was as a raw beginner. My brief time with him came before he had appeared in front of anyone except a few workmates and so could dwell only on his rank amateur days, rather than the era in which he created record television ratings and was known in every UK household – including the Royal household and both households of Parliament!

So I prepared to do my bit and talk about the 'fun' I had teaching Michael (as he was back then) microphone techniques with the long handle of my mother's Ewbank carpet sweeper, showing him how to use it to change the size of the people he was impersonating.

One of the most popular shows of that era, running from 1962-1974, was Ray Galton and Alan Simpson's rag-and-bone sitcom *Steptoe and Son*, starring Wilfrid Brambell and Harry H Corbett as Albert and Harold, father-and-son residents of 26a Oil Drum Lane. Michael was first to develop a brilliant comedic impression of the pair's outrageous facial and physical characteristics, but he couldn't get their difference in height and stature right.

The Ewbank created a perfect 'reference'. By speaking 'up' to it on one side and then quickly moving to the other to speak 'down', both impressions gained an additional element. This was just one of many 'tricks' I passed on to the enthusiastic ears of this very strange young man who seemed a long way from the world of showbiz. I'd no idea that he would become a star, but recognised extraordinary talent.

Fast forward to 2023 and I was driven to a house in Bredbury, Stockport, where I met David Howard, Rik Hall and crew, complete with lights, cameras, drones and researchers. I felt rather foolish getting out of the taxi clutching a carpet sweeper, until seeing that David was visibly surprised and delighted by this unexpected prop. My job was to welcome Mike's daughters, Charlotte and Clare, back to 'Yarwood Towers' and give them a demonstration of mic and size-changing techniques at the Ewbank Academy of Performing Arts.

I think I surprised everyone by admitting I wasn't that impressed with 'impressionists'. There were already more than enough and all doing the same characters... Ken Dodd ... Tommy Cooper ... Harry Worth ... Arthur Askey and so on, much of a muchness. What had so impressed me about Michael was his ability with ordinary people. He had an uncanny way of spotting mannerisms so small that even the individual wasn't aware of them before he honed in and blew them out of all proportion, much like a Gerald Scarfe cartoon.

Mike, a rare talent, had thoroughly entertained the customers in the tailors shop where he worked. They had a great time, but bought nothing! Thankfully, as it turned out, his boss did not appreciate his cruelly observant take on him, so needless to say he was fired.

The filming of the documentary went well. I enjoyed the warm company of Charlotte and Clare, especially as they remembered me from *This Is Your Life*, some forty years earlier. We even found time to record a selfie on Charlotte's phone to talk to Mike and remind him what a cruel impression he did of me, my northern accent and my pronunciation of the word 'funny'. The whole experience was indeed a celebration and I knew Mike would blush like a girl scout, but thoroughly enjoy the fun we all had in his old house.

Then, on 8 September 2023, came the announcement that Mike Yarwood had passed away. This news stopped me in my tracks. I was surprised to discover he was actually three months younger than me. I remembered all the good things about our working together.

Before coming to Thames, Mike really was a huge star on the BBC with many top rating series and Christmas specials to his name, on a par with Morecambe and Wise who, a couple of years before, had made the same cross-channel journey. So why, you may ask, was his use of a producer/director other than myself so personally upsetting?

Well, put simply, Mike Yarwood became a star in his own right, but not without an enormous amount of unpaid time and dedication from yours truly at a time before Mike had even considered a career in showbusiness. He says as much in his autobiography *And This Is Me!* (Jupiter, 1974) in which his parents recollect how I coached him from nervy shop assistant to *Sunday Night at the London Palladium*.

So there we were in 1981: Mike, a megastar moving from BBC to ITV, and me, having hoped, in fact assumed, that in the unlikely event such a thing occurred he'd choose me to help make the show, conceited enough to think I might get a phone call from Philip Jones.

My favourite maxim has always been 'assumption is the mother of all fuck-ups,' a view whose accuracy has never failed. But, do you know what? Who knows? Perhaps Mike did ask for me. Or maybe Philip had innocently promised it to someone else, not knowing of our earlier connection. Why would he? Was Philip misquoted re the BAFTA situation? I'll never know. However, someone who'll remain nameless wrote this to me recently: 'By the time Mike Yarwood came to Thames from the BBC, his sparkle had all but gone. If you had produced that series you may well have been credited for giving him a start, but also blamed for killing his career off altogether.'

There really is no business like showbusiness!

And now this extraordinarily talented entertainer is no longer with us, I will never know the truth about such a massive moment of disappointment in my life.

What I am sure about, however, is that if all those biblical stories about an afterlife are true, by the time you are reading this Mike will have perfected a caricature of the Big Man himself and no doubt be working on all the supporting characters in both books of the Bible.

With or without a Ewbank carpet sweeper.

3.
Three Creatures

LOOKING back, I realise that some of my most enjoyable working moments came when I was part of a team, albeit as the director. As we've seen, this was certainly the situation during the Seventies, when I directed approximately 150 episodes of *This Is Your Life*.

It was a strange animal in many ways. The more I learnt about the nature of the show and how it was protected and nurtured by presenter Eamonn Andrews, the more fascinating it became. One thing that stuck out from day one was that it carried no passengers. Everyone on the payroll was responsible for its outcome. It was not possible to shirk work or hide away; a kind of professional epiphany.

Up to this point, I had been bouncing around various senior directors, observing them in action and attempting to learn a craft that appeared less and less attainable the longer I studied it. As a member of the camera crew, or more widely the studio crew, I learned to take responsibility for my behaviour and actions. It would have been career suicide to attempt to deny being guilty of any misdemeanour because it was all so clearly visible.

Here I was, a brand new programme director in the company of some of the most charismatic household names, leading producers and directors who were feared and revered by most, if not all, studio crews. The very idea of a 'cock-up' was never considered. However, from my newly-privileged position of being able to watch their every move and observe their conversations, arguments and moments of mind-blowing creativity, I soon discovered that they did indeed make mistakes. The reality was that they had acquired certain skills that enabled them to camouflage their guilt by reframing it as a moment of creativity: i.e 'You can't be sure it will float until you throw it into the water.'

This 'asbestos' philosophy became another skill I had to master pretty quickly if I was going to survive as any sort of director facing studio crews and performers. Looking back, I reckon the key lesson I took from established directors was as follows: When working in new surroundings with new crews, the first couple of hours on the first day of studio rehearsals are spent by the entire studio staff finding out just how big a fake, you (the director) are!

The best example of this strange 'auditioning' phenomenon happened in 1972, when I arrived in the Fuji television studios in Tokyo about to direct an episode of *Opportunity Knocks* in Japanese.

Apart from anything else, there was a major language problem – I didn't speak one word of Japanese. I had an interpreter, but this splendid gentleman, Joe Miyasaki, was there to interpret words, not emotions or feelings. Words by themselves can be icy, and can create a barrier between two such fundamentally different cultures.

Joe and I tried to communicate with the wholly Japanese crew and it was evident we were being 'blanked' by a bunch of technicians who couldn't understand why one of their own wasn't directing this most prestigious show. I tried for some glimmer of co-operation but it wasn't to be. I became angry, but knew that if I allowed my anger to get the better of me the entire production could be ruined beyond repair. I suddenly noticed that two of the cameras in this alien studio were mounted on 'dollies', wheeled devices used to produce moving images either away from or towards a subject. I knew them inside-out from my days on the camera crew in Didsbury, Manchester, an era that here felt a million light-years away! Dollies were known as 'Vinten Pedestals', cleverly designed for the TV and Film industry.

One camera operator was particularly rude to me (via actions and gestures I quite wrongly 'decoded' at the time), but a slanging match was quite impossible via an interpreter. Seeing red, I walked up to his camera and depressed a large metal button on the base of the dolly with my foot while grabbing the steering ring and revolving it through 90°, effectively disabling the thing, gave its questionable operator the international two-finger sign and strode off.

To my sheer delight, instead of silence, there was applause from the entire crew who now recognised that this particular director had spent some time studying the Vinten Pedestal. Only someone who knew every aspect of this piece of equipment would know how to disable it so efficiently and quickly.

I had passed my audition! The rehearsal schedule kicked in and we proceeded to make a very unique television programme.

However, there were other bizarre obstacles for me to navigate before I could eventually relax. The first of them being what was, in every sense, a control room. In the UK, and I suspect most places outside Japan, there is nothing strange about a studio having one of those. But this one appeared to control every studio in the entire Fuji complex! It was vast, the noise deafening, primarily due to the cacophony of sound coming from the twenty or thirty people seated around the periphery, all oblivious to one another while yelling at their own particular bank of monitors.

As I attempted to get to grips with this scene I swiftly began to identify – from pictures on the monitors – each individual control area around this master nerve centre: 'News', 'Sport', 'Weather', two or three different types of 'Drama' and at least four different 'Music' shows. And finally, a row of blank monitors dedicated to my studio.

The moment I donned a pair of headphones the room became silent to me and, once I sat in the director's chair, I became oblivious too to the ongoing mayhem at my back.

My PA at the time, Bridget Moore, was very experienced in the role and had travelled with us from the UK. I'd come to see her as a person fazed by very little. There were very few things Brigette had not seen or done in the television industry, yet even she was dumbfounded by this set-up, especially on learning that the film we had previously shot at the Osaka World Fair (destined to be 'rolled in' to our final programme) was ready for her to roll whenever she liked. However, through excellent interpreter Joe, Brigette then learned that the pictures were on one machine and the sound, should she require it, was on another. They hadn't been 'married' as we hadn't specified they should be and now it was far too late for it to happen. To this day I am in awe of Bridget for coping with this challenge and so many others during her complex contribution to the show.

As for myself, restricted by having to wear 'cans', it soon became obvious that Joe's spoken interpreting services were going to be futile. He did, however, offer a suggestion that enabled me to direct this programme using the Japanese language.

Joe Miyasaki was a gentleman, orphaned as a tiny baby in 1945 during the annihilation caused by the nuclear attacks on Hiroshima and Nagasaki and subsequently raised by an American family in New Orleans. They were determined that his original culture would be maintained and, as a result, he was educated at the best Japanese college in America. So Joe had complete command of the language BUT as spoken by the Japanese elite. His accent and choice of words were that of highly educated nobility, which meant that every time he spoke in his native tongue those listening straightened their backs and took notice. He was a gift that kept giving. To this day, I doubt whether our Japanese experience would ever have happened had it not been for the extraordinary contribution made by this great man.

Joe already had experience of television production, which is why my London Agent, David Wilkinson of the Noel Gay agency, had organised for him to be our interpreter and guide. He had noticed that, actually, just a few key words of command were used during the making of a TV show. Talkback was not conversational, but a series of one-word précised commands that seemed to be just about the same in America and Japan (so why not the UK and Japan?).

These commands were the numbers one to ten followed by some technical terms: standby ... tighten ... loosen ... crab ... left ... right ... headroom ... push in ... pull out. There were also words to do with pleasantries or courtesy, such as thank you ... please ... nice ... and well done, about thirty words in total to help survive any television control room situation. Joe cleverly identified these utilities and had arranged the construction of a 'phonetic idiot board', to be placed above the bank of Japanese monitors for Brigette and myself. It didn't take too long before we had both mastered the use of this system, much to the delight of a somewhat bewildered studio crew.

1= ICHI	STANDBY= TAIKI SURU
2= NEE	TIGHTEN= SHIMERU
3= SAN	LOSEN= MAKETA
	CRAB= KANI
4= SHI	LEFT= HIDARI
5= GO	RIGHT= TADASHI
6= ROKU	PUSH IN= OSHIKOMU
7= SEBUN	PULL OUT=HIKIDASU
8= EIGHT	THANK YOU= ARIGATO ZAIMASU
	PLEASE= ONEGAISHIMASU
9= KYU	NICE= NIC
10= JU	WELL DONE= SUBARASHI

So, having made some headway in communication and, with Joe's help, explaining what *Opportunity Knocks* was all about and how popular our star host Hughie Green was to the British viewers, it was time to tackle another significant element – the show's music.

Before we flew to Tokyo our musical director, Bob Sharples, had for weeks been his usual nauseating self. He explained in graphic detail (and at every opportunity) that music was international and that he, unlike me, could prepare 100 per cent while still in the UK. Bob hadn't endeared himself to the small group of arrangers who, every week for years, had transformed contestants' tatty piano copy (which adequately served a local three-piece band) into a seventeen-piece arrangement for one of the most versatile orchestras in the country. These were good little earners because the chosen arranger could charge a rate based on 'per bar of music'.

But now, as this Japanese trip was the first of many exciting forays into the unknown, Bob decided that he, and he alone, would write them. Furthermore, each musician would have their 'part' written by hand, in Indian ink. Bob was very keen that each sheet of music would be regarded by the Japanese musicians as a masterpiece, thereby ensuring that they would never ever forget the great Bob Sharples. He signed each sheet personally, again in Indian ink.

If the name Bob Sharples is new to you I must explain that, by the 1970s, this Bury-born conductor, composer and bandleader had somehow manoeuvred himself into position as virtually the only musical director at ABC TV/Thames. It was much later in company history that other musical directors like Ronnie Aldrich and Geoff Love were employed. Bob was famed for supplying orchestral music for light entertainment variety shows. He even had a pseudonym, 'Robert Earley', under which he also wrote TV drama themes for such series as *The Sweeney* and *Public Eye*. Due to his powerful position at Thames, he didn't waste time being diplomatic and, as a result, wasn't particularly popular amongst his fellow musicians.

Take one incident during an *Opportunity Knocks* band-call. They were playing a funky arrangement (by Bernard Ebbinghouse) of the Average White Band's newly charted number 'Pick Up the Pieces' conducted by Bob. It was always good to offer modern music to a speciality act who, for years, had grown used to putting up with whatever the local church hall organist knew by heart!

Because of the strict tempo of this piece, the band was 'following' the drummer's rhythm. He was a character called Art Morgan who had a wicked sense of humour. Somewhere in the middle of 'Pick Up the Pieces', for reasons known only to himself, Art randomly hit the drums in no particular order and no particular tempo. Naturally, the band fell apart behind this 'fold-up'.

Bob Sharples, stunned by this act of rebellion, asked what the hell was going on. Art stood up and said: 'Bob, will you do us a favour?' Bob replied: 'Anything for you, Art. What can I do?' Quick as a flash the drummer responded: 'Will you please stop waving that white thing around ... we're finding it very distracting down here!'

Bob stormed off and the band went into an overdue coffee break. I just loved Art's use of the word 'distracting!'

I seem to have strayed away from Japan, don't I? Never mind. I felt it important that you should meet Bob Sharples! So back we go to our encounter with BS and his hand-picked Japanese Orchestra

A front view of the old ABC TV studios in Manchester, *above*. The view, *right*, is from the rear and shows the height of the 'flys' and 'wing space' above the revolving stage area. The name Capitol was replaced by ABC TV in the 1950s.

Studio One control room at ABC. Ted Kotcheff directs a live *Armchair Theatre*. Ted went on to direct *Rambo* and other Hollywood blockbusters. *Above left*, Sydney Newman, the man who introduced live drama and *Armchair Theatre* to British television.

The ABC TV Didsbury studio stage crew enjoy a pint in the late 1950s.

On the set of *A Night Out* in 1960, *right*. Harold Pinter is third from right with Philip Saville and Arthur Lowe.

Gene Vincent does his thing in Jack Good's Saturday night show *Boy Meets Girls*, starring Marty Wilde, the Vernons Girls and other stars of the day. Made in Studio One, Royston was part of the crew as it ran from September 1959 to February 1960.

The making of *Buckaroo* starring Tessie O'Shea and Lionel Blair at ABC Didsbury in 1959.

Diddy David Hamilton's birthday with, *clockwise from left*, Ray Fell, Bob Sharples, Roy, Freddie Garrity and *Coronation Street*'s 'Voice of Granada', actor Bernard Youens, aka Stan Ogden.

Rolling Stone Mick Jagger, *left*, most definitely NOT being told off by Royston Mayoh in February 1967.

Roy talking to guest Marty Feldman, *right*, during the making of Tyne Tees's *The Stuart Henry Speakeasy*, 1969.

Briefing for *Opportunity Knocks* in 1970. *Left to right*: Royston Mayoh; programme associate (and sister of Dame Alicia Markova) Doris Barry; programme associate Len Marten; Hughie Green; ace camera crew Dave 'Rocket' Barber, John Darnell, Peter Coombs, Bob Bierman, Chas Watts (dark hair almost totally hidden by camera) and John White Jones (sitting on crane).

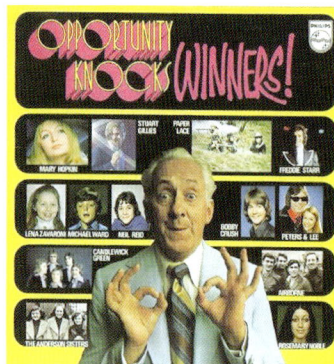

Above left: An invite to apply for *Opportunity Knocks,* following which an audition awaited with Roy, Doris and Hughie, *below*. There was no one on television quite like Hughie Green, pictured on a record album cover, *above right*, and hosting in Tokyo, *left*.

Roy and Milo Lewis, *above*, with a quintet of Grumbleweeds

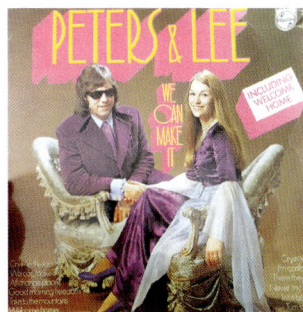

An *Opportunity Knocks* voting slip, *right*. Success turned acts like Peters & Lee into big stars

'Opportunity Knocks' Made Them . . . .

"OPPORTUNITY KNOCKS"

Fill in this form and place in box at bottom of gangway

I VOTE FOR

Few TV performers knew how to work an audience quite like Hughie, *above*, a much misunderstood man. In the background of the shot, *right*, is prop man Wilf.

Production Team.
Thames Television

Royston Mayoh
(Producer / Director)

Bobby Chapman
(Production
Assistant)

Barbara Dudley-Evans
(Production
Assistant)

DAVID NIXON

George Martin
(Everything to everyone else)

Aileen Vernon
(Stage Manager)

Nigel Cooke
(Floor Manager)

Ali Bongo
(Everything to Everyone)

Michael Minas
(Designer)

THE DAVID NIXON SHOW

Roy and Maurice Leonard with John Wayne, *above,* and Kirk Douglas, *below,* filming Patricia Neal's *This Is Your Life.*

Right: David Nixon

Above: Roy in *David Nixon Show* warm-up mode.
Left: Roy's running order for floor manager Pat Vance.

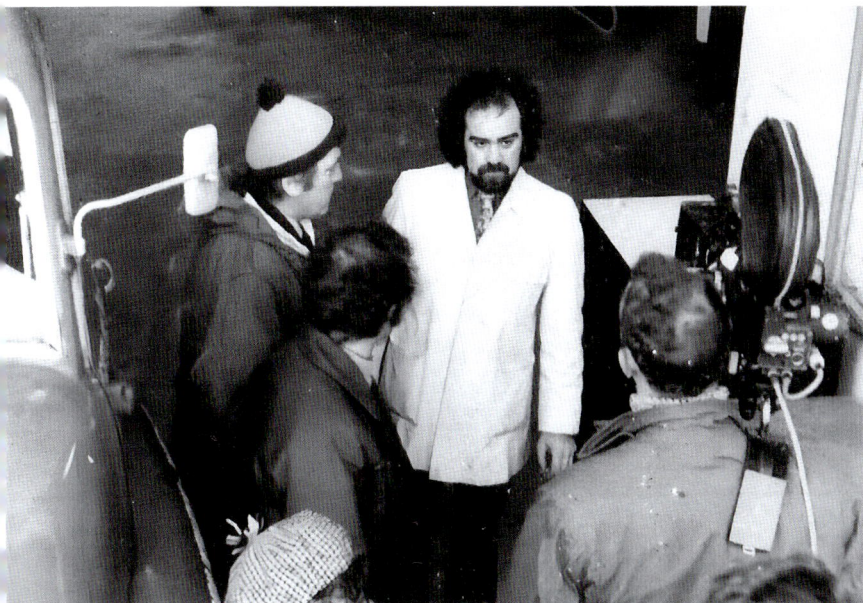

Above: The making of an episode of *This Is Your Life* in February 1972 when it was decided to surprise Hughie Green, who piloted his own plane. Host Eamonn Andrews pretended to be a disgruntled lorry driver carrying fuel to Green's Cessna 365 aeroplane.

Below left: A nice moment during rehearsals for *The Tommy Cooper Show*, in the papers.
Below right: Roy relaxes in the Thames TV bar with Maxton G. Beesley and Doris Barry.

Not like that!....Like that!

At least we think that's what producer Roy Mayoh must be trying to say at rehearsals for the new series of Tommy Cooper specials. Roy looks a little worried when Tommy Godfrey tries out his mallet-over-the-bonce trick in the studio. But look at Tommy Cooper – he's delighted. He's obviously just thought of that gag of his . . . My friend had a touch of water on the knee – so I gave him a tap on the head! Ba-Boom!

OPPORTUNITY KNOCKED

Above: As this picture montage clearly shows, Hughie Green helped to launch the careers of many future TV favourites.

Right: Hughie during his days as a childhood star.

Royston Mayoh

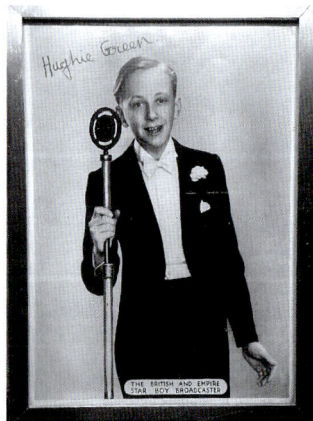

made up of the finest musicians to be found in that part of the world. It didn't go well.

Bob had numbered the pieces and been sure to place the music on the correct stands in the right order. He mounted his podium, did some weird oriental genuflection to the orchestra, picked up his baton and out-stretched his arms (a signal to any orchestra to pick up their instruments in readiness). He then loudly proclaimed 'four bars for nothing' and promptly counted his 'four bars for nothing' into fresh air, followed by a definite thrust indicating 'play'. Some of them did, some of them didn't. A disaster. Bob smiled, glared around the Japanese orchestra and tried again. This time a few more joined in, but not enough to constitute a 'tune'.

Joe Miyasaki promptly offered the help Bob needed, reluctantly accepted. After much chatter it transpired that the notation in Japan was different to that in Europe. Bob was reluctant to accept this until Joe produced a magnificently written Japanese score. All bets were off as Bob's face turned red. One of those irritating types who find it difficult to be wrong about anything, had he not been so talented he would never have got away with his annoying peccadillos.

Joe explained that sustained notes, staccato notes and grace notes were marked differently on a sheet of Japanese music and that there were many other anomalies as well. So much for Bob's assertion that music was an international language.

Trying to emulate Joe's 'idiot board' solution for Bridget and me, Bob asked for – and got – a chalkboard mounted on an easel. Using Joe in his official role of interpreter, Bob then attempted to 'teach' these distinguished musicians the European notation! The leader of the brass section was so angry at this act of British conceit that he threw his trumpet at the board and stormed out. It took the studio plumber a good ten minutes to remove the mouthpiece from the main body of the instrument before it was ready to be played again.

I tried to intervene, but by now Bob was grey with anger and determined to win this orchestra and its leader, the man with the broken trumpet, over. So I left him to it. After an official delegation from the band demanding an obscene amount of overtime, music was eventually forthcoming and, not so surprisingly, it was better than first class. The great Bob Sharples, meanwhile, never spoke of his Japanese experience again.

IT was some years before I encountered the Japanese culture again, during a series of rock shows made in London's Riverside Studios at 5.00pm and beamed live to Tokyo for transmission at midnight.

Each week the executive producer would telephone our London office with a list of people and bands we should try to secure for the following show. If a record company was promoting a new single or album they would bend over backwards to gain visibility in such an important marketplace, so these were easy to secure. The rest were a little harder.

One such request came in for a group called Three Creatures. We began our search for a band that none of us had ever heard of, but because our Tokyo-based executive producer had a firm grip on the European music scene it meant we had to try a little harder to locate them as soon as we could. We extended our research, but still with no luck. It looked like we would have to admit our inadequacy for the first time and that we had failed. At last he filled in a few blanks and Three Creatures emerged. It was such a relief. More of that anon.

There were occasions when a simple word being misunderstood would cause all manner of disruptions. Sometimes ignorance of the most obvious ones caused the blood to boil. On one such occasion, a form of words was uttered that completely took my breath away.

It was the mid-1990s and I was directing the pilot for a series of gameshow *Spellbound* for producers Action Time and Sky One. On the first studio day we were in the vast Studio 12 at Granada in Manchester, about to welcome an executive who'd travelled from Head Office, in fact the commissioning editor, a title created by the TV industry to describe a manager in charge of the overall budget and compliance of the many requirements imposed by the regulator.

The commissioning editor also employed and negotiated fees for the leading creatives employed on the show, including me! I'd never met this person but we'd spoken many times during the preparatory stages of planning. I was looking forward to meeting 'the boss' and we were well into rehearsals by the time she arrived from London. She came into the control room and, noticing that we were in the middle of a sequence, took a seat at the back, where we had arranged coffee and sandwiches in case she was peckish after her journey. We ended the sequence and I announced a studio break to re-set and to give me time to welcome her formally. She walked up to my place at the desk and uttered words that still make me smile, but the smile camouflaged how angry I was at the time.

'How lovely to see you,' she said. 'Having only ever spoken on the phone, it's great to see you working. I'm so impressed. How is it possible for you to watch all those televisions at the same time?'

That sentence said so much about how little this person knew about an industry she was now budgeting, casting and negotiating fees for. It may have been the word 'televisions' that struck my funny-bone with such force! Or was it the idea of looking at them all at the same time? Take your pick. From that moment on I never assumed that anyone senior to myself knew better. This was an odd discovery since up to that point – in 1994 – I had always enjoyed my superiors being, well, superior.

I've always been fascinated with words and how one, placed in an odd context, can rattle your cage so violently.

One night I went to the theatre. I arrived very early, people were still coming in. I was browsing through the brochure and wondering why I'd just forked out a fiver for such a naff publication when I heard a particularly loud female American voice say 'Have you seen Mavis?' She was obviously talking – or shouting – to a friend some distance away in the Stalls. 'No!' this other American shouted in reply. 'She came in before me. I don't know where she went...'

There was silence for at least ten frames when the first American then announced with glee: 'Oh! I see her. She's sitting a few seats away from that bald guy in the scarf!' I'd already decided to edit these voices out of my consciousness and find something in the brochure worth a fiver when a lady a few seats away yelled 'Hi!' To my horror, I realised I was the bald guy in the scarf! That word, bald, had never been used before by anyone to describe me – well not to my knowledge anyway. This conversation between two strangers ruined my evening. Now all I could think about was the price of the brochure and where could I buy a hat!

AS in any industry, television and theatre have their own unique terminologies and, sometimes, peculiar usage of otherwise ordinary words. However, within both there are many sub-cultures, each with their own idiosyncrasies. As a TV light entertainment director I had to cope with many of these sub-cultures, but none were so strange as the world of magic.

It's only natural to ask a magician: 'How did you do that?' But if the performer in question was stupid enough to reveal the simplicity of their method it would be a great disappointment and ruin the enjoyment of the trick forever. I have too much respect for the Magic Circle (and the many magicians still attempting to fake a living) to expose any secrets here. The use of the word 'fake' is intentional and will be enjoyed by anybody involved in the 'magic' industry.

Throughout my TV career I have never been far away from a magician, although my IMDb entry lists only two such television series: *The David Nixon Show* and *The Mind of David Berglas*. These though are two of the most influential names in the genre. Of course, many UK viewers will be more familiar with Paul Daniels or Steven Frayne (Dynamo). Paul began his career on one of my *Opportunity Knocks* shows, but he actually became 'a name' after appearing on a David Nixon show I did some years later.

My great friend Kenneth Earle (once of musical comedy double act Earl and Vaughan) was at the beginning of his latter career as an agent and asked if I knew of a chap called Paul Daniels. Paul had described himself as an 'Unusualist' (a word that's hard to forget). Kenny explained that Daniels was enormous in the north of England (mainly thanks to Johnnie Hamp at Granada TV), but that he was eager to spread his wings and become known throughout the UK. *The David Nixon Show* was perfect because it was a network show watched by the entire 'magic' community, including agents booking acts in and around Europe. I invited Paul to audition for David and our unbelievably knowledgable programme associate, Ali Bongo. I told Kenny there wasn't an illusion or trick that David and Ali hadn't seen (if not its original inventors). Kenny took this on board and reported back to Paul.

The audition was set for after a show, its audience invited to stay for an extra treat. Paul asked for three chairs and nothing more. He asked David to pick three members of the audience to come and sit on these very ordinary chairs. What followed blew everyone's minds.

The three participants were jumping out of their seats swearing they had felt a shock. Meanwhile, Paul was faking an introduction to a 'proper', although non-existent, trick while the random activity on the chairs kept interrupting him. It was a remarkable illusion that Paul repeated many times during his own show and for which there is still no formal explanation (although I bet Debbie McGee knows).

After David Nixon tragically died in 1978, Ali Bongo and George Martin (backbone of *The David Nixon Show*) joined Paul to make his show, undeniably the best on TV. At time of writing, it still is!

In the world of magic I had to sit through hours of people talking about things such as the Elmsley Count, the French Drop, a Mercury Fold, a Monte, the Rough & Smooth, a Sphinx, a Servante, a Raven, a Bentz, a Convincer, a Force, a Gimmick and a Lapping! These were/are some basic magic principles, the bricks and mortar of any trick that anyone can understand. However, a true magician will mix them up, swap from one to another without notice, and engage the patter (a more meaningful word than script) in order to misdirect the observer into thinking something else altogether is happening.

There is no instruction book for this heady mixture of skills, just trial and error and an inordinate amount of practise, practise and practise, one reason I remain in total awe of magicians, conjurers, illusionists and ventriloquists. When done properly, the latter are the greatest illusionists of them all, but none were so wondrous as the late Ray Alan (and Lord Charles).

Incidentally, if you asked me to describe any of the 'principles' above I'm not sure I could. They were told to me by Ali Bongo and I am still convinced it was total gibberish to shut me up. Nothing is ever as it seems when you are working with magicians!

'Nothing is impossible' was the phrase used when I produced *The*

Mind of David Berglas, a Channel 4 series in 1986. David was not just a big star in the UK, but revered globally as a successful and unique illusionist. He'd been the (magical) consultant on numerous James Bond movies and was regarded with awe by many 'big names'. Such was his reputation and the power of magic that it wasn't overly difficult for my co-producer Christine Williams to book an array of impressive guests ... Omar Sharif ... Christopher Lee ... Ingrid Pitt ... Arlene Phillips ... Peter Cook ... Ian Carmichael ... Max Bygraves ... Kid Jensen ... Willie Rushton. It was an unlikely list for any show, but particularly one made in Newcastle upon Tyne.

The series was a success for Tyne Tees and Channel 4 in terms of ratings and critical acclaim, partly because it was a magic show like no other. It was set in a castle (its studio set brilliantly designed by then head of design for Tyne Tees, Ash Wilkinson). Its opening titles consisted of an exterior shot of the magnificent Bamburgh Castle in Northumberland, shot during a particularly stormy night. The whole thing had an atmosphere of mysterious grandeur. David Berglas had a beautiful aura of tormented mystery about him.

The wardrobe policy was dinner suits or cocktail dresses for all guests. We successfully created an atmosphere of late-night, post-dinner relaxed-yet-thoughtful chat that involved some outstanding illusions created by David and previously unseen on British TV. The main set was a room furnished with luxurious Chesterfield sofas and chairs, plus a magnificent leather desk and matching captain's chairs.

The castle's mysterious alcoves and entrances were used to transit effectively into alternative studio set-ups pre-recorded in front of an audience of some two hundred and fifty people.

The sort of illusions David Berglas produced were truly unique. For example, he'd randomly select fifteen audience members. As each one arrived on set he'd man-handle them into a long row. David would start at one end and ask each person when their birthday was (date, not year). After six or seven answers, it slowly dawned on the audience that he had arranged these individuals in an accurate date order. The applause started around number six and got louder as David progressed. By the end there was a standing ovation as David asked the fifteen to return to their seats in the audience.

In another odd and rather worrying illusion, David invited two members of the medical profession from the audience to join him. He removed his jacket, rolled up his sleeves and asked the volunteers to grab a wrist each and take his pulse. They did this and, of course, their readings were the same. David then asked them to do it again while beating its rhythm with their other hand so the audience could also know David's pulse rate. After a few seconds the pulse in one arm slowed... and then stopped completely. Then the pulse in the other arm stopped. That pulse soon resumed but now his arms were alternating beats. Eventually the pulses returned to normal. David thanked the medicos for their assistance and they returned to their seats, accompanied by tumultuous applause.

Such things hadn't been seen on British television before and the final illusion always involved the special guest. With Omar Sharif, it involved a roulette table. Inevitably, David was able to predict the unpredictable. The series was a sheer joy to work on and I was always disappointed it hadn't been sold overseas or repeated a few times. That series of six was glorious to produce and direct and there was no need for me to know how the illusions were done. It was far better to be just as astounded as the viewers at home. After all, it's the TV director's job to represent their eyes and ears.

ONE of the great television entertainment producer/directors of all time was Ernest Maxin, probably best known nowadays for his involvement with Morecambe and Wise. I only ever worked with or for Ernest in my capacity as a camera operator for ABC TV, in Didsbury. He earned and enjoyed total respect from the entire staff, not just for his technical knowledge, but mostly for his charismatic personality and ability to see the funny side of himself.

Following those early ABC days in the late-1950s I became close friends with Ernest's younger brother, Gerry. We often reminded ourselves of a series entitled *The Ernest Maxin Show,* in which Ernest was not only the show's *raison d'être* but, with the designer and lighting director, initiated its unique backdrop. As director, Ernest was responsible for plotting camera moves and audio requirements necessary to turn a theatrical performance into a television show. He also chose to do his own warm-up prior to the 'as live' tele-recording. This extraordinary man made an entrance dancing from the control room to music written by himself! He tap-danced his way towards the audience in pristine top hat, white tie and tails. He was joined by numerous glamorous dancers in leotards and tall feathers, while accompanied by a thirty-two piece orchestra. He then performed a beautifully staged and choreographed routine before arriving at a solitary stand-mic to sing the last chorus, capped by a sustained 'top C' that brought tumultuous applause from an utterly bewildered audience.

After which, he would allow their clapping to fade to an uneasy silence, glare at two or three sections of the audience and, in a deep dramatic voice, address them directly. 'I am very displeased with this evening's entertainment,' he'd begin. 'You will have noticed on your ticket that it clearly says *The Ernest Maxin Show*. You have just met some of the Ernest Maxin Dancers performing a routine choreographed by me, Ernest Maxin, while listening to the Ernest Maxin Orchestra playing a tune also composed and arranged by yours truly. Tonight's show is produced, written and directed by myself, Ernest Maxin, and do you know what ladies and gentlemen, the first thing to go wrong and they blame me!'

The silence before the laughter and applause was magical. Sheer class! I will always believe that in the vast world of television entertainment there was only ever room for one Ernest Maxin.

I am very humbled to have worked with Ernest as a cameraman. Then, some time later during my time as producer/director of *The Kenny Everett Show*, I was thrilled to receive a letter from him (through the post!) congratulating 'me' on 'my' work! I doubt whether receiving an Oscar could have been more emotional.

I often wonder what lucky star it was that entered my life twixt being a very happy cameraman and very frightened trainee director, especially when I thought about directors I had worked with like Ernest, William T Kotcheff, Philip Saville, John Llewellyn Moxey, Alvin Rakoff, Piers Haggard, Shaun O'Riordan and Voytek! These and dozens more of the world's top TV drama directors had set a standard by their sheer weight of 'know-how', a standard that, while a cameraman, was a joy to be part of. But as a trainee director it was a very daunting prospect.

My life in that role began with a very strange interview board. It was so strange that by the time I'd walked back from interview room to my fellow camera operator crew room I was unable to remember anything about the questions they'd asked or what answers I'd given. I do remember that after the formal part was over a rugged time-worn old chap called Bernard Greenhead said to me, with an odd air of delight, that should I be successful in my application for this most important post I would be given eighteen months intensive training. If during that training or indeed after training ABC TV did not think that I was up to the standard required, I would not be able to return to my job on cameras. Before leaving the interview room I was made to sign a document to this effect.

Now the more cynical of my friends on the camera crew pointed out that this was a novel way of handing in my notice. They pointed out that I only need do a couple of weeks shadowing a proper director to be told: 'Sorry, you don't fit in. Bye bye!' This observation didn't faze me as the chances of my actually being offered the post of trainee director seemed very unlikely because all knew for certain that a charismatic young designer, already popular with the bigwigs, was going to fill the vacancy. It was even suggested it had been created especially for him. Such was the certainty, he'd already had a celebratory piss-up with the scenes and props crews weeks earlier!

So, imagine my heady cocktail of joy, confusion, fear, inadequacy, embarrassment, delight, happiness and wonderment upon being told by the controller of programmes (all programmes) at ABC, Mr Brian Tesler, that I had been successful in my application and would start immediately.

This meant many things. I was no longer a camera operator and never would be again. I was no longer 'staff' (which had meant income tax being done for you, paid holidays, sick pay and three weeks' notice if they wished to fire you – three weeks that wouldn't start until a lengthy union procedure had taken place, usually taking months). I was now freelance meaning, basically, I had no rights!

My lucky stars didn't desert me though. I was put with two female producer/directors, Margery Ruse and Margery Baker (aka the two Marges), from whom I learned discipline, what not to say or do, and humility. In later years the expression 'imposter syndrome' came into common usage. I was always glad my fear hadn't been given this name during my first few months as a trainee director. If it had been I might well have voluntarily visited a psychiatrist. As it was, I felt that the only way to reduce this fear was to acquire as much new knowledge as possible.

The two Marges knew me as a cameraman, so they already had an idea about who I was as a person. They were wise enough to tell me, over a pint in the Parrs Wood pub (directly opposite Didsbury studios) that they were as surprised as I was about my appointment. But they pointed out that their superiors had told them I was a good choice and worth teaching the ropes.

I thought that no amount of tutorship would result in my being competent or useful in the job. But what the two Marges were able to teach me was a need for planning, not just planning the potential effects it might have on my job but also the *effect* of planning, or conversely *not* planning, would have upon every single department involved in the complexities of programme production.

To me, the studio floor was where the entire programme was made. Everywhere else within the complex involved people engaged with administration, housekeeping, comfort or security, but not directly with the actual production. How wrong I was.

I knew about 'housekeeping' from my early student days as the part-time 'boy with the brush'. Then, with my boss Derek Pye, we had spent hours and hours mopping the studio floor to rid it of small patches of pavement, carpet, gravel paths etc, painted in emulsion around the scenery for some heady drama in the *Armchair Theatre* series. Part of my job then took me into hidden places in the studio, like a mysterious department called CTR (control transmission room). This was only accessible via an anonymous door halfway up the stairs to what used to be the circle when the place had been a cinema. In here, dozens of techie types pored over a vast variety of screens. There were five or six film projectors seemingly pointing nowhere and, as each remotely started up, someone would hurriedly change the film on the one that had just stopped. It was always busy and nobody seemed to have time to chat as I served them a variety of buns, sandwiches, tea and coffee. They simply didn't have the time to walk down to the canteen to take a break.

I'd sometimes been required to sweep the car park or, more often, the reserved parking place at the front of the building right next to the entrance. This was for the Rolls Royce Silver Shadow belonging to Mr Gerry Mitchell, general manager of the complex. I hadn't equated any of this manual labour with any of the artistic processes needed to make a programme until the two Marges had begun their tutelage of me! It was these remarkable ladies who introduced me to the distribution list and the crucial importance of displaying it in alphabetical order so nobody felt they had predominance.

This was well before computers, internet, wifi, email and mobile phones. To send a memo to a couple of dozen people involved making a couple of dozen copies (via a 'skin' on a Roneo machine) and posting them in the internal mail. It usually took a day. The memos were put into well-worn brown envelopes marked with a long list of people who'd previously received something else in it. All names were crossed out but could make for very interesting reading.

The two Marges taught me the fundamentals and during my long career I'd often go on to notice how many people in reasonably senior positions had obviously never had the benefit of this basic insight into the rudiments of TV production.

The lesson is simple. There is no 'i' in 'team', and a team includes everyone. The word 'everyone' meant everyone within the walls of the studio complex. If a crew had a bad experience in the canteen (with food or service) it could have an impact on their patience, concentration or general mood, which could then have an impact on their efficiency doing the job. The whole production could suffer! The same tumble-up effect could start with security, the receptionist or even the call-boy (call-boy being the name of a job borrowed from the theatre denoting a youngster employed to knock on the dressing room doors of performers and call them when needed).

These basic lessons in awareness and consideration for everyone stayed with me and afforded me many lovely memories of people who had traditionally been ignored. 'Every member of the studio floor has a moment in which their action could destroy the show if they are not doing their job properly!' I can hear it now.

These early lessons from the two Marges were added to those learned during my seven years on the studio floor as a cameraman, and all of them served me well. However there are one or two that are not doing me any favours while I write this book.

One such lesson goes back to my student days when my first boss, Derek Pye, took me to one side. 'You are going to rub shoulders with a lot of famous people,' he said. 'It is a firing offence to ever ask any of them for an autograph. And as for having a photo taken with them, well that is totally out of the question now and forever. It is the sign of an amateur, because now you are working among stars who are also working. You must never behave like a punter.'

That first lesson from Derek made me feel, for the first time, like a professional and it's stuck with me for fifty-plus years. Which is why this book is not plastered with photos of me and any number of stars beaming a forced smile and fake cuddle to camera. I could never bring myself to do it. That said, it is a shame that I don't have an album of me with all the stars I've enjoyed working with since my debut as a TV director in 1963 on the *NME* poll winners award concert from Wembley Stadium.

There were no books dealing with working in an ever-changing British studio environment, although American communications consultant Rudy Bretz's book about camera operation, *Techniques of Television Production*, taught me a lot of stuff that came in very handy early on. It gave clues about communicating without words, what headroom we were using, what lens (focal point and aperture), and what size of shot we were offering to the director. The gestures seemed very clumsy to us, though, so as early as the 1960s we (the camera crew) were toying with the idea of using BSL (British Sign Language) for silent communication in and around the studio floor. That notion never materialised, especially since radio cans soon became a reality, meaning that everyone wore a set and could silently communicate with ease. It would have been useful to have mastered

BSL and I regretted not learning it, particularly as, later in life, I found myself lecturing a class of twenty or so profoundly deaf students. Proficiency in BSL would have made the job so much more enjoyable had I been able to communicate using their language.

Although I was prevented from doing the job of directing during my training, an exclusively observational period, it seemed to be going well. I got a rude awakening, therefore, when I was passed to an extraordinary producer/director by the name of Milo Lewis who, from day one, sat me in the centre seat and asked me to describe what was in front of me.

It sounds far-fetched but every director will tell you the same... the first time you sit in that centre seat is the moment you are aware of the responsibility you have taken on board; it's a perfect mix of excitement and fear. This is the moment when every brand new TV director experiences that aforementioned 'imposter syndrome', together with a tsunami of cold sweat.

Milo threw me in at the deep end by having me plot some music numbers on paper. He demanded that I describe the entire song on a single page of A4 and challenged me to invent a treatment I could use for cameras, lighting, stage management and post production.

He asked me to do this while making it quite clear that such a document didn't already exist. Milo had bothered to find out about me and spotted early on that my love of both the bizarre, the mathematical and the ordered-form might well be enough to spur me on to inventing such a document. It's a format I have used ever since. The initial horror on people's faces is soon replaced by delight as they realise what a valuable tool it is – and there is no need to be able to read music.

Music is normally dealt with by utilising a musical score of sheet music. If the director or vision mixer cannot read it then a musical associate is employed to read the score and pre-warn the director about whatever instrument is coming up, so he or she can identify and cut to it at the appropriate moment. It's clumsy and not much fun. The purpose of my document was to make it enjoyable and keep control of the various shots used, especially as a good eighty per cent of the studio floor technicians couldn't tell a bass from a treble clef.

Training over and armed with a whole new viewpoint about priorities, communication and language of television production from a director's point of view, I suddenly found myself as assistant director to the already legendary Mark Stuart.

He'd been planning a massive outside broadcast from the Empire Pool, Wembley, and explained that my job was to create and make a 45-second title sequence for the event (that aforementioned *NME* poll winners award concert). I was given a budget to work with that included two full eight-hour days with a 16mm film crew including audio. There was also provision for post-production (i.e. processing, editing and finally the finished graded print), all to be rolled-in to the live transmission on the night.

After much soul searching for the brilliant scenario that would wow everybody, it dawned on me that one of the lessons I had learnt from the two Marges was always to cut the waffle and just tell the story, so that's exactly what I did. I booked a mixed bag of trendy young things who could simultaneously dance and look a million dollars. We picked a snazzy tune from our non-commercial, non-copyright library at Thames and set off to shoot a video in four parts.

Part one would be youngsters dancing in a club, interrupted by another over-excited youngster who'd just won a dozen tickets to the *NME* event. They leave the club and pile into a London black cab.

Part two would see them piling out of the cab at Baker Street tube station. The kids dance down the stairs, passing posters advertising the goings on at Wembley. A train is waiting on the platform.

Part three sees the youngsters dancing in a carriage, entertaining a bunch of smiling passengers.

Part four sees them leave the train and dance up Wembley Way, finishing on a large billboard announcing the *NME Poll Winners Award Concert*. The idea was then to mix from this to an already manic crowd within. This unique forty-five-second promo would be entirely my creation and my personal directorial debut.

Directing this ninety-minute live concert with six cameras was down to Mark Stuart, who planned to be situated around the Empire Pool. I had been studying the unbelievable complexities of that mammoth task but didn't loose any sleep over it because that was

Mark's problem – not mine! My mini-masterpiece had been edited to within one frame of its life. We'd graded it, colour balanced it and refused to run it again through any machine to avoid scratches until we transferred it onto video tape. Happily, it still looked like a grainy black and white newsreel film. I hadn't realised that 16mm reversal should never be processed to give an answer print in colour. Ah, the content still looked pretty good to me! You will still find it on YouTube under the 1966 *NME* concert, online, where you can make up your own mind.

However, if you do bother to look at this live concert, you may enjoy it a little more by knowing that it took place on May 1 and that Mark Stuart is in the director's centre chair of the spacious outside broadcast mobile control room. My job is over by now – or at least I thought it was!

The opening titles done, we are now into the concert for real with Jimmy Savile doing what we then thought he did best (40 years in the future we were to learn otherwise), ie being an irritating long yellow-haired buffoon with an irritating yodel. However, for some strange reason, he was liked by the kids simply because they'd seen him on television and he looked different.

This was no ordinary concert. In one way or another, all the best in pop music that year appeared. Headlined by The Beatles, it featured the Rolling Stones, The Who, Dusty Springfield, The Yardbirds, The Walker Brothers, Roy Orbison, The Spencer Davis Group with Steve Winwood, Three Creatures, The Shadows, Herman's Hermits and The Small Faces, all playing short sets of their current hits.

The reason it was never enshrined in mythology like other live events such as Woodstock or Live Aid was probably because of an argument at the previous year's show. Mark had already been told that neither The Beatles nor the Stones were willing to be filmed.

During planning, Mark had declared that while those two groups were on he intended to turn the cameras from the stage towards the 10,000 strong audience, for reaction shots. These could be edited into the show during the week following the concert and before transmission. If any artist didn't get the applause they deserved then they'd benefit from such insertions as were bound to occur that way.

Even so, he was livid about this legal argument the two bands were having with promoter Maurice Kinn, and hoped, right up to the start of the concert, that it would be sorted. It wasn't and this would be the last live concert The Beatles would ever play in the UK.

The concert was about four minutes in and I was sitting behind Mark watching and listening to his every move and directions when he turned around and said: 'I'm busting for a pee – jump in. I won't be a minute.' Dutifully, I did as I was told, leaping into the centre seat with a bank of monitors in front of me, which immediately became one huge de-focussed muddle of disassociated pictures showing everything going on in the arena!

I was about to go into panic mode when, in my head, I suddenly heard Milo Lewis say: 'As a Director, you are always the last to panic, never the first.' So I took a deep breath and focussed my attention on Jimmy Savile, who said: 'Now, guys and gals, here's no stranger to our charts, the first *NME* poll winner tonight singing her number four UK hit and the first of her six transatlantic Top 40 hits, 'I Only Want To Be With You'. It's Dusty Springfield...'

I realised there was a disappointing level of applause for the loud music, so changed the camera shot away from a wobbly full length shot of Savile to a wide shot of the entire stage. There was movement and I saw a picture on camera three's monitor of Dusty walking on. 'Great camera three,' I shouted, 'take three.' Vision-mixer Peter Phillips yelled 'on three' in response – and we were on our way.

Milo had taught me: 'Never hang about enjoying the shot on the transmission monitor. Instead, look for the next shot ... and then the one after that!' I was determined to make a good fist of it until Mark had relieved himself and returned to his rightful centre seat.

I was quite pleased with my work on Dusty Springfield, apart from one reaction shot of the audience who, sadly, refused to react! It flashed through my mind that Mark had already planned to edit-in audience shots from the Beatles or Stones, so I knew that I could replace this duff shot during the edit before transmission.

Anyway, Dusty finished and the concert continued with still no sign of Mark I asked the PA if we should be worried about him, but his PA said: 'No, keep your mind on his show!' I did just that through band after band, award after award, with still no sign of Mark. Eventually, I cleared a camera to the end roller caption machine, a long black card on which the names of all the contributors to the show had been painstakingly scratched with singular Letraset letters, a thing that took at least a week to compile.

And then, to my utter amazement there it was, the very last credit: DIRECTED BY MARK STUART and ROYSTON MAYOH.

Mark had been secretly planning this baptism of fire for weeks. I looked round and he was standing in the doorway of the mobile control room smoking a cigarette. 'I was watching every shot,' he said. 'If you'd started to bollocks it up I'd have been in like Flynn. Congratulations, you did a good job. Your training is over!'

It felt like receiving a knighthood; up to that point the greatest moment in my life. I can still feel the overwhelming rush of emotion.

Over the years, I've often been asked for the difference between a producer and director. The glib answer is always 'about £30,000 a year' (and if any statement was to place me in a specific decade that must surely be it). In the late 1970s and early '80s the accountants were busy saving money by merging the roles into one, namely the producer-director! The double job did attract a higher fee, but never reached the figure of one producer and one director separately.

There were occasions when I was offered such a combined role with an acceptably healthy fee, but the programme format, content, star involved, company offering the work (or combination of those) prevented me from going anywhere near it. To have accepted a P/D job for programmes I suspected were already full of anomalies and pitfalls would have been madness. Wherever these issues originated, in the end the buck would land firmly on my desk.

I always preferred the director role because it was hands-on and much more fun working with designers, lighting directors, sound supervisors, camera crews, sound engineers, props and scenes, wardrobe and make-up. The producer was mainly office-bound and required a pretty hefty organisational filing regime. It was much less fun and more managerial than I had trained for.

But back to this chapter's title, 'Three Creatures.' Having been totally flummoxed trying to identify this group (Heavy metal? Folk?

R&B? We had no clue), we plucked up the courage and asked our Japanese client to tell us a little more about them.

Fortunately, he was happy to oblige. Three Creatures, he told us, had first become known to him through hit song 'Congratulations' in 1968 and then, much later, a 1976 song called 'Devil Woman'.

Of course! The penny dropped. If your English wasn't too good, then Three Creatures *did* sound a bit like Cliff Richard(s).

4.
What's in a Name?

IN the 1960s, 1970s and 1980s, people knew my name. Not because I was famous. As I wrote earlier, eighteen million viewers regularly heard it on popular talent show *Opportunity Knocks*, as uttered week after week by its famous host Hughie Green. Anyone in the business would immediately have known, however, that Hughie did that for editorial reasons rather than out of any respect or recognition for me.

Green (as everyone called him in his absence – just plain Green) would change the subject and interrupt himself by saying something like 'Now, friends. I know our director, Royston, has a photograph he wants me to show you...' This device – there were many versions of it – allowed him to appear spontaneous. It also meant he could change the subject or foreshorten what he'd been saying at the time.

However, there was a downside to this semi-fame. My name may have been well known, but I certainly wasn't. On many occasions, people point blank refused to believe that I was '*the* Royston Mayoh' who Green seemed so deferential towards. I was a very young man for much of my time on OPNOX. I said goodbye to it in 1975, some ten years after I'd first directed the show. Come the end, I was still only 34.

I recall one occasion when the Thames company secretary invited me down to his office to go through a pile of suspect postal votes – postcards being the only way for viewers to pick their favourite and thereby determine the winner. One of Green's many catchphrases was 'Vote, vote, vote, because your vote counts,' subsequently used by every would-be impersonator, along with ... (*coughs*) 'Got a little frog there, friends, and I mean that most sincerely.'

Naturally some people thought they could cheat the system by sending in hundreds of postcards championing the same contestant. We decided that our counters would extract any dodgy ones until the final figure was totted up. Only then, supervised by the company secretary, would they determine whether these potentially rigged votes would have made any difference to the final result or not.

Occasionally the company secretary felt the need to inform the producer of a particularly brazen attempt at cheating, such as whole bundles stuffed into one large envelope (to save on postage!) ... or hundreds of identically printed ones with the same sender's name ... or even hundreds of separate votes with the same handwriting. It was really important that these improper entries were retained and correctly recorded in case of any future legal dispute. The popular press was always eager to uncover some anomaly about OPNOX, so we (Thames TV and The Hughie Green Organisation) were on full alert for any attempt to influence the result improperly.

Anyway, on this occasion the dodgy-looking votes had been held back before the winning declaration. I had no idea what was about to happen. The company secretary had an office within an office, his outer office was run like clockwork by his own personal secretary. When I entered the outer room there were other people waiting to see him. As soon as she saw me, his secretary said 'Ah, yes! He's waiting for you', opened his door and, most unusually for this very proper lady, shoved me inside, where the company secretary told me not to be alarmed or ask questions. 'Trust me!' he said. 'I'm trying something out!' He then asked me to go back to his outer office, pick up a large parcel form his secretary's desk and bring it to him. He also asked me to apologise to the other people for keeping them waiting. I did as directed. He took the package from me and asked me to wait back outside for a few moments myself. I did that too and heard his secretary say into her telephone: 'Certainly, sir', and then to the other people, 'You can go in now.'

I sat in that outer office for about five minutes, just long enough for my imagination to start working overtime. I had no idea what this was all about, particularly since it seemed far too cloak and dagger for such a usually reserved fellow. The company secretary himself then opened his door, saying: 'May I ask you to bring the other box in please.' His secretary pointed to another load of votes on the floor, hidden from general view. I now grabbed that box and walked back into his room.

There was silence as I placed this second box on a side table. 'It's been very rude of me to keep you waiting,' he told the assembled group. 'I'm sorry, but have you met this gentleman [me] before?' Nobody responded. Turning to me, he said: 'Thanks a million for bringing the boxes through, can I contact you in your office in about an hour?' I was thoroughly confused and about to ask his secretary what on earth was going on when she put a finger to her mouth in a 'keep quiet' manner. Taking the hint, I returned to the relative normality of my own office, albeit completely bewildered.

After almost exactly an hour, the company secretary rang to tell me that his visitors had been a young lady, her parents and a legal representative. They were there to make an official complaint that she, the young lady, had been made pregnant by the producer of *Opportunity Knocks* ... Royston Mayoh!

I had unwittingly taken part in an identity parade in which the visitors had been given ample time and opportunity to identify me as the man they knew by that name. They hadn't done so. Asked to describe said scoundrel, the young lady had described him as much older and shorter than myself with a North East accent.

Some months later the real culprit was located, who admitted to gaining entrance to a club in Middlesbrough by falsely using my name. Then, still calling himself Royston Mayoh, he had sexually abused this under-age young lady. I was horrified, going cold at the thought of what damage this outrage had done to her and might have brought upon me, the *Opportunity Knocks* brand and Thames Television as a whole. It was the sort of story every torrid tabloid newspaper would be itching to get their hands on – accurate or not!

At the end of that memorable day the company secretary invited me for a drink at The Anglers pub, next door to Teddington Studios. He explained that while he was quite sure she had been duped, he needed to demonstrate the truth to her, her parents and her legal representative without any shadow of doubt. I could not thank him enough for being so wise in staging this extraordinary scenario.

DURING my early years as a new TV director I met a man with the most improbable name who was to have a great influence on me. He was Billy 'Uke' Scott. No prizes for guessing what instrument this extraordinary man played. I was introduced to him by Peter Dulay, a well-established producer of variety shows (whose father, Benson Dulay, was a top-of-the-bill illusionist of yesteryear). At the time I was directing the series *Comedy Bandbox (The Autumn Years)*, beautifully produced by Peter, at ABC TV's Studio on in Didsbury.

The venue's history as an old cinema – stalls covered over and levelled out to the height of the stage, dress circle unaltered, but with original cinema seating – made it ideal for any TV show that needed the audience sufficiently separated from the studio floor to enable a proper sound balance, like Jack Good's 1960s live rock 'n' roll shows *Boy Meets Girls* and *Wham!!* for example. In *Comedy Bandbox (The Autumn Years)*, we used its original proscenium to emulate a theatre. Peter, no doubt calling on his father's influence, had gathered an array of Music Hall stars whose names were still recognised but who hadn't been seen for many years due to the arrival of pop music and a very different type of performer now wanted for television.

To me, these people were heroes. As a boy I'd heard them on the radio and seen them in films, but never dreamed I'd ever see them live or, more bizarrely, meet them in person. They seemed to live on a different planet! Purely because it gives me pleasure, I will try to list as many as I can remember, and I do urge you to learn a little more about them to understand why I was so starstruck at the time. The extraordinary talent in this wonderful show included (in alphabetical order) such legends as: Albert Modley; Anne Shelton; Arthur Askey; Arthur English; Betty Driver; Billy Dainty; Billy 'Uke' Scott; Bud Flanagan; Cardew Robinson; Chesney Allen, with the Crazy Gang; Doctor Crock and His Crackpots; Eartha Kitt; Eve Boswell; Fred Emney; Freddie Frinton; Harry Worth; Hetty King; Hylda Baker; Ida Barr; Jimmy Clitheroe; Jimmy Edwards; Jimmy James; Eli Woods and Company; Jimmy Jewel and Ben Warriss; Joyce Grenfell; Ken Dodd; Marie Lloyd Jr; Max Wall; Mike and Bernie Winters; Nat Jackley; Norman Evans; Old Mother Riley; Randolph Sutton Jr; Robb Wilton; Ronnie Ronalde; Roy Hudd; Ted Ray; Morton Fraser's Harmonica Gang; Tommy Cooper; Wee Georgie Wood; Wilson, Keppel and Betty. All of these performers appeared in one guise or another throughout 26 one-hour shows carefully – and lovingly – curated by Peter Dulay and directed by myself.

If these black and white recordings existed today they would constitute a major record of a bygone era that can never be re-visited. Yet tragically they were all incinerated, together with countless other classic TV shows of the 1950s and 1960s to make room in the 1980s for the introduction of a whole new method of management.

Due to his close connection with The Grand Order of Water Rats, Billy 'Uke' Scott was able to contact these old-timers, many of whom having retired decades earlier. Billy himself appeared on *Comedy Bandbox* performing a section from the *William Tell* overture on his ukulele, a feat that I doubt will ever be witnessed again. Peter made him our assistant producer! During this amazing period, I got to know Billy, an expert on his era and its legends, so he and I learned the television ropes at the same time. We became very close friends.

We all knew Billy was the undisputed champion of the uke – and that included George Formby. Anyway, Formby played *banjo*leles, all tuned differently so he needn't ever change his fingering for songs in different keys, just the instrument! Billy, meanwhile, was a true musician who had completely mastered the microscopic fingering required on his tiny instrument, changing key whenever he wanted.

It wasn't music that I learned from Billy, though, but a whole new way of thinking and behaving as a person. There was much more to Billy 'Uke' Scott than the name implied. I admired him and acquired a code of conduct of professional honesty and trustworthiness that has remained with me ever since.

I also discovered that Billy had spent some time in a monastery before marrying his beloved Ann, an experience that instilled him with inner peace and a calm focus I had never seen in a man before. Billy was universally admired by his peers, a proud member of The Grand Order Of Water Rats (Rats is STAR spelt backwards and that's what Billy represented), the British entertainment industry fraternity and charity formed as long ago as 1889 in The Water Rats pub, Gray's Inn Road, London. Only performers of real stature were invited into its membership. Billy was a much-valued, high-ranking member.

Sadly, when I became a divorcee in 1979, Billy and I parted ways. The whole concept of divorce was against everything Billy stood for and he found it impossible to take sides, as a result removing himself from both our lives completely. On numerous occasions I tried to reignite our friendship but alas, such was Billy's conviction that as long as I subscribed to the reality of a divorce a reunion was never going to happen. However, my story would not be complete without mentioning the gift Billy 'Uke' Scott gave me, and it's a gift that I will always value ... the removal of my imposter syndrome.

ANOTHER name I will never forget is Gerry Mitchell, general manager at ABC TV from 1956-1960, although it was years before I learned who he really was. However, before I reveal that, let me say that I owe my entire professional existence to the guy.

As a sixteen-year-old student, gainfully employed as casual 'fish and chip boy' on £1 a day, doing everything from serving coffee to sweeping the car park to acting as call-boy to the stars, I'd begun to get ambitions. Studies over, part-time work was longer good enough. I requested an interview with Gerry, hoping to go full-time.

He listened patiently to my passionate request to be a permanent fish and chip boy before explaining that it would be impossible, since the minimum age for new staff was 21. I still don't know what it was that changed his mind but after stroking his chin for what seemed like ages he then did the most bizarre thing. Going to his enormous leather desk, he opened the centre drawer and handed me a self-tie bow tie. He asked if I knew how to tie it. I told him, honestly, that I had never seen one before, let alone knew how to put it on. He told me to go away, learn, and come back to his office in an hour.

Who on earth could I ask to teach me? The only person I thought might know was the sergeant on duty in the main reception area. George was very proper and very posh, so I figured he might be familiar with this mode of dress. After all, he was a member of the Corps of Commissionaires (a global movement created to employ veterans of the Armed Services). If anyone knew, he would.

Except that he didn't – but knew someone who did, a formerly elegant man who was now the resident drunk at the Parrs Wood pub directly opposite our Didsbury studios. The resulting lesson cost me half a crown, or more precisely three pints of Boddington's best bitter.

I duly returned to Gerry's office in a yellow and green floral bow-tie with one side slightly larger than the other (to show it was self-tied; a bonus tip from my drunken saviour). Impressed, Gerry asked me to take it off and put it back on again without the use of a mirror. Miraculously I managed to do so, even remembering to create the correct imbalance at the sides. He told me to wear it always, behave older than I was, and gave me a week in which to prove myself.

Extraordinarily, he also soon organised a month's work for me in each and every department (except for make-up which, back then, was an all-female domain). At the end of this unofficial, but very demanding, period Gerry then decided the area I was best suited to. He decreed that my best match was to be part of the camera crew.

For the past 59 years, I have regarded Gerry Mitchell's decision as affording me the best possible time any working man could ever have hoped for. I was therefore thrilled to come across this article, written by Lloyd Hubbard-Mitchell, which appeared on IMDb many years after Gerry had left ABC TV.

GERRY MITCHELL. Born in Ancoats, Manchester to Charlotte Hubbard (née Anderson) with three sisters, Gerry was raised by his step-father Joseph Mitchell (whose surname he later adopted) before entering the Xaverian College in Manchester. Upon leaving the Xavarian College, Gerry joined the Kings Own as a regular soldier and witnessed the 2nd Sino-Japanese war, capturing important strategic images on his Box Brownie. These original photos are held by the Imperial War Museum, London.

After returning to the UK from the Far East, Gerry was recruited into the new Royal Armoured Corp which formed part of the British Expeditionary Force campaign against Nazi German forces in France, where he was injured; later to be rescued by a boat which contributed to the flotilla of 'Little Ships'.

During R&R from his duties, Gerry courted Betty Cooper and ultimately married her. Whilst recuperating, Gerry's immediate bedfellow neighbour suggested that, when released from service, Gerry should follow him into the British Film Industry. This he did and, in 1945, his first production was on nationwide release, *The Man from Morocco*.

Gerry continued his film career until 1956 when he retired from movies. He immediately started working on television as production manager at Granada and later with ABC working on *Oh Boy!* and attending the concept meeting for the new 'man in the street' production which was to become *Coronation Street*. In 1968, he retired again after a disagreement over the new independent television licensing rules, turning down the position of first controller of London Weekend Television, offered by David Frost of the London Television Consortium...

I'd no idea Gerry had such a distinguished military and film career. I did know he was once photographed from behind walking towards his Rolls Royce Silver Cloud Convertible clad in his signature riding breeches, hacking jacket and bowler hat. That picture became the publicity image for Lord Rockingham's XI, a group of British session musicians employed by Jack Good on *Oh Boy!*, *Boy Meets Girls* and *Wham!!* In 1958, they had a number one hit with 'Hoots Mon'.

So it might be accurate to say that Lord Rockingham gave me my first break! However, I do remain forever grateful to the anonymous drunk and Gerry Mitchell for helping me to grow up overnight.

ANOTHER name I enjoy thinking about is 'John of the Street', who also afforded me one of my most satisfying career challenges. He is from Belgium and far prefers his Flemish name: Jan Vanderstraeten.

Jan had been commissioned to create an event to mark the launch of VTM, the first Flemish and second commercial television channel in Belgium after the French-speaking RTL-TVI, scheduled to air on 1 February 1989. He was directing and producing corporate videos and graphics at the time, but hadn't a clue how to make a basic programme, let alone an opening night spectacular. He was looking for an experienced executive producer and was introduced to me.

From day one, Jan Vanderstraeten and I saw eye to eye and spent most of our early weeks doing a lot of laughing. Jan had also secured the services of a writer who was himself a celebrity in the UK, Tony Bilbow, the BBC's first anchorman on *Film Night* in the early 1970s. The three of us immediately became a team and began discussing the package we'd been given to play with, a daunting task indeed. It became more daunting the more we developed the idea and realised how massively important this would be for the Belgian TV industry.

At the time, Belgium had two national networks: VRT (Flemish) and RTBF (French). For entertainment, Flemish-speaking viewers watched Dutch channels. VTM – Vlaamse Televisie Maatschappij – aimed to change all of that from Flanders. Tony Bilbow and I were reliably informed that this was a massive gamble as nobody in the media, and most northern politicians, believed it could survive let alone be a triumph. Only the Liberal Party supported the initiative.

The ever-smiling Jan made no secret of the fact that we were in unknown territory. There were no facilities available in Flanders: no lighting, no outside broadcast units or mobile studios, no expertise for the production of a great event. The biggest show ever in Belgium had been the 1987 *Eurovision Song Contest*, organised and produced by the RTBF after Sandra Kim won it in Norway the year before.

The more we learnt about the job the more bizarre it became. For example, any programme of importance needed heavy duty pre-publicity and on-air promotion, which was not possible here because the very first thing VTM viewers would see was this show, which is why it was called *Het Openingsgala,* in English *The Opening Gala.*

The programme would be recorded on Saturday 28 January and launched on-air (after editing) the following Wednesday. If anyone tuned into the channel before 7.00pm all they'd see was a test card accompanied by an oscillating tone of unbelievably dull proportions.

Very soon after beginning this momentous task we learned that the usual problems associated with producing any television show were to pale into insignificance. We also realised this *Openingsgala* had unique boundaries and limitations. The top four being:-

1. The show would not be made in a studio, but in the Ostend Casino.
2. The audience wouldn't be the general public but invited advertising executives who would judge the show and VTM by either using or not using their cheque books.
3. Afterwards, these VIPs were to be given a mammoth champagne hospitality party.
4. The show would effectively be a huge promotion spot for the new channel. It would feature every genre of programming VTM would be offering their viewers, not just light entertainment.

So within the confines of our allocated three-hour slot we were duty-bound to include news, sport, current affairs, daytime magazine, children, feature films, soaps, American imports, comedy, music, documentary and education.

What's more, the new Board of Directors added and subtracted items every time they met. At one point we were convinced they were meeting ten times a day. The list of demands seemed never ending. With each incoming item so disparate, the three of us would end our day clutching a cold Duvel brew in one hand and a totally unrecognisable draft of the running order in the other.

It truly was like nothing I had ever tackled and I still look back with pride in the sure knowledge that our *Openingsgala* did the job of launching VTM as the most popular TV channel in Flanders.

And, oh, that humble test card! It had been playing on my mind. I kept wondering how, when it came to the exact moment for VTM to become a reality, we could visually move away from this boring technical graphic to the interior of 'Casino Oostende'.

Everyone would expect the test card to fade and be replaced by a new shiny VTM logo. So how to make such a transition in the most unexpected way? We toyed with numerous ideas already in the lexicon of special effects and therefore to be expected. Until it suddenly struck me that everyone, including me, assumed that a test card was a computer-generated graphic.

What if, instead, we made a twenty foot wide by fifteen foot tall (4:3 aspect ratio) test card and stood it on the centre of the stage in the casino, so that when the audience came in they might assume that this was the actual test card they'd been looking at on their sets for the last few months? This basic idea appealed to our small but perfectly formed production team.

We decided to develop the idea even further and soon settled on the notion that someone, who would look very small in front of this huge piece of scenery, ought to walk on and announce the birth of VTM. But who would be the right person to do this? The Prime Minister? The MD of VTM? A pop star? All the ideas seemed to get further and further away from the original purpose, which was to hero VTM. So who should it be? This question nearly scuppered the whole idea. Should he or she have political importance? What would they say? How big a speech should it be? The entire idea threatened to become a non-starter before it had even begun. Out of context, and over a glass or two of Duvel, somebody mentioned the brilliant comedic talent of vaudevillian mime artist George Carl.

George was a massive international talent who became famous after Johnny Carson invited him to appear on his iconic *The Tonight Show* in America in March 1985, when Carl was 69. He was a clown without traditional make-up and had many elements to his act, but the most memorable was his uniquely complex routine of walking on and simply adjusting the height of the mic-stand. Seconds later, his thumb would 'inadvertently' get caught in his jacket buttonhole, trapping the mic cable between the stand and his body, which he then tried to correct by lifting the stand over the wire, thus making the situation a hundred times worse and all in total silence. These and many more corrective actions, involving arms and legs, then grew ever more complex and were made still funnier by his deadpan expression. Eventually, gloriously and quite accidentally, he would somehow rectify the situation and walk off stage, leaving the mic-stand exactly as he had found it having uttered not one word.

Suddenly we had a tag. This was to be our opening sequence, from silence to laughter with no music or words required, and all taking place in front of the test card. We thought it inventive and memorable at the time and I'm unaware of anyone trying it, or even having the necessity to try it since 1989 when, at precisely 19:00hrs, we would invisibly mix from the computer generated graphic of the card to an exact match, but now the shot would be of a huge photo blow-up replica designed by Erik Van Hemelrijck. This transition would take place in the centre of the Ostend Casino stage.

The moment we made this visual changeover, the audio would also switch from the oscillating test tone to the ambience of a live audience impatiently waiting for something to happen. Following a couple of seconds of this ambient sound, George Carl would walk in front of the scenic test card, unannounced and without applause, carrying a microphone stand. As people slowly caught on, the sound would go from silence to peels of laughter from an audience of 2,000.

VTM was on the air and, in Belgium, it remains an iconic image.

Naturally, following this visual gag on both the viewers at home and those present, the Eric Melaerts Orchestra struck up big music, Alan Harding's *Summertime Special* dancers danced and we were underway with a fast-moving show, featuring many European stars like aforementioned *Eurovision* winner Sandra Kim; jazz musician Toots Thielemans; singer Viktor Lazlo; comedy double act Gaston Berghmans and Leo Martin; crooner Willy Sommers; Won Ton Ton ('The Dog Who Saved Hollywood'); and Belgian bands Clouseau and Soulsister. From Portugal we had singer Linda de Suza, with The Italian classical chamber orchestra Rondò Veneziano. America's Robin Beck, Glenn Medeiros, Randy Crawford and Howard Keel appeared, as did the UK's Jane Seymour, Clive Webb and Tom Jones.

The only thing in place before Tony Bilbow and I were invited to join Jan were the arrangements for the lavish hospitality reception, designed to win over advertising executives who would hopefully buy airtime. This entire post-show event, together with exclusive car parking arrangements at the casino, had been the sole responsibility of Jan and his small team. No wonder he needed extra help.

During the show's development from a blank sheet of paper, we had to keep reminding ourselves of our original brief – to produce a spectacular entertainment Show that introduced and established VTM as the 'must-watch' channel of both the present and the future.

The new board reacted well to our ongoing and ever-changing, work on the daily drafts. Amazingly, they actively chipped in with suggestions and, more importantly, funding. Their business plan fully recognised the importance of this launch and had unofficially made provision for initial costs to be recovered after twelve months of trading. Remarkably, after only one month, they had a return on their investment. VTM was a huge hit proving all the critics wrong, an unprecedented success story by any standard.

This very first show, though, was also designed to introduce, in an entertaining and memorable way, the frontmen and women who would host a long list of unfamiliar programmes – and we had just under three hours to achieve it. We also had to introduce overseas imports and, it was hinted, doing so without lapsing into the use of pre-recorded promotional clips. One such was *Dallas*. Following a song from *Eurovision* favourite Sandra, a giant screen was lowered centre-stage and projected on it were the soap's opening titles. These then mixed to a ranch interior where international star of stage and screen, Howard Keel, spoke directly to the camera.

'Hi there, across in Belgium,' he began. 'The entire cast of *Dallas* just wanted to say how thrilled we all are that you're going to be watching our show on your new Flemish channel, VTM! I apologise for speaking English, my Flemish is a little rusty!' Keel then started to walk towards camera and it pulled back with him as he went on. 'Although Dallas is nearly 5,000 miles from Ostend, we thought it'd be nice if we could make that journey to share in your celebrations.'

Under the screen we see the behind of a camera operator walking backwards. Then we see Howard Keel ... still talking and walking. The audience quickly caught on to the illusion. There was massive applause as they realised they'd all been suckered into thinking this was just a very unimpressive filmed promotion spot.

Keel was met on stage by one of the more well-known faces who'd joined the presentation team. They chatted about the occasion, Keel wished VTM every possible success and sang 'Send In The Clowns', before we linked to a fully-blown promotional film of *Dallas*.

At this point I must relate one of Jan Vanderstraeten's favourite anecdotes concerning Howard Keel. Our writer, Tony Bilbow, had loved the idea of surprising the audience in such a way, so wrote the most beautiful intro for the actor to consider, together with a full explanation of the surprise to be sprung on our live audience. This was 1989, remember, so well before emails and mobile phones and so on. So Tony's words were sent to Keel's management via fax machine. We all waited anxiously for a reply or acknowledgment at least of receipt, but nothing came. When Keel eventually landed in Belgium, Jan and Tony were at the airport to welcome him and bring him, via stretch limo, to Ostend Casino for the start of his rehearsals. After a few pleasantries in the car, Jan ventured, 'Mr Keel, Tony here wrote a long suggested text for your entrance. Did your management ever let you see it?' Both Jan and Tony were astounded to learn that not only had he received the fax, but that he had learnt it – word for word! As Jan recalls, that was when he realised that 'stars do not become stars by chance.'

The point of this entrance (apart from sheer entertainment value) was to establish a personal connection between VTM and *Dallas*, and this, we decided, would be our aim with every new programme introduced to VTM viewers during the *Openingsgala*. At one point in the running order we featured, for under a minute, a silly throw-away item from a well-known game show presenter who stepped right out of his comfort zone and performed a magical illusion. He used a chalkboard, divided into twelve squares, and randomly gathered the dates of three audience members' birthdays which he then entered into the top three squares (21–18–6). He put the date (1 February 1989) into the next three squares as the numbers 1–2–8, arriving at the single digit '8' by adding the year eight and the nine together to make 17, then adding one and seven. Each column added up to 22–20–14. He pointed out that these numbers seemed to be meaningless until you realised that the alphabet's 22nd letter is 'V', the 20th is 'T' and the 14th 'M'. He received a huge round of applause and linked into the first commercial break of the evening!

Each performance and item in some novel and unpredictable way had a direct and exclusive connection to VTM. The show was the success that we had all hoped for and VTM became (and still is) an important player in the Belgian television industry.

All of which meant a lot for me because I was a part of a process that every TV producer dreams of ... that magic moment when you realise there is a blank sheet of paper that needs to be filled and you have no idea with 'what'. However, the 'how' is even more daunting.

In this unique case, the whole process was a joy because the people I worked with were involved and dedicated to making the end product as perfect and entertaining as possible. To any creative, this sort of opportunity is manna from heaven, made even more exciting because such opportunities are so rare! Our *Openingsgala* was one of those extremely rare opportunities.

Before we leave *Het Openingsgala*, one particular moment moved me to tears of sheer joy. It was during the finale, when the audience gave a standing ovation to the entire cast assembled on-stage.

My attention was drawn to the front row of the circle, where a group of technicians (who I knew to be of different nationalities) were standing with their backs to the scene but applauding just as enthusiastically as everyone else. This was a moment that made me catch my breath. My eyes brimmed as, not for the first time, I realised what a bizarre and wonderful industry I was fortunate enough to be making my living in. Let me elaborate.

A few weeks earlier, during initial groundwork, I met with the Dutch Cine Video Group, already contracted to facilitate the event. Although this was essentially a Belgian production, it had been felt that the best technical know-how was to be found in Holland. So I was in touch, for the first time, with a Dutch OB unit consisting of lighting director, engineers, camera and sound crews. After a fairly straightforward start, the conversation came around to the lighting director and how he was thinking of producing a rig that could give the show a wide variety of atmospheres and moods. At this point, none of us knew what the show would contain, but we did know the stage would need to be lit in as many ways as possible. I was keen to ensure that once our content was finalised we would have enough scope to be able to ring the changes without any more equipment.

This Dutch guy was very impressive. He showed us a few sketches demonstrating various options. I asked him where he was proposing to hang his lights for this most impressive array of possibilities and he replied, quick as a flash, 'on scaffolding.'

I was horrified and unfortunately expressed my feelings in rough Mancunian. I pointed out that the reason we were doing this show in such a casino was because of its beautiful setting. There was little point in moving out of a custom-built studio if all the audience and cameras could see was 'bloody scaffolding!' The meeting came to a sudden halt and I found myself, with my 'boss' Jan Vanderstraeten, in the back seat of a car speeding back to Brussels airport, slightly more than miffed that I'd blown this first meeting.

Experience had taught me that it was of paramount importance to create a good working relationship with a crew from the word go, and this I had failed to do. I felt annoyed with myself. So I was more than surprised that 'John of the Street' had completely agreed with me and was more than happy to look for another lighting director who would comply with our wishes. I then boarded a plane back to Newcastle upon Tyne which, at the time, was still my home despite my having been fired from Tyne Tees a good while before. What can I say? I loved living and working among the Geordie people.

During the flight from Brussels, my mind suddenly focussed on another lighting director I'd worked with in the north east, who had a real flair for invention. He'd been with Tyne Tees since being a lad and had in fact risen in the ranks to become senior lighting director. Recently, he had been given 'involuntary redundancy', which is a very cruel way of telling a 55-year-old man he is no longer of value. I knew what a devastating effect on self-confidence such news had as the very same thing happened to my father who, following his own 'involuntary redundancy', became an old man overnight. I knew this chap, Bill Padgett, would feel just as low and unwanted.

Upon landing at the airport I was determined to find Bill and ask if he fancied acting as a consultant in helping me to solve this Ostend conundrum. The following Monday morning, at 6:00am, I was on a flight back to Brussels accompanied by the astonished man himself.

As both head of entertainment and a working TV director at Tyne Tees, I'd found myself taking on many odd jobs. One was being involved with the religious department, not because I'm particularly devout on that front, it was more that I rather admired the head of religious programming, Max Deas. He was used to being allocated trainees to make his output and I felt he deserved better, so when the time came for him to record a batch of fifty *Epilogues* – those five-minute late-night pre-shutdown (remember that?) talks which older readers may recall (a contractual obligation imposed by the Independent Broadcasting Authority) – I mentioned to my favourite designer, Peter Bingemann, that I'd like to invite Bill to light them. It wasn't a particularly demanding job, consisting mainly of a vicar sitting on a chair against a black background. The most recent batch had looked flat, washed-out and extremely boring.

Peter said I'd never get him to do it, which was a red rag to a bull. Over a pint in the Rose And Crown opposite the studios, I confided in Bill (who at this point I hadn't even met) that evangelical preacher Billy Graham had agreed to provide Tyne Tees exclusively with ten five-minute talks, but they had to be recorded in secret and that this information must not get out. The charismatic American speaker and persuasive God-botherer would fly into Newcastle the following week, incognito, come to the studio, record his pieces-to-camera and return, still incognito, via a private aeroplane back to the States.

I explained to 'our' Bill that I wanted the mid-shot on the 'other' Bill to be lit in the same way that the best possible portrait artist would light such a massive celebrity. He agreed and promptly made plans in our smaller studio for this mid-shot to be lit with 'sides', 'fill', 'back-lights', 'up-lights', 'modelling lights', 'filters' and everything but the kitchen sink. In fact, I believe he'd one of those standing by too.

I suspect you've already guessed that on the allocated day there was no Billy Graham, but a dozen or so very grey members of the clergy. Well, grey they might have been until they sat in Bill's lights, whereupon they suddenly looked like film stars.

Bill was far from angry with me and agreed that had I asked him to light an ordinary session of *Epilogues* he'd have refused. He also agreed that he wouldn't have thought of making it special had I not done a 'Billy Graham' on him, referring to the incident on future occasions as the best lesson he ever had on what was important and what was not. Thereafter, we became firm friends, which had given me the opportunity to involve him in our *Openingsgala*. Jan trusted me on the call, accepting Bill (and return airfares) without question.

Having arrived in Belgium, Bill asked us to leave him alone while he wandered around the Ostend Casino, making notes. Having done that he asked: 'And where exactly will Billy Graham be standing?'

So Bill Padgett was engaged for the job and promptly engaged specialists involved in the use of the most modern and experimental lighting equipment on the market. These were known as 'Star-Lites', the first generation of computer lights, imported from Germany.

In 1989, this technology was above state-of-the-art and involved personnel and equipment from many different European countries. They were fitted to the front of the dress circle and operated by a bank of computers also situated there. As a result, the number of seats available to the audience was slightly reduced, but not to the detriment of the spirit of the show. The VIPs occupied the stalls, the general public occupied the dress circle, so all this equipment was out of the line of sight of those who might invest in the channel.

At the time of writing, some 33 years later, our *Openingsgala* is still the most expensive show ever produced in Flanders. It was a truly international production involving a crew of technical experts from the Netherlands, France, Britain, Germany and others, all working together in perfect harmony under Jan's leadership.

And it was at the end of this spectacle that the Star-Lite operators in the dress circle all turned around to join in with the standing ovation and applaud their boss – Bill Padgett – who had coordinated the entire thing from his position a little further back. He often told me that was his proudest moment; it was certainly one of mine!

A postscript to this tale is that Bill was in constant employment as a freelancer thereafter, working on some of the biggest shows in Belgium. What's in a name? In VTM, his own became synonymous with excellence in television lighting. He made the journey from 'not wanted' to 'must have' – and all thanks to *Het Openingsgala*.

DURING my career there have been unpredictable and unexpected situations that occurred out of the blue which, because they were so bizarre, were usually connected to an unforgettable name. One such was Gunnar Bemert, an extraordinary man by any standards.

Years before I actually got to meet Gunnar, I did receive a phone call from him asking about my availability. Having discerned the nature of the job, which he described as creating 'a large box with sides that, when removed, could be transformed into four or more different rooms or scenes', I'd done myself out of a job by suggesting that the person he really needed was Peter Bingemann, a talented young designer who had just become available as a freelancer.

It would be another twelve years before I actually got to meet and work with Gunnar, a 'larger than life' character to be sure. In 1998, I visited MBC (Middle East Broadcasting Corporation) to meet this most remarkable Swede who was then MBC's senior producer, based in London. Gunnar had initially become involved in the Middle East as an underwater photographer whose impressive coffee table book, *Red Sea Coral Reefs*, displays the magnificence of marine life.

This glossy title (ISBN: 9780710300072) had found its way onto the desk of one of the senior royals in Saudi Arabia and word soon spread around the 'House of Saud'. As a result, Gunnar was invited to present private slide shows in assorted palaces around the kingdom and these made Gunnar very popular with the royal family.

One of the keenest admirers of this ebullient personality was Sheikh Waleed bin Ibrahim Al Ibrahim, a brother-in-law of Saudi Arabia's King Fahd, and owner of MBC TV. He utilised Gunnar's undoubted talents in visual communication by making him head of production at MBC. Sheikh Waleed introduced him to the governor of the Asir Province, Prince Khalid bin Faisal Al Saud, who was also the man behind the annual six-week Abha Music Festival. It was after meeting and becoming friends with Prince Khalid that the course of Gunnar's life changed from being a production manager to becoming a television producer.

The Abha Music Festival was introduced as a result of Prince Khalid's interest in promoting artistic culture across the Kingdom, but he wanted to extend its visibility by televising it across the MBC network to the entire Arab World. Gunnar was, therefore, charged with the responsibility of delivering this annual event on TV.

It took place in Abha, capital city of the Asir province, some 340 miles south of Mecca. A picturesque location up in the hills, it was full of fresh cool air for those who could afford it, and those who had just completed the Hajj pilgrimage. Offering the very best in live Arabian folk music and culture, it was a male-only event however. Gunnar was the executive in charge of recording and transmitting it from the MBC's London base in Battersea. It was there, during our first meeting, that he asked me to be its director.

Gunnar worked closely with the official Saudi TV units and had grown to understand their idiosyncratic ways. We all listened and learned from a man who seemed to get more outrageous every day. Whenever we arrived at Abha international airport, all eighteen stones of Gunnar, rugged and unkempt, enjoyed walking up to the taxi rank and asking for transport for us all – in Swedish.

Naturally the taxi drivers spoke to one another in Arabic and wasted no time discussing how they could take this fat European and his equally naïve group for an almighty ride. Gunnar would bide his time and then, in perfect Arabic, read each of the taxi drivers their fortunes – and then some! (I always suspected Gunnar's Arabic of containing traces of language he'd picked up from the royals as whenever he spoke in Arabic there was always silence).

Gunnar was our passport to perfect service; the Arab population respected him wherever we went without question. I was fascinated by his knowledge of the culture and loved listening to his many stories over a bottle or two of fine wine. For several years I looked forward to this annual culture shock and learning even more about this unique human being.

Gunnar and I were finalising plans for *The Saudi Arabian Music Awards*, a much grander televised event. We were also well into the making of a documentary commissioned by Crown Prince Abdullah celebrating the achievements of King Fahd. Had it not been for 9/11 in 2001, I'm sure we'd still be paying our annual visit to Abha and I would still be enjoying the company of one of the most exciting individuals I have ever met. What's in a name? Gunnar Bemert has occupied a large chunk of my happy memory bank for many years.

You will have gathered by now that in this job you go where the work is – near and far. When first invited to direct commercials, I had the good fortune to work alongside Ronnie Fouracre, a director who had vast experience of the world of advertising (a whole galaxy away from the television world). He'd also earned a good reputation as a television director on *Coronation Street*. Ronnie invited me to be his stand-in on a contract with a national grocery retailer (I'm reluctant to say the name for reasons that may become apparent further on and, anyway, I don't want to lose my 'divi').

I told Ronnie that commercials were new to me, but his words 'don't fret about it, the crew in Molinare [a studio facility in London] know all about it, you'll soon pick it up...' had the reverse effect. In the TV world, a director needs to know everything about a job before even setting off from home. This was like going back to square one.

Ronnie explained that he'd already made the master commercial and all that needed doing was to 'draw' a couple shots from the master, add a few more, together with different price tags, and then make thirteen versions for thirteen different regions with thirteen different voice-overs. If that wasn't daunting enough, there was also another upsetting aspect ... the job had a daily fee way in excess of anything I had the remotest chance of earning in television.

Giving in to my latent imposter syndrome, I started to worry that they'd expect much more from me than I was capable of giving. So, riddled with self-doubt and not knowing what would be required, I entered the Molinare facility just off Carnaby Street.

A wonderful 'First' (floor manager) approached me as soon as I walked in and said: 'We've just heard that Palethorpe's Pork Sausages have got a special on in the Anglia area.' My blank expression prompted him to continue: 'We need a new pack-shot and strap!'

The definition of a TV director's job might be to make something look 'better than it is'. On many occasions in my career I have been challenged and, am pleased to say, have usually succeeded in doing that while thoroughly enjoying the process. However, to make a tray of sausages look delicious is perhaps the hardest thing I'd tackled up to that date. The more I rearranged them, lit them, changed the shooting angle and tried numerous filters, the more they looked like turds. And when it was casually mentioned that they should look hot and delicious, things got even worse.

In desperation, I must have been heard to mutter 'I didn't know what else to do with them' when a prop-man shoved his head around a piece of scenery, held up an orange rubber glove with a sausage shoved down each finger, and shouted: 'This any good, Guv?' It was a magical moment, completely defusing the tense atmosphere I had caused in the studio.

After a few moments the same bloke came out with a new tray of 'bangers', arranged beautifully, dressed with parsley and looking somewhere near edible. He said: 'Ronnie couldn't sort the soddin' sausages out either'. I'd passed my audition and the rest of that day was both very productive and great fun. I later learned that Ronnie Fouracre, who died in 1983, had purposely prearranged my entire nightmare introduction to Molinare and the world of commercials.

In those early days of telly, ads that had an urgency to them were very popular. Some retailers were using TV to promote special offers or, in the case of the tabloids, an exclusive and controversial article. Such commercials were made quickly and in secret.

Competition was brisk! It was quite usual for an ad agency to pull a commercial together from scratch within 24 hours of transmission. This normally meant working through the night in readiness for the morning's breakfast show, a variety of programming that launched on the BBC and ITV during the year of Ronnie's death. Experts in this were the remarkable producer and copywriting pair Hugh David and Bob Maddams.

I loved the process of having to be meticulous with every frame and truncating as much information as possible into one piece of action lasting less than a third of a second (eight frames). From the team of Hugh and Bob I learned how complex writing voice-overs that ran to perfect time, while being informative and entertaining, was. They also taught me about the massive difference in working practices between the telly that I had been trained in and this brand new world. For instance, one day Hugh asked me for a 'chat'. He walked me from studio to car park and asked how I thought it was all going. We were able to take this time-out because I was well ahead of schedule. The crew and I were cooking on gas and naturally I was incredibly proud of this, which I relayed to Hugh. He pointed out that at the speed I was driving the studio we'd be wrapped well ahead of our scheduled time. I very proudly agreed.

It was at this point that I received a lesson I never forgot. It was simply that the job had been costed and the schedule agreed on well before my involvement. If I were to show that it could have been done cheaper and quicker, then those people who sat behind their desks number crunching would reduce both the budget and the scheduled hours on the next one! And it might be far more complex to complete. Also, all our fees were based on a percentage of the budget so it would have been madness to do anything to give those 'mid-managerial toss pots' a reason to reduce future ones. The less they knew about the process the better for all concerned.

I was made very aware, in no uncertain terms, that this particular commercial was just one in a whole series and, after all, 'one swallow does not a summer make!' I also learned that the client is always right, even when they're not, especially within the fundamental idiosyncrasies involved in the dark art of production management.

Any assumptions that the world of producing TV commercials had anything to do with the world of producing TV programmes were soon dismantled after just one brisk walk in a car park, arm in arm, with Hugh David. He made all future commercials contracts as a director a sheer joy to tackle, because he had a total grip of the production aspects, including the budget.

My initial training in TV budget control had been in the 1960s and had a totally different set of criteria. It involved a 'taking from Peter to pay Paul' methodology. To explain...

If, one week, the make-up department under-spent, I had the authority (as producer) to pass on that differential to the wardrobe department (as they had a heavy spend that particular week). Each aspect of the production had a cost heading and before the massive sea change in the way budgets were handled, all these cost headings were the sole responsibility of producers. If the orchestra incurred overtime one week, it was possible to correct that over a few other programmes by diligently monitoring and reallocating funds.

This system worked and meant any money assigned was seen on the screen. Because of this constant monitoring of expenditure and savings it was more than possible to bring a show in on budget as an 'individual' entity. More importantly, it was possible to bring a whole series of, say, twenty-six programmes within the parameters. Until the early 1980s, that is, when a mixture of Milton Friedman, Margaret Thatcher and Sir Keith Joseph began to re-invent it all and every aspect of life suddenly had to be formally 'managed'.

This impacted programme budgets because over approximately a decade they were now to be overseen by a whole army of managers. Each heading within the budget (lighting, wardrobe, design, make-up, music, contributors etc) would eventually be a stand-alone item supervised by a middle-manager who liked to see their particular cost heading showing positivity (or, if you prefer, in profit).

So, before each department head's budget was published, a chunk was held back as contingency. This meant that the budget initially allocated to by the programme controller was reduced at source before the programme had even begun to be made.

It is plain to see that this new philosophy replaced the 'take from Peter to pay Paul' methodology with a false picture of what was being spent and where. This new army of middle managers needed paying too, so the reorganisation became self-defeating and meant only a fraction of allocated funds found their way onto the screen.

As a result budgets were increased to eye-watering levels and the whole art of making a TV show was replaced by a mind-numbing battle with people who knew nothing about the 'art', but who did have a degree in 'managing' anything from tinned beans to tanks. Some were even heard to remark that they would 'rather not know about any issues as being made aware of the problems surrounding the job would make their role almost impossible.'

So, what's in a name? Well, anyone whose name is followed by the word 'manager' remains a phobia of mine to this day!

However, such 'management' is now a reality and, it seems safe to say, future generations will be even more manager-oriented. That is until someone, probably not yet born, comes along to expose and repatriate the vast amount of dead money tied up in the margins of complex spreadsheets hidden away in some digital cloud in Silicon Valley.

What's in the name 'manager?' Now, there *is* a question!

Royston as Darcy's butler in Death Comes to Pemberley, *a 2013 BBC Christmas series based on the novel by PD James.*

5.
A Dog Without a Bicycle

WHILE surviving a precarious, turbulent and sometimes cruel TV industry for over fifty-seven years, I always imagined retirement would be unacceptable. What a surprise then to have arrived safely in the land of the eternal arthritic concessionary pass to find that retirement is not only impossible, but far from unacceptable.

Oh yes, there are aches and pains in places I'd forgotten I had. I understand that many of my contemporaries suffer from short-term memory problems. Still, I'm pleased to say I have no recollection of these problems.

Now, where was I ... short term memory loss ... that's right...

My personal life is blissful and full of love, thanks mainly to my incredible wife, Sarah. My professional life seems far more enjoyable than I ever thought possible and for this I have to thank my agent, Alex Priestley. Alex is a young person, as most people are to me these days, but she has the wisdom only to put me up for acting parts well within the parameters of my limited talent.

So far I have played Raymond Robinson, an arrogant restaurant owner in *Emmerdale*; a bumbling farmer extracting a string of 'runner turnips' from the frozen earth in a Farm Foods commercial; a half-sozzled company chairman for the Co-op Funeral Service; a dodgy old butler in the BBC series *Death Comes To Pemberley*; a sad old chap in a Christmas edition of *Emmerdale*; plus a wise grandad for Ben Turton's Stockport community project film about debt and money lending. And grandad roles don't stop coming. I played a clumsy one in *Infomercial,* a web-streamed family soap; an aged sage in Tony Boffey's short art-house film *Cache*; one silly old soul with an inexplicable desire to go scuba diving; an aged client languishing in one of Her Majesty's Prisons; a drugged-up care home resident who befriends a serial killer ... oh, and another butler, but this time to Manchester-born rap star Aitch, in an attempt to flog energy drinks to his admiring public. Is there no end to this constant re-affirmation of my evident credibility?

It is a total joy for me to note that all of the above – together with a wealth of unsuccessful, but still joyful, auditions and self-tapes (thanks to the 2020 Coronavirus pandemic) – were conveniently intertwined by Alex into the simple life of an old-aged pensioner.

But to start a fuller look back over my present career as an actor, I think I will begin with my longest role to date.

For me, *Off Their Rockers* started life in 2011 as just one of many auditions. I was asked to do an ad-lib sketch with an unsuspecting member of the public in St Ann's Square, Manchester. I couldn't help recalling that fifty years earlier it was me asking Jonathan Routh and Bill Kelly to do much the same for a new series of *Candid Camera*.

Weeks after the audition, it transpired that I, along with another ten OAPs, had been chosen to form the core cast for a pilot. It was a while before it was accepted, but eventually a series of six *Off Their Rockers*, produced by CPL Productions, was commissioned by ITV.

Months of filming all over the UK culminated in a fantastic array of outlandish and irresponsible pranks that would eventually form the content for a series of six shows. The producers decided that each half-hour episode should comprise at least twenty diverse scenes, so the job was to produce at least one hundred and twenty high quality sketches. The first one aired on 7 April 2013 and we were all thrilled to watch as viewers ourselves and witness the magnificent job CPL had done in interweaving our pranks with the most unusual and entertaining pieces of popular music.

The viewers liked it too. Everyone connected with the show was over the moon to see the ratings soar. The programme was described as comedy gold in the popular press.

That first series was followed by a second series and then a third with a much expanded core cast. At this point, the production house decided that the show's success meant they could start cutting back on staff, scripts, props and travel. There ended up being twenty-eight episodes in all, over four series, and a special. A fifth series never happened because *Off Their Rockers* shot itself in the arthritic foot!

This crazy TV experience, though, did allow me to feature in hundreds of pranks, taking on dozens of guises as a solo performer, for which I will always be grateful. It also taught me that the business of making television programmes had changed beyond recognition, a business I would no longer survive in as a producer *or* director.

This realisation served to make me consider my retirement with even more glee – especially as I realised that it could also provide me with an indescribable amount of fun. Long may that last.

My earlier working life had taken place in an era when it was traditional in broadcast television to have one producer, one director or just one producer/director. The thought of multiple producers and directors hadn't entered anyone's head, thankfully, so the lines of responsibility were logical, recognised and respected by everyone.

It was, simply this. The buck stops with the producer.

The idea that one day several people would share that buck had never crossed my mind until retirement. I found the idea amusing for a while, until I became involved in *Off Their Rockers* and saw, first-hand, this 'modernised' system's many disadvantages.

After many early shoots I'd return home to Sarah only to moan and groan about what I had just experienced. I'd launch into a gripe about this, that and next thing connected to how shooting had been organised or administered. Oh, I realised that as an actor these technical matters were no concern of mine. The problem was that I found it harder and harder to relax, or fail to notice how some of its various directors were blatantly unaware of how to create a comedy atmosphere, talk to their 'talent', or even shoot a simple scene.

Sarah, having the patience of Job, was reasonably happy listening to my waffle, but also fearful that I'd blow my cover one day and chip in during the shoot, a move that would effectively, and quite rightly, have removed me from the cast. She gave me a wristlet to wear that she made from a black zip. Having this on my wrist during shooting days would serve as a visual reminder to keep my mouth shut about what was happening behind the camera and concentrate on what I was doing in front.

In other words: zip it!

Every time I spotted this wristlet out of the corner of my eye I was forced to inwardly smile, ignore the mayhem and give 100 per cent concentration to what my character was supposed to be doing. It worked wonders and if the four series of *Off Their Rockers* are ever repeated you'll be able to see this zip-wristlet in many of my scenes.

So here I was, having learnt to get on with my job of performing yet able to stand well outside the internal politics of the production and see something go pear-shaped without any need to get involved! However, I was still fascinated about how the buck was being passed around, kicked from one producer to another and then another until said buck disappeared altogether.

Sadly, however, a production without a buck is like a dog without a bicycle. It soon became apparent the production was out of control and, understandably, in a relatively short time *Off Their Rockers* became a thing of the past. The entire experience though did provide me with some much-needed acting practice in both role playing and ad-libbing. It also taught me a lot about myself.

Turning a blind eye to the many gaffs the various producers and directors were guilty of did make me wonder about how many times I had unwittingly done similar in the days when I called the shots. Certain moments flashed before my eyes. *'Did I really say that?' 'Did I really do that?'* I shuddered to think.

I had to remind myself that I'd come from good stock, by which

I mean experienced life as sweeper-upper and technician on the studio floor before operating as a programme director. So empathy in that direction must have played some part in preventing me from making an absolute 'horlicks' of it.

Thames TV's Head of Department was Philip Jones, who we met earlier in this book as a very knowledgable man of most distinctive character. The *Daily Express* once ran an article, by comedy and light entertainment historian Louis Barfe, in which the following extract appeared: '*Opportunity Knocks* producer Royston Mayoh remembers Head of Variety and Comedy, Philip Jones, chastising him for listening to audition tapes too loudly. "Can you please keep the music down?" Jones asked, "Anyone would think that this was a place of entertainment...". In the same article, Barfe went on: 'Mayoh also recalls a despondent Les Dawson in 1971, wondering why he was not allowed near the Terrace Bar at Thames Teddington. The answer was that it was full of his family and friends, all there to see Eamonn Andrews ambush him during his guest appearance on *Opportunity Knocks* to feature him as the subject of *This Is Your Life*.'

Les loved a pint and was uncharacteristically pissed-off by this embargo. I suddenly found myself lying through my teeth to a man who was my friend. This would be a good time to tell you why and how I first met him.

One of the strengths of *Opportunity Knocks* was how it featured amateur and semi-professional acts whose ambitions were less about wanting a career in TV and more about boosting their profile, and therefore income, in a very vibrant pub and club culture. Boasting that they'd been seen on TV would automatically double, sometimes triple their usual fee. Professional acts, on the other hand, didn't want to appear as they possessed no willingness to be dubbed amateur or semi-professional. In fact, an appearance on our go-as-you-please show could bring their earnings down!

In all our audition sessions we would rope off an area behind our production desk so that any professionals, such as friends of Hughie or ourselves, could sit and chat with us between auditions. One such audition session was in Milton Hall, Manchester.

It was a day like any other, the room packed with people waiting for their chance to get on the telly, standing room only. I noticed one chap perched just inside the main entrance, who I thought I recognised as one of those professional comedians who came out of nowhere, stormed the working men's club and cabaret circuit, and then vanished as fast as they arrived. And assuming this, I thought I'd invite this professional entertainer to sit in our VIP area.

Having waited for a suitable lull in proceedings – a piano was being moved from the centre of the floor back to where it belonged as unseen backing for the show's many singers – I walked from our desk over to the crowded entrance door and began to ask this fellow over to join Hughie Green, our production manager Doris Barry and myself when a lady I now know to have been Meg, his first wife, interrupted me, saying her husband was here to audition.

And thus I had my first meeting with a very grumpy Les Dawson.

I was dumbfounded, thought they were likely to be a double act taking the mickey, so played along, explaining: 'Well, you can't just turn up here and expect us to see you. You have to write in, wait to receive an application form and send it back to us ... we then decide whether we can fit you into a very tight schedule of auditions at the time and date you've indicated as convenient on your application form before we send you a formal invite...'

'We've done all that,' said Meg, wafting an invite in my direction.

'Hang on a minute,' I said, before nipping off to ask our PA, Cindy Winter, to find the application form for this professional comedian called Les Dawson so we could get him up to do his audition asap.

Cindy spent quite a while shuffling through the comedians, but couldn't find one for Les. Eventually she gave up. There wasn't one. 'Oh, hang on,' she then said. 'I've had an idea,' and after a couple of minutes found it. It had been in the 'pianists' stack not 'comedians'; someone in our Thames office had written 'pianist – Lesley Dawson' on the top of the form. An inauspicious start, I'm sure you'll agree.

The confusion, of course, had come about because Les also played that instrument, so I asked our pianist, Jack Dove, to give me a hand shifting our piano to a central position. 'Oh, no!' said Hughie Green. 'Not another pianist. Can't we have a comic to liven the room up?"

I didn't respond, just shouted: 'Mr Les Dawson, please...'

Les walked up to the stool, sat down, lifted his arms to play, but then swivelled around, leaned on the keyboard, stared Hughie Green straight in the eyes, and said: 'In 1875, Hamish McDonald walked, single-handed, around a mountain. He had to ... one leg was shorter than the other. Hamish was the man whose great grandad on his mother's side, at the Battle of Bannockburn, had gone behind enemy lines with nothing but a bag of radishes and a yard of rubber tubing ... his mission ... to put the wind up the English.'

By now the show's host was in tears of laughter, just like the entire room full of auditionees.

Les continued with this wonderful nonsensical story full of totally original gags, until suddenly stopping, shaking his head and staring, glumly, at Hughie: 'Sorry about that,' he said. 'It just shows how the mind wanders when you're panicking.' After more peels of laughter he continued: 'No, I'm here to play a little known piece by Ludwig van Beethoven ... the very last piece he composed before he passed away. Ladies and gentlemen, The Beethoven Symphony, OPUS 33...' Les then played one long, very dramatic note, turned to Hughie and said: 'Then he died...'

Les Dawson first appeared on *Opportunity Knocks* in 1967, won it and soon afterwards became a huge star in the UK, eventually going on to host the show himself. His story really was rags to riches. Prepare to read more about this remarkable man later.

Readers already aware of my name will more than likely associate it with *Opportunity Knocks* due to Hughie's habit of mentioning it on air, as referred to earlier. You have also read by now how he wasn't everyone's cup of tea, referred to by most of our team as not 'Hughie' but 'Green'. Nevertheless, I considered him a friend and my job was to produce a top-grade transmittable show, ensuring it complied with the various union restrictions (ie: musicians' union, Equity, NUJ and BECTU), plus any other restraint and recommendation made by the ITA/IBA and government office, Ofcom.

Occasionally, he and I would come to verbal blows over a piece of content he wanted to include in one of his links. But Hughie knew that, as producer, I was the representative of the company employing both of us (Thames), technically 'publishers' of content transmitted under its name. So Hughie and I would argue the toss over almost everything and at such times I had to ensure I was in possession of all the facts. If not, he would be, and wipe the floor with me. This, thankfully, didn't happen very often, but there were occasions.

It's no secret to anyone who knew or worked with Hughie that he was politically radical, simultaneously left and right wing. He was passionate about many things and felt his presence on the nation's TV screens gave him the right to express extreme views now and then. Hughie always felt that his programmes were a 'force for good' and would get a bee in his bonnet over issues he felt were either unfair, unforgivable, unethical, unreasonable or just plain unjust.

He would phone me (any time day or night) in a raging tirade about something he had just seen or read, and I had to listen. I called these 'one-yard-phone-calls', because you had to hold the phone at least a yard away from your ear. They would be immediate too. My phone would ring, I'd pick it up and – without any form of courteous greeting – Hughie would go straight to his point.

He even made such a phone call at 03:30am which began: 'Are you watching this crap on the box?' I asked him what channel. 'It's on that tape Doris gave me...' When I pointed out that his VCR was only playing for him, he laughed 'What a dick-head!' and rang off! I do not doubt that every producer in his career would have been subjected to similar over-enthusiasm.

Whenever we argued about something within the content of the show I was unsure about, I had to point out (every time) how I'd need to get clearance from the regulator and/or my boss Philip Jones OBE. Sometimes I would gather enough self-confidence to confront Hughie head-on, knowing it would end up in a screaming match. I can honestly say I have had more arguments on the phone and face-to-face with Hughie Green than anyone else in my TV career.

So why did we stay good mates all those years? It's because I understood him and his lack of self-esteem. Mr Charisma on screen and with an extremely confident style in public he may have been, but in private he was a very different – and lonely – man.

I understood this better than most, especially after my extremely messy divorce in 1979. I had to keep up appearances professionally, but inside there was a massive gaping hole of loneliness. I filled it with booze and partying, neither really doing the trick because, like Hughie, I was surrounded by acquaintances not friends.

It wasn't until many years later when I met Sarah in 1991, going through something similar in her life, that I found a real soul mate. We have been best friends ever since and in 1998 we married.

Prior to then, I knew something of Hughie's pretence and he saw it in me too. We too were soul mates. Frankly, I was fascinated by the man and his extraordinary history.

Aged 14, Hughie had been a star in Hollywood – see him in a 1935 adventure film *Mr Midshipman Easy*, co-star Margaret Lockwood. As such, he never ceased to remind me that it was he who 'gave the great Carol Reed his first break as a director' (having previously been a first-class film editor). Hughie rarely mentioned however that he had also been a Squadron Leader in the Royal Canadian Air Force during World War Two and the youngest 'Boy Star' to grace the top theatres in Great Britain as 'The British and Empire Star'. I refer you to his book *Opportunity Knocked* (Fredrick Muller Ltd, London, 1965). His days before British commercial TV success were astonishing.

Often, when Hughie was feeling particularly low, he'd tell me how his years as a TV performer were a backward step from Hollywood. And I must say that, although he was ITV's biggest star at the time, I understood exactly where he was coming from.

Hughie Green couldn't act, tell a joke or sing songs, but he had charisma in bucketloads and an excellent eye for how the general public wished to be entertained. This talent for knowing what most viewers wanted was handy to producers, directors and broadcasters if they chose to listen to him. Sadly there were those who believed that his TV image defined the man – how wrong they were.

In those days, audiences were measured in number by JICTAR (Joint Industry Committee for Television Audience Research) whose figures were all about the number of households viewing a particular channel at a specific time. Nobody bothered about the nature or number of people occupying those homes in terms of their ages, gender or status. The requirement to identify and serve more specific demographics came with the birth of Channel 4 in November 1982, when it was decided that six basic demographic groupings reflected viewership – no point trying to sell a Rolls Royce to a train driver, was the theory. Sooner rather than later, the obvious shortcomings of this new system resulted in those too being broken down into even more detailed categories like gender, race, age, location, social background and education. Later, the gender heading was itself subsectioned into LGBTQ+. Ratings that previously helped to identify marketing targets became a whole new ball game for advertisers, influencers and marketeers. What had been an art form had become a science that eventually made rating the success of a TV show via mass viewership numbers impossible, thereby rendering its very existence worthless, since the target audience was no longer the general public but very small and extremely specific groups. And because the entire income of ITV came from selling commercial airtime, programme makers became totally influenced by paymasters who were, in effect, the advertising industry.

The odd thing is the BBC already knew who their viewers were (licence fee payers), but chose to ignore serving this database with programmes to suit such a mass audience in favour of competing with an ITV network that had a totally different business model and financial *raison d'être*. Yet another dog without a bicycle!

When advertisers then began to demand audience detail in terms of specific demographics (i.e. age, sex, marital status, occupation, social grade etc.), they were soon only purchasing air-time during programmes which favoured their specific target audience and the overall number of people watching became academic.

In terms of business strategy, ITV chose to make programmes that appealed to advertising agencies and sales departments. And as methods of creating a profit became more and more sophisticated, those showmen and showwomen who knew how to put 'bums on seats' were now less in demand.

The model of what and why certain programmes were made and when they were transmitted seemed to make less and less sense to those of us who had been in at the very start of commercial TV and thought we knew what was peak-time and what was not. Suddenly, our pre-Channel 4 thinking was outdated and redundant.

ITV became, first and foremost, a money-making enterprise, producing a whole new way of going about the task. Unfortunately, Hughie Green was one of the decreasing number of showmen who couldn't accept such a situation. This – together with some terrible advice – caused his downfall just before his death in May 1997.

As I said earlier, Hughie was my friend and I will go to my grave believing that the announcement at his funeral that he was the father of Paula Yates may well be genetically true, but Hughie himself never knew it while alive. He could never in a million years have kept that a secret! And nobody has come forward to say he knew about Paula, who had thought herself the daughter of *Stars on Sunday* presenter Jess Yates, simply because the fact is Hughie himself had no idea.

There will always be those who prefer to remember Hughie in a less than favourable way and there is nothing I can do about that. However, I do wish he could be remembered for being the reason so many significant newcomers enjoyed brilliant careers in show- business. How about this for a list: John Miles, John Parr, Mud, Aswad, Mary Hopkin, Peters and Lee, Showaddywaddy, Paper Lace, The Real Thing, Grimethorpe Colliery Band, Berni Flint, Tony Monopoly, Middle of the Road, Les Dawson, Tom O'Connor ... hang on, while I get my breath ... Cannon and Ball, Little and Large, Frank Carson, Freddie Davies, Maxton G Beesley, Freddie Starr, Russ Abbot, Pam Ayres, Bobby Bennett, Paul Daniels, Darren Day, Su Pollard, Ruth Madoc, Bonnie Langford, Tony 'The Muscle Man' Holland, Bobby Crush, Lena Zavaroni, Bruce Thompson, Millican and Nesbitt, Neil Reid, Shag Connors and the Carrot Crunchers! And it does not, by any means, include all those who owe their start to *Opportunity Knocks*.

In 1994, I was busy producing and directing *Catchphrase* (hosted by Roy Walker) for Action Time, a brilliant production company headed by Stephen Leahy, co-creator of *The Krypton Factor*. After a busy day in the London office, I decided to take the train home to Manchester. However, I decided this on the spur of the moment and was therefore late arriving at Euston. It seems odd now, but in 1994, although smoking was an acceptable activity, it was just beginning to be frowned upon. The smoking carriages were purposely situated at the farthest end of the station, obviously by a non-smoker!

Being late, I found myself running along the platform (a sight rarely seen) and after what seemed like a mile arriving at the door of the train. Still not on board, I was breathlessly trying to talk to an equally breathless fellow passenger. Neither of us could make sense of the other but were both trying, like gentlemen, to give way.

We were complete strangers, but once in the carriage flopped into a pair of unreserved seats facing each other. After getting our breath back, we both suddenly saw the humour in the situation, started to cough and laugh in unison and, after a while, introduced ourselves.

Dick Evans was the principal of a further education college in Stockport so we had nothing in common, yet the two-hour journey seemed to take fifteen minutes. A few weeks after this serendipitous meeting I received a letter (emails were still in the ascendancy) from a Dr Richard Evans inviting me to consider becoming a member of the Board of Governance at Stockport College of Further Education.

I immediately wrote back, attempting to explain that my job as a producer/director was such that looking into the future any further than a couple of hours would be folly. I could never be sure whether I'd be available, let alone in the country. I added that I was flattered even to be considered for such an important post, but suggested he should offer it to someone with a more predictable lifestyle.

Dr Dick was insistent, so eventually I found myself co-opted onto the board, specifically sponsored by the principal himself. He was a remarkable man with four doctorates and a great sense of humour whose vast knowledge, perspective and radical opinions on further education I couldn't help but admire. That, plus learning about his extremely unexpected love of canal longboats and the music of Chicago blues singer, guitarist and harmonica player Howlin' Wolf, made him the most fascinating man I'd met outside showbusiness.

At the time I found this strange addition to my CV amusing, as I'd attended the same college as a night-school pupil forty-three years before while working at ABC-TV Didsbury in 1958. Back then my subject had been electrical engineering and a ninety per cent pass was essential if I was to qualify as a Grade B camera operator. This upgrade from camera assistant to Grade B was massive and involved not only a rise in salary but also the ceremonial burning of a pair of disgustingly filthy cloth gloves (camera assistants wore those because their main job was keeping the heavy one-inch-thick camera cables away from the feet of the camera operators).

Fast forward to 1994, and as I took my place as a new member of the Board of Governance around a large round table in the carpeted posh part of Stockport College, I couldn't help pausing to think how far away it was from scrambling around on a dirty TV studio floor reeling cables into neat figures of eight, this episode being one more example of how unplanned, unexpected and serendipitous most of the events of my life were in reshaping it and earning me new and diverse friendships for years to come. To say I was out of my depth at that first meeting is an understatement of epic proportions. For a start, every speaker packed their statement with a thousand and one acronyms, which to the totally untrained in the world of education turned all their speeches into gibberish.

The clerk to the chairman gave me a pamphlet identifying such acronyms in alphabetical order. Had I looked I'd have realised that I'd already received this info in my far-too-big-to-study welcoming pack and never read it. I'd have been no better off if I had! I promised myself that I would learn them, but never did get around to it.

Before long, I was able to participate but mostly came away from those two-hour meetings wondering what had been achieved aside from agreeing on the next meeting's agenda. Even after the very first, where I was welcomed and greeted like some alien being, I had a sense of foreboding that would eventually manifest itself.

Being on this board did allow me the opportunity to walk quite freely around the vast college site to meet and appreciate the work being done by the fantastic teaching staff. I'd been there quite a while before I dared venture into such a labyrinth of learning. I began to recall that, back in 1957, the college was known as Stockport Tech and associated more with the vocational than the academic.

I walked past piles of bricks in the Built Environment Dept and half-constructed cars and bikes in the Motor Vehicle Maintenance Dept and began wondering if I had unwittingly wandered into an entirely different college. Somehow the hustle and bustle, laughter, vibrancy and the 'muck and bullets' of this college seemed to have nothing whatsoever to do with the place we were attempting to govern in that plush boardroom so far away in the admin building.

Over a couple of weeks I found myself meandering in this way, beginning to realise why the college principal, Dr Dick, was so at odds with the managers and members on the board. He was a very down-to-earth man. His priorities tended more towards practical than academic and, while his string of doctorates and qualifications suggested otherwise, he was less interested in paper qualifications and far more concerned with the students' frame of mind and ability to earn a better living after leaving the college.

Eventually my presence on the board became less observational and I found myself chipping in and, naturally, increasingly in breach of standing orders (which always seemed infinitely more important to the chairman than any of the 'content' being discussed). The last time the guy invited me to interject with a point of information, I didn't make myself at all popular by identifying that if anyone were to check the minutes of the last three meetings they would find that the one word missing in all those meetings was 'student'. I'm sure they were glad to see the back of me as I followed the only person I understood, respected or made any sense of, Dr Dick, out the door.

During my many exploratory trips around the site I happened across an area situated in the bowels of an older part of the building that looked remarkably like a television studio. Having discovered this hidden treasure I quite wrongly found myself showing more interest in it than the others. But, fortuitously, that was before this fascination would become a problem for me.

In my absence the board chose to rid themselves both of Dr Dick Evans and, of course, myself. I was appalled at the injustice; like just about everything else to do with this board of governance it was all about political expediency, nothing to do with further education.

It was good to reflect, though, that throughout all of this Dick's popularity with teaching staff and his attitude towards students was in complete contrast to that of the board. This body (including a lot of aged semi-pro committee meeting goers) saw their function at a college of further education in an entirely different light to him.

A few years before, I had decided formally to retire from being a full-time freelance TV producer/director and I often think I chose to retire from the industry a tad before the industry had the chance to retire me... we'll never know. By now, I was living in Manchester with Sarah and finding retirement less than acceptable. I realised I needed the stimulus of a challenge to stop me from going completely bananas. And as time went on, my mind kept returning to that hidden treasure within the walls of Stockport College, its TV studio.

Then I noticed that the college was advertising media studies as one of its courses. Thinking 'why not?', I applied for a teaching post. To my utter astonishment I was interviewed and soon found myself in the same studio as a new 'Point Five College Lecturer', teaching a bunch of young adults the magic of broadcast TV production.

The pay was appalling, however the satisfaction of passing on some of the tricks of the trade to a group of wide-eyed youngsters more than compensated for the hours of unpaid preparation needed to ensure that my few hours of actual paid teaching were valuable.

Of course, I had a fixed curriculum to adhere to and the modules had to be taught within a strict framework set out in the academic model. Still, I was able to stray away from these parameters and, hopefully, bring the subject to life, adding a little of the magic I had enjoyed during my time doing the job.

During those few years teaching at the college it was always a thrill to see students graduate. Initially, the qualification was the HND (Higher National Diploma). After a couple of years 'academic brains' decided that an HND wasn't sexy enough to attract fee paying students to the place, so they renamed it a 'Foundation Degree'. They even managed to do a deal whereby any student who passed this degree with a good grade had the chance to be considered for entry into a proper university for a further two years, to qualify for a BA.

Suddenly, this vocational college had become a mini-university. The curriculum was re-written to contain more academic essay-writing and seminar-type tuition, practical workshops almost disappearing altogether.

I'm sure this re-branding had the opposite effect to that intended. It frightened young people and their parents away. But that's just another thing I'll never be able to prove.

I had learnt during my first couple of years teaching this course that, in the main, the students were young people who for whatever reason had been less than successful during their school years and now wished to learn a trade in order to get a job and earn money.

Yes, there was more than a little truth in the popular theory that people chose media studies as the easy option. However, many students have since told me that, having signed on, for the first time in their lives they were given psychological tools that motivated them into creating and communicating in equal measure.

I'm still very proud of every student I was able to help complete their two-year media studies course. I remain happily in touch with many of them who are now earning a good living, some even in the media, which I hadn't ever imaged would be the case.

Years earlier at NEMTEC (North Eastern Media Technology Education College), Sarah and I found ourselves teaching media to a dozen or so miners who had been so cruelly made redundant from one of the north east collieries.* These men had been forced (by the Government) into applying for and attending a college, any college, of further education in order to get their dole money. They'd looked through the subjects on offer and decided that media studies seemed easiest. So, as a bunch of passive and belligerent students, they came into our lives. Over the years, Sarah and I often reflect on those days and think how lucky we are to have met them, a group of people who'd had their credibility ripped from them! One minute they were bread winners and national heroes. The next they were unable to provide for their families and seen, by some, as national villains, unceremoniously and psychologically castrated! And here they were, up from the pit, to learn about *what* again?

Sarah and I began to enjoy sharing anecdotes with them, playing with the notion of saying something, anything, in visual form. They gradually opened up and, after a few weeks, started to regard Sarah

---

* *I'm not about to bang on about the Miners' Strike, or Mrs Thatcher's heartless stupidly and cruelty, because I want this book to be more about positivity. There is enough written by far more qualified people than I about it – put 1980s Miners' Strike into Google and stand back.*

and I as friends, albeit drinking friends, but soon we'd earned their trust. We announced they were going to make their own programme on video tape and, suddenly, they no longer regarded media studies as easy but instead started to see the possibilities of telling stories via modern technology. Stefan told me that before college he'd been turned down after a particularly bad interview, due to nerves, for the post of car parking attendant in Newcastle. He told us this over a pint in the pub next door and insisted on buying it as he had just heard that following another interview (no nerves now, due to what he learned about himself at NEMTEC) he'd got a job. Only not as a parking attendant this time, but as manager of that same car park.

The most memorable and glorious part of the miners' story came on the final day of their time at NEMTC. They had devised, written, shot and edited their own story on videotape. A chap called Ernie, being the most senior of the group, had bagged the role of director and some of them had taken on dual roles, or in one case five.

On the final night, these miners invited their wives, partners and friends to see what they had been up to; wives, partners and friends who were convinced they had been doing nothing except go through the motions of turning up in order to qualify for their cash.

Consequently, our lecture room was packed and I was surprised to see that our students had positioned themselves as a group in the front of the bleachers and not, as expected, with their guests. But hey, this was their gig. They seemed to know what they were doing.

Sarah and I made a brief introduction on behalf of the college, dimmed the lights and cued the playback of their documentary. It was dreadful. However, throughout the playback there was utter silence and as the credits started to roll, starting with: A 'Redundant Miners' Film – 'Written by ...' and so on, the applause began and got louder and louder as each name came up. When the credits finally ended on a director credit for Ernie, the entire audience stood as one and whooped and cheered as at some amazing movie premiere.

I looked at Sarah, she was in floods of tears! Sarah looked at me, I was in floods of tears! The miners all stood up and took a bow... more whoops and applause and emotion. It had been the most exciting night of their lives. The course had done more for these miners than any academic body could have possibly planned for or imagined. It had won renewed respect from their wives and families.

OUR time at NEMTEC was to come to a sudden halt as someone somewhere ordered its closure. We never found out why. As far as we were concerned, we had fulfilled our remit to the students, some of whom went on to do much greater things.

However, we always felt that the two of us had benefitted more from the NEMTEC experience because we had learned a lot from the miners about priorities. And then even more from a group of a dozen profoundly deaf students, to whom we gave seminars on unlikely subjects as chosen by themselves.

The pros and cons of sound effects in TV quiz shows was one such. To prep for that was a nightmare, given that it was pointless to utilise any sound effects. Again, the students themselves provided all the answers and exposed all the areas of mystery while blowing massive holes in the official national curriculum published for their course. Another learning curve, and again it was us – particularly me – who was doing most of the learning.

I knew my time in the education industry had come to an end when, towards the final months of my tenure at Stockport College of Further Education I was told that my entire rationale was wrong and that the purpose of college was simply to deliver a qualification. What any student chose to do with that qualification was of no concern to the college as they were 'not an employment exchange'!

And here was I, thinking it had all been about preparing students to discover and join a workforce. That told me! I left both the college and teaching profession, but only after serving a whole year's notice so I could help my final year students reach a satisfactory conclusion.

It's a joy, through the oddities of Facebook, Meta, Instagram, WhatsApp and LinkedIn, to follow the career paths of some of the more successful students. I was even employed by one to voice a character in a radio play that he'd both written and successfully managed to get on air. The character was a late-night radio talk show host unremittingly beleaguered by the eponymous character Barry

Pigeon, a rather strange nightwatchman who has precious little to watch! The script (by talented Kurt Brookes) was fresh and a joy to perform. Like most of these occasional jobs, it was fun to deliver while having little or no effect on my fast-dwindling bank account!

One job, however, did positively affect my finances, although it did cost me, momentarily, a dip in credibility. I think the realisation that the fee paid to portray the character countered any permanent damage to my reputation. After appearing in the opening titles of *Off Their Rockers* stark naked, running across the screen and asking two young ladies to photograph me, I thought nothing I did later could damage what little of that I had left, so 'The Scuba Diver' came as a shock to my system.

I was on my patio pruning my interminable ivy when my agent Alex phoned to ask whether I could be in Eccles in an hour. Since Eccles is about six miles from my home this was totally doable.

Some weeks earlier, I'd attended an audition where the director asked me out of the blue if I could walk across the room as though wearing flippers. Naturally I obliged, to peels of laughter and a very solid thank you, which left me in no doubt that this funny walk marked the end of my chances. This moment of sheer silliness had completely disappeared from my memory, though, until, dutifully, I presented myself at the Eccles swimming pool an hour after Alex's call. The director of this obviously big shoot was the very man who had asked me to do the funny walk, Chris Cottam, a most eminent director of high end commercials more recently known for his TV work with the likes of Romesh Ranganathan and Sue Perkins. Chris walked over and said that frocks and props were waiting for me in the dressing room... could I please put them on and report back to him as soon as possible.

Quickly donning the Bermuda shorts, loud shirt, scuba diving snorkel and enormous yellow flippers, I waddled back poolside, where Chris handed me a piece of script and asked me to deliver a line to a camera mounted on a giant transatlantic crane. I said it, Chris was happy, thanked me, and said that I was free to go.

This whole Eccles swimming pool experience took me eleven minutes. Before I knew it, I was on my way back to pruning the ivy.

Alex called me while I was driving home and said that if they used this one-liner in the final edit (and it was a big *if*) the fee would be £350, plus a buyout, but that I shouldn't 'hold my breath.'

The ivy got pruned and life returned to the bliss of retirement with Sarah. It never ceases to amaze me how stress-free my life is nowadays. Most of my previous relationships had some element of concern about whether I was behaving properly or spending enough time with the other half. There always seemed to be an unfulfilled something causing friction. Not with Sarah... no friction and no stress. What could be more blissful than that in a relationship? 'You did what?' I heard Sarah say, in a way which nevertheless accepted, unreservedly, the stupidity of this foray into bit-part acting. 'Are you sure, this wasn't *Candid Camera*?'

Two days later, Alex phoned again to say they were using this one line and could I attend a photographic session the following day. She also informed me that the fee was indeed £350 for the day (eleven minutes' work), plus a buyout of £7,500!

When I arrived at the stills studio, I was greeted by a woman carrying a pair of Bermuda shorts, a loud shirt, scuba diving snorkel and yellow flippers. Once again, it took me less than a minute to don this ridiculous outfit and a further half-hour posing to camera and giving my all, thumbs-up, a salute, beaming smile, okay gesture with finger and thumb, and all manner of absurd actions required.

I was astounded that this entire process, demanding no effort, earned me £7,850 (less commission and tax). I wasn't quite prepared, however, to see a still of me in every newspaper, every weekend, posing in said scuba outfit while advertising holiday insurance! This story would normally end there except that just under one year after making this outrageous commercial, my agent phoned again out of the blue to say they had taken up the option for another year with the commercial, so there was another cheque in the post for £7,850 (less commission and tax).

Again, the story would normally end there, except this happened for a further four years and three months. I'll let you do the sums, but based on the fact that this entire job took eleven minutes, it worked out at something like £2,900 a minute. Needless to say, this was a one-off and I should imagine will remain so. Nevertheless, a very welcome moment in my new acting career.

On the subject of income, I was once directed to a site on Google, which asked 'What is Royston Mayoh worth?' The answer, according to the site, was $5million. I wish! Not even in pounds! I can't imagine how they came to that conclusion, where they got their info and why it was a very definite $5million, not $4million or $6million! I already had enough evidence of Google being less than accurate, so this new revelation only served to renew my already sceptical view about anything web related.

There was a time in my early career when I earned an obscene amount of money. I use the word 'obscene' because my dad was still working a forty-hour week and making pennies relative to my basic income. Although I was a freelance television director, thankfully I enjoyed a regular renewal of contracts which gave me the illusion of constant employment.

My dad was a strange chap! He had worked all his life at the Shirley Institute (British Cotton Industry Research Association in Didsbury, Manchester). The Shirley Institute was a research centre dedicated to cotton production technologies and had employed him since before World War Two. He had dedicated his life to Shirley, so when one day he received his redundancy notice it knocked his self-confidence and security for six. Especially as he was regarded as one of the leading experts in cotton and man-made fibre ring spinning machines. So, not long after this devastating turn of events, he was both relieved and thrilled to be offered another job. However, this one had a title that could have been invented by one of the country's top comedy writers: Head of Quality Control for Brentford Nylons.

Only those of a certain age will see the irony. For those who don't, let me to explain. Brentford Nylons was one of the best-known and least-loved names of the 1970s. It never shrugged off the image of electrostatically-charged bedsheets and a particularly nauseating advertising campaign starring the disc jockey, Alan Freeman.

My dad was surprisingly naive about businesses and greed. He genuinely thought his job was to enable Brentford Nylons to make a better product – bless him. He'd mused long and hard about how this could be done. He slowed the machines down and altered the way this man-made fibre was spun, so it produced less static. He also changed the settings on the machines, so they would produce a far wider and more user-friendly product.

The R&D department was overjoyed with dad's alterations in his quest to fulfil his role. However, the board of Brentford Nylons had noticed a distinct drop in the amount of bedding coming out of their Cramlington factory in the north east. It was pinpointed directly to their head of quality control, who had wholly misinterpreted the word 'quality'. Brentford Nylons had wanted dad to increase the volume of cheap bedding coming off the machines, not decrease it. But it was all too late. The damage to the brand had been done and sales figures began to plummet. Following lousy publicity, Brentford Nylons were in 1976 bought out by Lonrho from the receiver, but even Lonrho became a thing of the past soon after.

Dad, completely disillusioned, retired with mum to a new home and garden in Morpeth. During this time of upheaval in his life he was constantly seeing his name (Mayoh) on the end credits of some pretty mind-numbing gameshows and quizzes. He could not, in any way, imagine my job being stressful, tiring, exacting or demanding. After all, he sat and watched his telly for half an hour and naturally assumed that it had taken me half an hour to make it – why not?

When all is said and done, that is exactly the illusion that we, the production team, had spent such a long time trying to achieve. The best editor is the person who can edit a programme so that nobody would ever believe it had been edited. It was the same for production teams. The idea was to make our programmes easy viewing, which often took some doing. My dad took a very dim view of both me and the profession I was in. He was convinced that ITV had no future and that it was utilising the services of staff who had either been rejected from or would never even be considered by the BBC.

He didn't have a good word to say for anything to do with ITV, but he did like Max Bygraves. So when I found myself producing and directing a series of Max Bygraves shows I thought it might be an excellent opportunity to show my father that I wasn't a complete waste of space. I arranged a flight from Newcastle to London for my parents, together with cars and hotel. The big day came when I could sit mum and dad down in the VIP seats between the control desk and the bank of monitors in Studio 1 at Teddington Studios. The show went amazingly well and Max (during one break in recording) even welcomed mum and dad to his show. My dad was so chuffed he went bright red (most unusual for him).

We finished recording the programme and I saw my dad put his coat on. I waited for some sort of 'Well, that was very impressive...' or 'I hadn't realised how much it took to put on a show like that...' or some other positive observation. None was forthcoming, so after an awkward pause I ventured an attempt at getting some positive feedback. 'Well, dad. That might give you some idea of what I do for a living?' I said. 'Yes,' he replied. 'Very interesting. I see you had six cameras situated in different parts of the studio. You could talk to them and they could talk to you? Right?' I agreed, pleased he had taken notice. 'So your job is to choose any number from one to six ... seems straight forward to me. Come on Linda, let's find a cup of tea.' And that was that.

My entire training, years of learning on the job with the constant awareness that I had much, much more to learn ... all weighed up, compressed and shoehorned into one short and simple sentence.

No wonder dad was bitter. It has to be said he went to his grave never knowing the joke about being head of quality control. I was convinced he hadn't taken the slightest interest in my career until well after his funeral, when we discovered three suitcases packed full of scrapbooks and newspaper cuttings, including *TV Times* billings for every programme I had ever made. He was proud of me after all.

I wish I'd known that while he was alive.

Ali Bongo, Programme Associate on The David Nixon Show, *above*

John Christie, winner of Opportunity Knocks – Australia *in 1972*

6.
There's No Business Like...

IT was only after writing a few chapters of this book that it occurred to me I was omitting some of the more irritating moments in my lengthy career for reasons of trying to stay upbeat. To present them as causes of heartbreak, or even sadness, would be to enter into the realms of embellishment and hyperbole. They were nothing of the sort. However, upon reflection, I thought I should document a few.

As a very young man in the magical world of television, I'd been taught that there was always a possibility that the most horrendous things might happen to you. Therefore, to survive and remain sane a methodology was required and it had a crucial word – 'context'.

As camera crew, we were alerted to the many external factors that could ruin your best efforts. It was unspeakably stressful to see a shot ruined as a result of some external action (such as an actor being off their mark, a vision mixer mistakenly cutting your camera to line, someone tripping over your cable during a shot ... you get the idea). It was drilled into us to 'let it go'. In other words, not to allow external incompetence to affect our overall body of work.

These lessons included an awareness of the total waste of time that emotions such as temper, petulance, tantrums or just plain old-fashioned anger are when working on a studio floor.

One of the more graphic explanations of this attitude involved the realisation that a moving TV picture was made up of twenty-four frames every second. So, in a ninety-minute drama there were nearly 130,000 frames, or moments when something could go wrong. If such a scenario eventuated, therefore, it didn't matter whether it was your fault or someone else's, the secret was to forget it as soon as possible and make the most of the next opportunity (i.e. the frame to come). And while you were on air live as a camera operator these opportunities were coming thick and fast.

This is not to say that mistakes or moments when something went disastrously wrong were to be denied or even glossed over, but to remember that there was a time and place to display emotions. Those times and places rarely had anything to do with the other members of your crew or production team who, for all you knew, had their own personal nightmares to deal with. If so, they certainly didn't need your issues on top of that.

So this chapter is about those nightmares – those moments that demanded a clear mind regardless of every nerve in your body shouting 'fight'! A self-help lesson in how to manage annoyance.

To begin with, let's return briefly to Hughie Green and the query that has followed me over the years: 'Was he a c*nt?'

It was always a loaded question, usually asked in the expectation of both confirmation and insider titbits. I always replied in similar terms to the previous chapter ... banged on about his knowledge of the viewing audience ... his eye for talent ... how he could walk out of any studio straight to the airport, qualified to fly a jumbo jet!

Apart from our friendship, my approach also had a lot to do with a principle I'd been taught in my earliest days as a studio attendant, simply: 'What happens on the studio floor stays on the studio floor.'

Following Hughie's death in 1997, aged 77, the BBC chose to make a drama documentary about the man. In my opinion, *Hughie*

Green, Most Sincerely, duly broadcast in April 2008, was a disgraceful misrepresentation of his character. I understand the use of dramatic licence and the necessary embellishments to make a point, but this programme, like no other, reduced me to tears. The tears were not sad tears or happy tears, but tears of disbelief.

By the time it went to air, I was well and truly retired. So apart from my long-suffering wife/best friend, I'd nobody to talk to about this desperate sense of injustice, certainly no one who could make any difference. One full week after transmission of this garbage my irritation still hadn't gone away. Even I was sick of hearing myself rant like a demented rap star. The only thing to do was write to the Director General of the BBC with my reasons for thinking that Hughie Green had been grossly misinterpreted.

Here is an edited extract of that letter:

To: Mark Thompson
6/4/2008
Re:'Hughie Green, Most Sincerely'

Dear Sir,

The recent BBC4 docu-drama, starring Trevor Eve in the title role, was perhaps the finest example of how a person, after death, can be so cruelly misrepresented.

It must be established from the outset of this letter that I am certainly no apologist for Hughie Green.

Most, if not all, of the people who worked with Hughie Green and myself as the producer/director of both *Opportunity Knocks* and *Sky's the Limit* will recall many occasions when he and I came, quite literally, to blows.

He was, undoubtedly, a difficult man to work with; he was opinionated, stern, undiplomatic and loud. On many occasions, a complete pain in the butt. BUT for all that, he knew better than most how to make a TV show that would attract the maximum television audience in the early evening slots, which would enrich and create a healthy 'inheritance' for those shows starting at 19:30.

He was a household name and, along with Michael Miles, a pioneer of 'Real People' TV. Since Hughie Green's death there has been a constant stream of malicious misinformation.

Having watched the programme with horror, it was quite apparent that no attempt had been made to check the facts or verify the assertions. The programme was simply a visual version of a book written by Christopher Green designed to destroy the memory of his father for all time.

The depiction of Hughie Green by Trevor Eve was skilful but, like a large part of the content, quite defective. Green had a great sense of humour, something that Eve failed to portray, along with Green's considerable charisma.

At Green's funeral, Christopher seemed just as shocked and surprised at the Paula Yates revelation during the eulogy as the rest of us mourners were. All the controversy at the wake proves that both he and his sister were unaware of the Paula connection before that awful day at Golders Green Cemetery.

The amazing thing, to me, is that the BBC, especially after Gilligan and the Hutton Report, should be guilty of happily publishing unverified material.

Other great swathes of alleged plot were distorted. Was this poetic licence? Or just plain misinformation? If it was poetic licence then one should calculate the benefit to the actual story. In the case of the relationship between Hughie Green and Jess Yates the truth, as a storyline, is far more interesting than the pointless gibberish presented in this production.

I should imagine the depiction of the incredible house-keeper Mrs Carr in this BBC production would be distressing to anyone who had the pleasure of meeting her, and especially her family. The notion that this lady would even know what the 'V' sign meant, let alone using it behind Green's back, is beyond belief and quite unfair to the memory of a wonderfully quiet, gentle and charming lady who ruled the Baker Street apartment and Hughie Green with a Scottish Presbyterian rod of iron.

There is no way that Christopher, or anyone living, could be sure that Hughie Green's mother was unceremoniously shagged, doggy fashion, whilst a young Hughie looked on with

Left: David Essex, Kenny Everett, Barry Cryer, Ray Cameron and Royston Mayoh prepare another surreal episode of their show, 1981.

4.20 Razzmatazz
ALASTAIR PIRRIE
SUZANNE DANDO

The weekly pop show packed with music, madness and mayhem. Today, Ali has a chance to make a hit record and Suzanne comes face to face with Giant Haystacks. Studio guests are Depeche Mode and Kate Bush. Plus, the brand new pop game, Chartbuster.

RESEARCH ADELE EMM,
POSY HARVEY, KEN SCORFIELD,
ED SKELDING
DESIGNER PETER BINGEMANN
SERIES EDITOR ALASTAIR PIRRIE
DIRECTOR/PRODUCER
ROYSTON MAYOH
Tyne Tees Television Production

TV Times MAGAZINE Be sure to place a regular order

7.30 The Kenny Everett Video Cassette
with Arlene Phillips'
HOT GOSSIP
THE PRETENDERS

It's a bumper bundle tonight with Billy Connolly, Cliff Richard and Tom O'Connor joining Kenny Everett in magic comedy items. Anna Dawson appears as the lovely Carla, partner of the intrepid Captain Kremmen. The Pretenders sing a new number and Arlene Phillips's Hot Gossip show off their biceps in Muscle Bound.

The show is written by Ray Cameron, Barry Cryer and Kenny Everett with music by Alan Hawkshaw. Music director is Geoff Westley.

See Inside Television

DESIGNERS BILL LASLETT, PETER ELLIOTT : DIRECTOR/PRODUCER ROYSTON MAYOH : ASSOCIATE PRODUCER BRIDGET MOORE

Thames Television Production

Alastair Pirrie, *above*, with his *Razzmatazz* (1981-1987) co-host Lisa Stansfield before stardom, and a couple of TV mag listings.

Left: Royston introduces Alastair to the Duke of Kent on the *Razzmatazz* set in 1983, just before the show went on to win the prestigious Gold Award in New York, *below*.

1983 GOLD AWARD
PRESENTED TO
TYNE TEES TELEVISION
for
"RAZZMATAZZ"
PRODUCED AND DIRECTED BY ROYSTON MAYOH
International Film & TV Festival of New York

Above: The *Make Me Laugh* team including host Bernie Winters, writer Garry Chambers, producer Heather Ging, director Royston Mayoh and Jeremy Fox (Action Time).

Above: Roy inside a container pimped by designer Peter Bingemann. Travelling by road between major cities, it magically appeared on TTTV's *Get Fresh* as a spaceship.

Left: Warming up for Bonnie Langford in 1985, before she pays tribute to music hall star Vesta Tilley on *Supertroupers*. *Above*: Celebrating her 21st birthday with Bill Pertwee.

The paperweight, *right*, was presented to guests on *The Mind of David Berglas*, a memento of an illusion. Each one had a mind-blowing personalised prediction under the base.

Below: Tyne Tees made *The Mind of David Berglas* for Channel 4 in 1986. Here we have a wide shot of the studio. Can you spot a certain 'producer' having a rest and lying down, in the red jacket? David Berglas, meanwhile, is taking the applause.

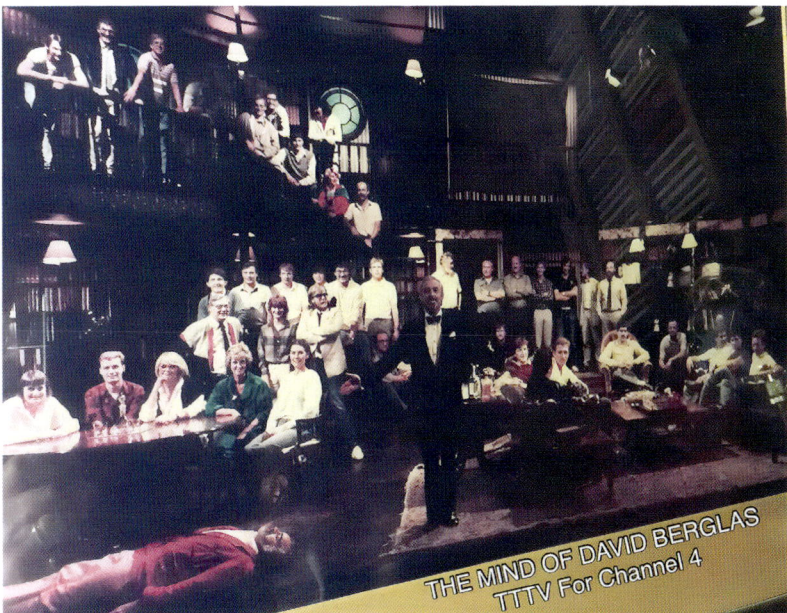

THE MIND OF DAVID BERGLAS
TTTV For Channel 4

Above: A profile pic from a magazine feature in 1989 about the making of Channel 4's general knowledge quiz *Fifteen to One*, which originally ran from January 1988 to December 2003.

BRONZE · AWARD
" TIMEKEEPERS " (Titles)
Experimental Film & Video:
- Computer Generated -
ACTION TIME LIMITED
1995

Above: George Carl gatecrashes the transmission card as the very first live image to appear on the Belgian commercial Flemish channel VTM in February 1989.

Left: Royston Mayoh with presenter Bill Dod before an episode of *Timekeepers*, an award-winning series produced by Action Time for the BBC, 1995-1996.

Above: The view from Roy and Sarah's hotel window in Bombay, now Mumbai.
Right: The couple pose at the Taj Mahal.

Left: Presenter and film actress Divya Seth on the set of *Aao Guess Karan*.

Below left: Presenters Desikan and Vandana Ranganathan on the set of *Jaane Kya Tune Kahi,* with Andrew Pemberton and Royston. Both shows were directed by Shoojit Sircar, *below*, now a Bollywood director, and produced by Siddhartha Basu (Synergy), with executive producer Royston (Action Time).

Top left: Bollywood, 1996-2001. Home to India's first lottery show *Khelo Number Khelo*.

Above: The main junction box for the entire studio power ... and not a health and safety officer in sight!

Centre left: Outdoor set building.

Below: Roy mid-flow during construction of the set.

Below left: A sewing machinist fashions a 200-foot Cyclorama.

Left: Technical director Karan Prabakaran and production manager Lesley Davies.

Above: The very moment when Pavorotti kicked the football during the Three Tenors promotional video. It was for the 1994 World Cup and directed by Royston Mayoh, produced by Rocky Oldham, *inset*, and commissioned by Time Warner.

Left: Royston Mayoh busily making one of hundreds of self-taped auditions. His chances of success, he has calculated, are similar to his chances of becoming the next Prime Minister.

Right: The most important moment during the second International Indian Film Awards in Sun City, 2001. Having noticed this French acrobatic act's anchorage hadn't been completed, Roy ordered a break in live transmission so they could be mended – a vital decision that cost him the 2002 gig!

Left: Some of the original cast of *Off Their Rockers*, namely Royston Mayoh, Seb Craig, Rosie Bannister, Sonia Elliman, Rosemary Macvie and Iris Sharples.

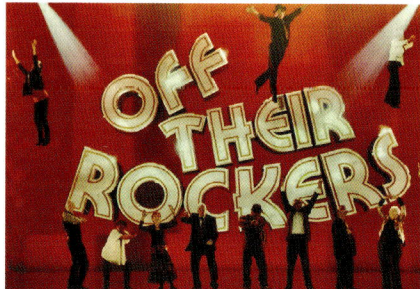

the Major weeping in the background. This was a scene that was utterly offensive to any of us who knew and met Mrs Violet Green ... it was a shocking, valueless and pointless intrusion. Certainly neither Major Green nor Violet herself could have related this story. The only other two people there would be the stud and the young Hughie. Unless this primary research came from the stud then it only leaves Hughie as a boy, and if Hughie ever related this story to a member of his family then, in all decency, that is where it should have stayed.

The un-verified defamation of Hughie Green's mother was inappropriate. If it was only included to demonstrate why Green was wary of women, then the message could (and should) have been generated via some well written narrative dialogue. But I rather feel that it was included for pure cheap sensationalism.

There is no doubt that a documentary based upon the complexities of Hughie Green would make great television. There is no doubt that sections of such a documentary would depict a man without a conventional family life, a man committed to his on-air persona and, in many instances, a pain in the butt. An authentic portrait of this 'larger than life' man would also feature his charm, humour, charisma, popularity, and 'other life' as an aviator (his company was G&M Air Interests). It would also surround Green with the advisors and 'friends' who played such a major part in his busy and productive career.

I'm sure that had Trevor Eve been made aware of the width and depth of the character he was asked to portray, as a highly talented actor he'd have tackled his interpretation differently.

Hughie Green was not the best of dads. Hughie was the first to know that, but I remember quite a few times when he went out of his way to help his son. As I was only slightly older than Christopher, Hughie would seek my opinion on his son's actions and problems. I'm afraid I was of little help. Hughie Green was a man who was desperately sad that he couldn't get near to his son and, for that matter, his daughter.

I am no apologist for Hughie Green, but I must try, via this letter, to redress the injustice meted out to him by the BBC.

Royston Mayoh

In short, Hughie Green gave more to the independent television industry in the United Kingdom than almost any performer of that period in broadcasting history. And no, I never did receive a reply.

Actually, Hughie and I were involved in two programmes.

Along with the first national television talent show *Opportunity Knocks*, we also worked together on *The Sky's The Limit*, a re-vamp of *Double Your Money* which, also hosted by Hughie, had been ITV's first quiz show when it went to air days after the commercial channel's launch in September 1955. Prior to then having been on Radio Luxembourg, *Double Your Money* was itself based on the American radio quiz show *Take It Or Leave It*, from where we get the saying 'That's the $64,000 question'.

Produced by Yorkshire Television, *The Sky's The Limit* had a straightforward quiz show format too and ran from 1970-1974, virtually a replica of the much earlier programme that had, in effect, launched ITV in the UK along with Michael Miles's *Take Your Pick*.

Hosted by Hughie with co-hosts Monica Rose, Audrey Graham and Katya Wyeth, contestants answered questions on their specialist subjects, correct answers increasing their cash pile. In round one, the value of a right answer rose from £1 to £100 (roughly equivalent to not far short of £2,000 nowadays). Whether or not they answered a further 'special question' correctly dictated qualification for further rounds in which contestants entered a soundproof box. As the show went along, the questions became more complex – the final round question coming in five parts. Winners bagged 21,000 miles of travel and £600 in spending money (equivalent to £10,000 now). I directed it and our producer was Peter Holmans.

Opportunity Knocks meanwhile, was first broadcast on the BBC Light Programme in 1949 and thereafter on Radio Luxembourg in the 1950s. It had come to ITV in June 1956. It would be eight years, however, before it was given a firm television berth and a long one at that, broadcast on the channel and hosted by Hughie from 1964-1978. In 1987, it would be revived by the BBC and hosted for two years by Bob Monkhouse as *Bob Says Opportunity Knocks!*, before dear Les Dawson fronted a single run in 1990. I worked on the show from 1966 to the end of Hughie's stint in 1978, when it had a forty-five minute Monday 6.40pm timeslot, serving to build the sort of early evening viewership that led to top soap *Coronation Street* attracting upwards of 18 million viewers, another ITV programme valued for its weekly celebration of regionality.

During my tenure, *Opportunity Knocks* strayed from its normal 'six new acts' and 'all winners show' on a few notable occasions and did a few specials. Among them was the first colour production from Channel 9 in Melbourne, Australia, included in the UK as just one programme in the standard series of twenty-six, which meant the UK winner from the previous show had to travel down under to compete again, while the winner of the Australian show headed to the UK to defend their title. That Aussie winner by the way was John Christie – the singer, not the serial killer – who won a further five times and became a West End star as lead in the musical *Time*.

And in another innovation, new and aspiring writers from the viewing public were invited to contribute a five-minute sketch. These plays were then brought to life by some prominent actors, including Garfield Morgan, Patsy Rowlands, Peter Madden, Rita Webb, Anthony Jackson, Anna Karen and Jack Smethurst. Every one of the successful six went on to make a career as a professional writer.

Another *Opportunity Knocks* special came from the Trident nuclear submarine, moored in Clydebank. This particular show became a political hot-potato well-documented in journalist and historian Chapman Pincher's book *The Secret Offensive: A Saga of Deception, Disinformation, Subversions, Terrorism, Sabotage and Assassination* (St Martin's Press, New York, 1985). Although the programme had been openly discussed for months within the Light Entertainment department headed by Philip Jones, on the eve of our scheduled filming day our normal planning stages were brutally interrupted by the special interest of the British Security Services. The UK press immediately assumed Hughie had become political, which upset Thames TV, the IBA and a Government that was under the premiership of Edward Heath.

This very public and unfair row didn't do Hughie's reputation with his audience any good either but, somewhat bizarrely, boosted the viewership.

We were waiting in a hotel near Glasgow. 'We' being a skeleton two-man 16mm (reversal) crew (camera operator/lighting director and sound supervisor), for Hughie's arrival. Then, as in a scene from a poorly-cast pastiche of James Bond, a very tall and handsome man in sunglasses (honestly) joined our company at the bar and began to ask some very random questions like: 'Whose idea was it to film on Clydebank?', 'Who gave permission?' and 'Who is in charge?' Naturally, I stepped forward and asked this bizarre stranger to introduce himself and explain why he was asking so many questions.

To my utter astonishment he explained he was from a section of the security services and would be overseeing our activities. I never found out his name or from which particular section he was from. However, I did overhear one officer on Trident refer to him later as 'Commander'. He was a mystery then and remains a mystery to this day. Throughout filming, he would step in and stick gaffer tape over the faces of dials (whether these showed sensitive information or not didn't bother us) and such attempts at secrecy only added to the excitement of filming there.

Hughie, meanwhile, was soon on top form interviewing various technicians within the sub, each interview ending with a link to an act who then performed live in the studio. This meant that all of the footage shot in the submarine could be edited, hopefully approved, and cleared by the Commander.

The show itself contained the same level of performing talent as any of the other twenty-six programmes in the series, but Hughie's submarine links were dependent upon the Commander finishing his removal of shots he didn't care for, thereby removing any sense of geography within Trident and several bits of interesting footage. After he'd finished with his scissors it was quite obvious we could have built a wee set in the corner of the studio and saved the expense of going to Scotland and putting up with the constant strain of censorship. But that's showbusiness!

The Commander had rendered the whole concept worthless, undoubtedly the point of the exercise. It also stopped any other idiot thinking about utilising the UK's premier nuclear deterrent as generic television talent show fodder.

Opportunity Knocks had a format that happily lent itself to venue changes and none more bizarre than our trip to Fuji TV in Japan in 1972, as expanded upon in chapter three. It was also a programme that not many TV directors seemed eager to work on. Firstly, there was the 'stigma' of being associated with amateurs, as if in some way it made the directors themselves any less professional. And second, the popular belief that Hughie was the devil incarnate!

This flowed from an underlying belief that if he were to express a dislike for a director, it was effectively the end of their Thames career in Light Entertainment. This absolute belief was nonsense and rather underestimated the power and professionalism of our boss, Philip Jones, who knew Hughie better than most.

For me, *Opportunity Knocks* provided a more than pleasing way of life for well over 200 programmes. Demanding and challenging, it provided regular visibility on a national network and paid well. The nature of the format (six diverse acts, plus a winner each week) gave me seven weekly visual challenges within a tiny budget. Added to this was the reality that each act really had little or no experience of performing in a TV studio. So the first job was always to create an atmosphere in which each act could feel as relaxed as they were when performing in a pub, club or other everyday environment. This aspect of the job can be even more demanding when working with top professionals, but more of that anon.

SHOWBUSINESS. That's both 'show' and 'business'. The clue is in the name. It's no secret that putting on a show is all about bums on seats or, in the case of television, viewers choosing what to watch. It is also a fact that without a show there could be no business. The show must have prominence.

My initial training and entire TV career took place during an era before satellite broadcasting ... or home recording devices ... or digital platforms ... and all the other recording paraphernalia that today render paper and ink listings magazines irrelevant.

You could be forgiven therefore for thinking that as an old timer I preferred the halcyon days, but you would be wrong!

Yes, live TV, as a director, technician or performer, was incredibly stressful. That stress manifested itself as excitement and motivation. However, now I am a viewer like everyone else, I love the freedom provided by catch-up TV of being able to record an entire series to binge watch or just store. As I do the option to pick and choose from any genre or channel. I have to stop now and again to appreciate this new digital age, especially during those rare moments when I get angry that there is too much to choose from. What a fantastic dilemma for any television viewer, anywhere.

Having spent a lifetime with programme makers and production companies, I can't help but attempt to follow the ever-changing trends and popularity of those eager to make it big in a constantly evolving industry. There will always be competition between the programme makers for dominance but it's most likely these days to be about which programme maker is bankable enough to invest in, or which original format (naturally with provable IP) has potential for both longevity and international sales.

Already programme formats have become currency on the international market. It's widely recognised that ones which deliver a relatively poor performance in their country of origin can, when suitably adapted, provide massive popularity elsewhere. The 'show' is still needed ... just. But the business aspect has overtaken it. Here in 2023, it's the 'business' that has prominence.

As a keen mathematics student back in the day, the accountancy side of showbusiness offered me considerable enjoyment, creating self-calc' spreadsheets and playing with existing figures. But the fundamental idea of buying something for a pound and selling it for two always stuck in my throat as being immoral, unjust and unfair. No matter who tried to convince me otherwise with a perfectly good justification that buying something for a quid, improving it, and then selling it on for two, the basic notion of that transaction in my mind remained as being fundamentally immoral.

You are forgiven for reading that and thinking: 'How naïve, Royston.' I would agree with you, but this overwhelming dislike for profiteering came from my father. As an only child, I was brought up to be scared of my own shadow. I was told, repeatedly, that I was the result of the only time my father got drunk. It was also clear that the arrival of this accidental baby had effectively ruined both of my parents' careers.

This was 1941, during World War Two, so with sirens and air-raid shelters to contend with it's understandable that children were disciplined by their parents to do as they were told, be seen and not heard. That was certainly the case for me. Naturally, I had no concept of anything else (such as the existence of brothers or sisters) and as people respected my father, I unquestioningly believed all he taught me. The immorality of profit was one of those thoughts injected deep in my subconscious and, 81 years later, it's still there!

Sometimes, I do wish that it wasn't.

It's for this reason that the word 'business' has always seemed to be a field of study easy to avoid. Of the two, I majored on 'show', which offered far more potential for enjoyment. Now retired, I think about the difference it may have made financially to my pension had I shown more interest in 'business', but then I think to myself that I have all I need in abundance, so probably made the right choice.

As you've read, showbusiness fascinated me from the moment I walked into that mysterious space called a 'TV studio'. I met people laughing about their time in a German concentration camp; people just back from the Korean war with limbs missing; young men much older than their years simply celebrating being alive.

I saw actors in the canteen ordering 'egg under toast' (an egg cost 3d, a slice of toast 3d, but egg *on* toast 8d.) I heard singers limbering up, watched musicians maintain instruments and dancers queue to see Nurse Willy for bunion plasters! The spectre of showbusiness backstage took my breath away with excitement every time I walked into this magical world. Most mornings, I actually ran to work.

My introduction to this wonderful world, via its beginnings as a 'fish and chip boy' and eventually in full-time employment, further included the three extraordinary weeks between my school years and first studio job when I joined Robert Gandey's United Circus. This was a time when I probably learnt more about tiredness, hard work and physical pain than any other comparable period. The whole experience was a shock to every system in my body, to this day I regard it as one of the most pivotal times in my life.

I still have numerous pictures of clowns around my home, they serve as a constant reminder of days when show and business were painfully entwined. They also serve to remind me that showtime and real life are rarely one and the same. I can quite understand why people suffer from coulrophobia (fear of clowns), but for me their look doesn't generate fear. Instead it brings to mind a time when the colourful make-up was a perfect camouflage for rookie innocence.

As a 16-year-old white grammar school youth, I was utterly unprepared to be subjected to racism. I'll never forget the indignity and horror of being judged and assumed guilty, however, simply due to being part of a small group of offbeat and exotic people. Yet for circus boss Joe Gandey and family this was an everyday occurrence they'd learned to live with for many years and accepted as the norm. I considered it an unbearable assault on my illusory loftiness! It took a long time before Joe could get me to a state of calm where I could accept his explanation and the reality of the situation.

Joe explained that circus people were an easy target for anyone looking to blame someone for a robbery or any unexplained local breach of the law and having listened to his wisdom (endorsed by his wife Mary and the rest of the group) I began to understand something I'd never considered or even thought about before that moment. Without realising it, I had been guilty of racism on many occasions prior to this auspicious day and was ashamed of myself.

For many years, Robert Gandey's United Circus had proudly boasted that it was 'England's Largest Single Mast Circus' despite it being small and involving very few people. Due to its size, it could move relatively quickly from one bit of common ground to another a few miles away (having gained the appropriate council permissions and rental waivers), which effectively meant it could attract a brand new local audience every time it moved, rarely staying at one site for longer than three days. The circus would also offer an afternoon matinee in addition to its evening performances, which meant very few vacant seats. A small business, it was still a viable concern.

Even so, shifting it from one place to another was no mean feat, especially as moves always began following evening performances. And the people who were physically involved in the move were the same who just performed both matinee and evening performances.

The entire tent, plus all its contents, including seating, had to be stowed away, while the very last thing to be disassembled was the central 'king' pole. The journey from one site to the next was taken before the evening meal or sleep were even considered. At first light next morning, Joe would be first to emerge from his caravan before conducting the traditional time-honoured shout: 'King pole, Calor gas, khazi..!' As it was deemed to be extremely bad luck to pitch the king pole in the same position as a previous occupant, he would then examine the ground and declare the exact spot. That done, the Calor gas which meant a proper breakfast for people and animals, and after breakfast, well, you can probably guess.

Those three missions accomplished, the tent would be erected and secured, followed by seating, performance area and box office. The last job of the morning was to drive into town and announce, via a loudspeaker, that 'The circus is in town...' Then it was time for lunch, make-up and standby for the matinee.

Between matinee and evening show there was time for maybe an hour or so's relaxation. Following the evening performance, bed (or if it was the last day the beginning of the move again). I've detailed all that purely to illustrate that being a part of this small circus was no walk in the park. It was exhausting, even for a 16-year-old, and we must have looked unkempt when not in costume and make-up.

It's easy to see how the locals must have viewed circus people with suspicion. The strange and wondrous thing was they didn't associate those performing in the ring as being the very same untidy lot who mingled with them in town. Such was their suspicion that circus people were always first in line when there was a breach of the law.

In the minority, they met with bigotry. However, when the same human beings performed in the ring they were greeted with whoops of laughter, applause and delight. Ever since, I have viewed such prejudice as pure ignorance and stupidity.

Gandey's Circus also taught me to appreciate the vast amount of work always necessary to put on a show. The expression 'there's no business like showbusiness' never applied more than it did in those three weeks of hard physical graft. However, the many moments of sheer joy always provided the solution to restoring the body to normality. And that joy came from performance.

Joe Gandey gave me a name, Cha-Cha, make-up and an act. It was only a two-minute act but, to me, it was a Royal Command every time. Its purpose was to provide a distraction from the activity needed to set up the next turn: Joe Gandey and his performing geese. These geese were called Arthur, Jane and Mary. Although they had a mind of their own, Joe was able to pre-empt their movement to make it appear they were following Joe's orders when, in reality, the reverse was true.

To prepare for this sure-fire audience winner, the geese had to be kept quiet while being ushered into their opening position and the only way this could be achieved was by putting them in the dark until needed. Which is where my act came in. During the applause for a juggler, all the lights were turned off, leaving a single spotlight on me (aka Cha-Cha the Clown). A disembodied voice then came over the loudspeakers: 'Cha-Cha! There is a present waiting for you to open...' Cha-Cha would then mime a few bewildered responses as if to say: 'Who? Me?' 'I can't see any present.' 'Can *you* see a present?' And then finally: 'You mean this here..?'

The present was a large trunk placed there moments before. Cha-Cha eventually found it and became excited as he tried to get it open. That done, he pulled out a large floral dress and floral hat. The disembodied voice came on the loudspeakers again: 'They're all yours – try them on! Do you think Cha-Cha should try them on?' Naturally the audience shouted encouragement that he should.

Once Cha-Cha was dressed he embarked upon an exaggerated lady's walk before returning to the trunk where he pulled out two large balloons. The voice came on the loudspeakers again. 'They're all yours – try them on! Do you think Cha-Cha should try them on?' Again the audience obliged.

Cha-Cha did as he was told and stuffed the balloons down his front before continuing his extravagant stroll around the ring. About three-quarters of the way round, though, he did a 'cod-trip', fell flat on his face and burst both balloons. Naturally (don't ask me why) there was hysterical laughter from the audience and music played to signal the bit was over. They broke into spontaneous applause just in time for the lights to go up and reveal Joe with Arthur, Jane and Mary – the performing geese made much better use of the trunk!

The odd thing is that if a clown cavorts in a dress nobody gives it an 'unnatural' connotation. A clown has nothing whatsoever to do with 'normality' which is maybe why so many people find them creepy and somewhat sinister. A clown of many years experience once explained to me that they let children believe they are suddenly the sensible ones. Clowns do all the things kids aren't allowed to.

I left the circus forever after my three-week stint of exquisite purgatory. The experience, however, stayed with me throughout my career and served as a constant reminder that nothing is achieved without considerable – and usually invisible – effort.

THEATRICAL agent Kenny Earle was a very dear friend of mine for over fifty-five years, but there was one particular day in 1980 when, just divorced despite the best efforts of Mr Clutterbuck my bank manager, who you met earlier, I was enduring the emotional anguish of involuntarily parting with my house and a lot of money.

If you recall, I lived in Newcastle upon Tyne, having accepted a job paying far less than I was used to at the time, sitting in a newly-acquired flat that was being re-wired and re-plumbed. My phone rang and on the other end was Kenny from London Management.

I confided in him that life was shit. I was missing my daughter, our lovely house in Rickmansworth, my bank account and freedom of mind necessary to enjoy working as a TV Light Entertainment producer/director in London and Elstree. Our conversation was brief and one way ... me to him, but that's what friends are for, right? Kenny listened, said something complimentary, made me feel a little better, put the phone down and continued with his job of booking acts for Butlin's holiday camps.

Half an hour passed and my new front door bell broke its silence.

I opened the door to be confronted by a fully-clad clown. He said: 'Good afternoon! I do hope you are Royston Mayoh, because if you are I have been sent by your friend, Kenny Earle, to entertain you! You see I'm a PULLYOURSELFTOGETHERYOUTWATAGRAM!'

So saying, he entered my flat and for the next half hour or so, entertained me and eight workmen with magic, balloon sculpture and ventriloquism, finishing with a ditty he called: 'Everyone's got a right to be miserable, but you are taking liberties!'

He left to huge applause and cheers from me and the workmen, who had been magically transformed from a bunch of grey middle-aged men into a gaggle of pre-school kids without a care in the world. It was a moment that I will never forget and a story that typifies the sort of friend I had in Kenny.

The PULLYOURSELFTOGETHERYOUTWATAGRAM worked wonders. It demolished my depression, in fact could be said to have cured it forever. I can say so with conviction, because even thinking about that afternoon, over forty years ago, I can't help but smile. If you could see me now, I'm still smiling at that fantastic gesture.

Our friendship was well known in our wide showbusiness circle and we stayed mates until he passed away in 2017. I am still very close to his wife Carol and three kids Tabatha, Juliet and Simon. Sarah and I regard them all as part of our family.

Over the years, I was often asked: 'Why isn't Kenny your agent?' My reply was always that had we been involved in the 'business' bit of showbusiness our friendship would have ended immediately after the opening bars of the intro! I valued his humour, anecdotes and positivity too much to chance discovering he was as good at doing business as I was. It was the 'show' bit of 'showbusiness' that we both enjoyed too much to allow the 'business' side to ruin it.

To people not actively engaged in it, 'showbusiness' has always brought forth images of glamour, starry-eyed youth, success and wealth. However to those working in it, the images are more to do with survival, fear of failure and finding the next job. I wouldn't want you to think that it is anything but the best business in the world, however. No, I definitely wouldn't want you thinking that.

But, please do remember, there really is no business like it.

For one thing, it's always been – and continues to be – associated with charitable campaigns. One of the oldest is The Grand Order of Water Rats, as mentioned earlier in relation to Billy 'Uke' Scott. It is a male-only organisation although there is a parallel charitable fund for women, the Grand Order of Lady Ratlings, founded in 1929.

Both of these charitable funds provide essential succour to fellow performers like Billy who fall on hard times, usually due to the vagaries of advanced years and their inability to perform any more. And both organisations display showbusiness at its best.

I first became aware of the Water Rats in the 1960s as a new TV director working with a wide range of variety artists. I noticed that some of the more successful ones wore a small gold emblem on their jackets and soon realised it was on all occasions, even while wearing a dinner suit. I also learned that should a member of the GOWR be seen in any circumstance without it, a hefty fine would be incurred.

They also hold an annual ball, usually at London's Grosvenor House Hotel. Its most crucial purpose, aside from raising funds, is to declare the result of a secret ballot announcing those members of the Order who will become officers for the coming year. The top job was – and remains – King Rat. It has been my pleasure to know and work with many who have filled that prestigious position over the years like Ted Ray (1949/1950/1964), Tommy Trinder (1955/1965), George Martin (1971), David Nixon (1976/1977), David Berglas (1979), Len Lowe (1983), Henry Cooper (1980), Les Dawson (1985), Roy Hudd (1989), John Inman (1993), Roger De Courcey (1994), Paul Daniels (1995/1996) and Duggie Brown (2020/2021).

During my time producing and directing *The David Nixon Show* from 1973-1977 – which, by the way, having debuted on ITV in 1972 also went on to fill the *Opportunity Knocks* Monday night slot of 6.40pm – its host, the eponymous and widely admired magician himself, proposed me for Water Rats membership. His proposal was seconded by another past King Rat and also the writer of the show, George Martin (not the Beatles producer, this one was best known, among other things, for his work on *The Basil Brush Show*, *The Keith Harris Show* and *Tonight with Dave Allen*). I'd never have known had it not been for a close friend, who told me how livid David was that his proposal had been unsuccessful. I might have been hurt by this rejection had it not been for the fact that they rejected Terry Wogan at the same time. I felt I was in good company.

The David Nixon Show was a sheer delight to produce and direct. Its team was David, George, Ali Bongo (magic associate) and myself. Our weekly meetings took place at David's Marble Arch flat and it was always up to me to bring the milk. We worked on three programmes in advance and at each meeting dealt with all three in their various states of preparation. We began with the furthest away from production with wide brush strokes, then the next furthest, and finally that week's production.

Due to a relative lack of studio technical rehearsal time (one eight-hour day only) and necessity to record the programme 'as live' (no stopping or editing), it was essential that running orders should be practical and run to time. We always had a stand-by item ready to go at every recording in case anything went so wrong it was rendered un-transmittable. This involved Ali Bongo's mother. Or to be more precise, Ali Bongo's mother's handbag.

At every recording, Ali's mum would sit anonymously in the audience. The show would be recorded and then Mrs Bongo would be escorted home in a company car. I would love to tell you what the illusion was (it involved the handbag), but if I did I would have to saw you in half and pull a rabbit out of your ear.

Owing to the nature of the programme, camera angles and shot durations needed to be rehearsed to absolute perfection. As little as 1° to the right or left of a performer and an illusion could be blown by exposing how an object was hidden from view (sometimes called 'cheats'). During rehearsals, performers were as likely to tell anyone how they did it as they were to disappear up their own nostrils.

As the director, I only had one option – to position the cameras in such a way as to provide a 'front' that the illusionist/conjurer/magician could work to and feel secure with in the knowledge that that 'front' would always be the same. This involved a strict code of conduct with camera crew and vision mixer to ensure the performer felt 100 per cent confident that their cheat was not being exposed.

Working with skilled performers and technicians is a privilege few get to enjoy. The most important aspect is to earn the trust of those relying on you to turn their specific skill into televisual reality. I often refer to this as providing 'a secure physical and psychological environment in which skilled people can feel free to excel.'

It was during rehearsals for one of my first *David Nixon Show* productions that I failed to deliver on this rule. I had only just come out of technical training and was about to learn why it is vital.

At this point I have to expose one of the tricks we often used in *The David Nixon Show*. It involved the desk or counter David stood behind while interviewing guests or presenting a piece to camera. To any viewer it was just a simple desk; in reality an amalgamation of complex trap doors operated from below by a skilled prop man.

On one occasion this job was being done by Wilf, a very able man I'd known since walking into my first studio. Wilf had known me as a student working as a studio attendant (sweeper-upper). He had seen me promoted to trainee cameraman and then to the exalted position of trainee programme director. He knew me better than any of my birth family and we had earned each other's trust and respect over a number of years. On this particular day he was under the desk receiving and pushing various items in and out of the concealed trap doors hidden on the surface. This had to be accomplished with split-second timing and to a complicated script delivered by David above the desktop. He wasn't just a magician. He had the remarkable ability to deliver lines as if they were total ad-libs, so anyone could be forgiven for forgetting it was a very tight script. Perfecting such routines is, of course, what rehearsals are for.

This particular sequence involved multiple items not just being sent down the traps, but also being sent back up a different trap positioned some feet away – and not necessarily in the order they had descended. David knew his lines from the word go. He had performed this minor miracle dozens if not hundreds of times over the years, so knew it backwards. Wilf was doing this complex routine for the very first time. David and Wilf had practised away from the studio floor in order that the trick could be performed to the amazement of the crew when it was first gone through on camera.

Take one was followed by take two ... and three ... and so on up to a point where I felt it necessary to come out of the control room to have a word. 'What the fuck is going on, Wilf?' I asked. 'If you're finding this all too much just say so and we'll re-allocate the job to someone else.' Wilf sheepishly assured me that he'd get it right, so I wandered back to my ivory tower.

When I got there I realised that I'd been followed by David Nixon, who quietly said: 'Roy, could I have a word with you?' He walked me out to the empty scene dock where he gave me one of the worst (and best) dressing downs of my entire life. 'Wilf is doing his best and at least two of the cock-ups were my fault. If you ever speak to a technician like that ever again I will refuse to work with you any more.' Initially I was shocked, but as the day went on I realised that David Nixon was correct. I learnt a very important lesson that day.

The David Nixon Show taught me an openness and honesty that I have tried to take with me throughout my entire career.

Ali Bongo too was one of the kindest and most professional people I have ever worked with. He was also an inventor of magical illusions, the very epitome of 'show' (or not show!) in showbusiness. Ali was a great character and a giggler. He'd react to most things with a nervous but charming giggle. A dedicated member of the Magic Circle, he never openly talked about the details of the methodology used in creating illusions to anyone outside that organisation.

When it became necessary for Ali to explain a trick in planning meetings for *The David Nixon Show* he would do so using a stream of strange expressions. These were headings describing the complex mechanics used in creating illusions, known among professionals as 'principles'. Of course, David understood every word spoken by Ali. George Martin and I would simply look at each other and start our own conversation made up of total gobbledygook.

Ali never offered a solution to a query immediately, but preferred to go away and think about it and then answer that query with the help of a detailed drawing or practical example. Usually this was in the form of a cardboard model produced from one of the many carrier bags that always accompanied Ali wherever he went. We did try to interest him in a briefcase, but he wasn't convinced.

Ali was in awe of Robert Harbin, inventor of the ubiquitous Zig-

Zag illusion, as was David Nixon. When they started to talk about Robert in hushed tones, George and I would repair to the kitchen and engage ourselves in the production of a pot of tea.

Ali was a personable but very private man, characteristics that don't often accompany each other in the business of 'show'. His on-stage performance image of a barmy pantomimic Far East nutcase could not have been further from this knowledgable and gentle man.

It was a privilege to call him a friend and I will be forever grateful for the insight he gave me into the world of magic and for teaching me the principle of the 'The Paddles'!

It took him five minutes to show me how it was done, and it then took me another twelve months of private practise before I had the courage to perform it in public, although not before auditioning in front of David and Ali to gain their approval. Having mastered the physical illusion I thought I was on my way, until George Martin strongly suggested I work on the patter.

There's no business like...

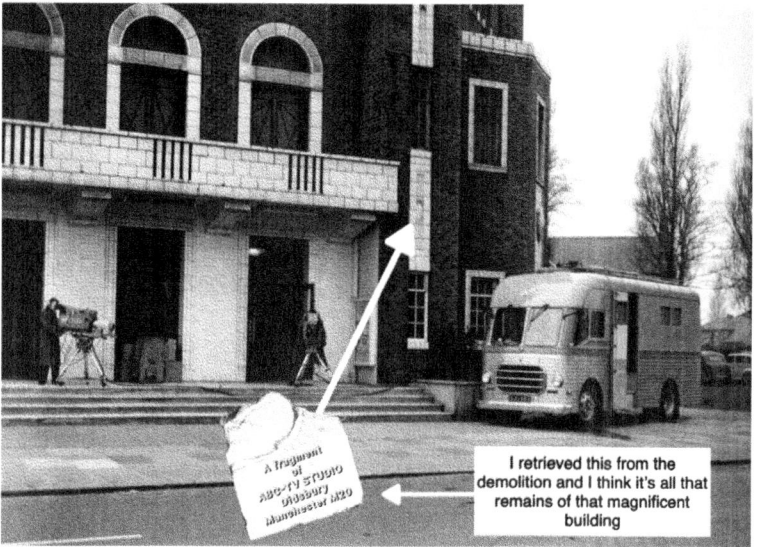

Roy's precious fragment of the ABC studio in Didsbury, Manchester

7.
Climate Change

IN 1964, Bob Dylan wrote that people ought to 'come gather 'round' wherever they roamed, accept that soon they would be 'drenched to the bone', start swimmin' quick or 'sink like a stone' because the times, 'they were a-changin'...'

Ok, like most men Bob had trouble with the 'G' spot, but his song generated awareness among youngsters that this was our moment and there was absolutely no need to regard the conventions of our parents' generation as the norm any longer. 'The Times They Are a-Changin'' gave us official permission to be perverse.

At the tender age of 23, Dylan certainly connected with me. Although a relatively inexperienced newbie TV director, I was living the dream, earning well above the average wage. For Royston Mayoh the swinging sixties really did swing – and then some!

Some of you may be disappointed to learn that I am not about to document all my over-indulgences, indiscretions and, as redefined some forty years later, general bad behaviour. Some are sprinkled around this book with attempts at justification that are invariably work-related and never simply excused as 'Well, it was the Sixties'.

That always sounds to me like a very lazy but convenient cop-out. I reference Dylan because I believe his expression, 'The Times They Are A-Changin', has been misused in every decade since. What was once a positive lyric heralding the birth of a new vitality has become more associated with negativity, as if anything new will be the thin end of a wedge that will make life worse, rendering all that went before passé and to a large extent redundant.

By the end of the 20th century, the underlying message of the song was increasingly interpreted as not so much inducement, more discouragement. Instead of suggesting 'you pull your finger out' to prevent getting left behind, the new meaning became 'stop rocking the boat with your blind enthusiasm... do as you're told. Toe the line!'

The first years of the new millennium were not a good time to be in British television. It was quite heartbreaking to see gloriously quirky, if not oddball, people become tamed, demotivated and also demoralised before being moved sideways into a variety of junior managerial positions far removed from all the creative juices and responsibilities to which they were so addicted. Later, some became senior managers due to being willing and able to do as they were told, even when those orders came without warning or explanation. Others were so sickened by the entire experience that they left the established TV industry to join the growing independent sector, or worse still, departed the business altogether.

My unscheduled exit from Tyne Tees in the mid-1980s, referred to earlier, was one such moment, a painful experience that contained all manner of intrigue, double-dealing, lies, denials, face-saving and an unexpected outcome. However, during the ordeal and for some time later, gossip mongers and busy bodies quickly jumped on the 'No Smoke Without Fire' bandwagon, making it virtually impossible for me to find anyone to take a gamble on me, just in case.

To be stuck with this stigma was something I'd never experienced before. Suddenly, my agent of the time (not my current one) became too busy to take my calls due to a sudden increase in her need for meetings. This was quite understandable since most of my trusted business friends and contacts were also in meetings and couldn't come to the phone either.

If ever there was a moment that shouted 'all change' – this was it. Yet, unbeknown to me, it was actually the beginning of a new and totally unpredictable and beautiful chunk of my life. After spending valuable horizontal time convalescing, following a much needed laminectomy (surgery to remove bone spurs and tissues associated with arthritis of the spine), every day seemed to be a new adventure. I met new people, went to new places and found my way into new genres of programming and work experiences.

The times, they were a-changin'.

As I got out of a car in British Columbia, to be met by six US secret servicemen with matching white plastic ringlets hanging from their ears, I thought: 'What the fuck is going on here?', unsure that I wouldn't rather be back in the comfort of my office playing head of entertainment. But as the cold fresh air of the Rockies hit my face and a voice said: 'Hi, I'm Mike Reagan!', I soon realised this was what I had been longing for... daily change.

Back in those formative years as a young cameraman at the ABC TV studios in Didsbury, I'd taken for granted the beauty of knowing that no day would resemble its predecessor; even the shape of the workplace would be different with new people working alongside. Such was the magic of having one large studio and one small. Shows would be turned around overnight, so opportunities abounded.

But now, in 1985, here I was in Canada and about to meet 'King of Gameshows' Ralph Edwards, who'd devised a bizarre one called *Lingo*. The prospect of meeting the man was in itself daunting. Here was someone who had narrated silent Laurel and Hardy films for 20th Century Fox and been in the film *I'll Cry Tomorrow* with Susan Hayward. Most famously, way back in 1940, he'd invented probably the first meaningful game show in America, *Truth or Consequences*, which ran on radio and television for thirty-eight years. In 1948, he had also invented and presented *This Is Your Life* which, in 1955, he brought to the United Kingdom, as outlined earlier.

So Ralph was not just any old bloke, but a true icon of American TV. The very thought of working with him filled me with awesome anticipation. But the light entertainment manager sent to supervise me, Bob Louis, was neither bothered nor impressed having never worked in television before. Ralph died in 2005 and may well be the only person I have ever met with two stars on the Hollywood 'Walk Of Fame' (one for radio, one for television).

I had flown to British Columbia to watch and learn, first hand, how this show called *Lingo* worked and be introduced to the detailed breakdown of its rules ... plus the ins, outs and couple of thousand contractual obligations that any UK franchisee must sign up to before even whispering the word 'action!' as presented in a specially produced book confirming the originator's continued creative and financial ownership of the concept. Usually these documents are extremely thick and irreverently called 'The Bible'.

It's always amused me that when newcomers to gameshows first hear this rule book referred to as 'The Bible' someone usually finds it offensive. And inevitably that very same person will be first to sing its praises. They soon realise it contains every question they might wish to ask that they hadn't thought of yet ... are required to answer from contestants ... technicians ... accountants ... directors ... producers ... sound and lighting engineers ... in fact just about every aspect of the show is dealt with in great detail within its pages.

What's more, The Bible must constantly be updated as sets of new circumstances call for necessary adjustments and that, of course, means change. That's why, along the way, no one has attempted to round-off or finalise the information; hence no index or break-down into logical chapters.

The curse of any gameshow format is that surprise anomaly. Most producers have discovered that, just when they least expect it, one of these accursed anomalies will leap out from nowhere and bring the production to a shuddering halt. This is normally when all the lights go on in the control room to allow a dozen or so people to tower over the one copy of The Bible in an attempt to find a rule covering it, or better still provide a solution the problem.

But back to Canada. My manager, Bob Louis, was a hell of a nice guy but neither a showman nor programme maker. This sudden introduction to the team of someone who had not been trained in any aspect of TV production was a revelation. He had been told he had the power of veto, an enormous change I would eventually and reluctantly have to come to terms with. Back then, new managers had been introduced to virtually every department. Called PPOs by most senior lighting directors, sound engineers and senior cameramen (an acronym for Programme Prevention Officer), their appointment led to a whole series of irreverent jokes which all stemmed from the original:

QUESTION: Why do managers think they are television experts?
ANSWER: Because they've got one.

The jokes, however, ceased to be funny when it turned out to be nearer the truth than anyone could have predicted. At that time, I'd no idea what nightmares this addition of passionless managers would lead to for we producer/directors. Had they all been as personable and eager to learn as Bob, then perhaps the imposition might have been regarded as a bonus.

For me, this marked one of the key negative moments in television industry history. It marked the moment of realisation that TV production could become obscenely profitable, but only for an elite few. Unfortunately those 'few' didn't have among their number any people who actually made programmes. There were, however, quite a lot who acted as administrators and/or managers.

In British Columbia, Mike Reagan introduced himself to Bob and I, backed by six butch chappies wearing plastic ear danglies. We then walked into a quaint wood cabin that looked very small indeed when backed by a vertical forest of extremely high fir trees and magnificent vista of the snow-capped Rocky Mountains beyond that. Bob and I looked at one another, our eyes saying: 'Wtf is going on?'

Suddenly, Mike and the curly-whirly six moved simultaneously, like a Red Arrows air display, peeling off into a restroom that actually had a stag horn display screwed to the door with a Mountie's hat hung haphazardly over one horn signifying a gents loo. The ladies, meanwhile, had a large pair of earrings dangling from the ears of a decapitated deer over a very pink door. Yes. This was a misogynistic mystery tour – ouch! Let's move on...

Bob and I had our first opportunity to ask each other who exactly this Mike Reagan was; no relation to the US President presumably? Was he Ralph Edwards's assistant? And who and what were these six

Bengal Lancers? Later, throwing caution to the wind, we decided to ask a member of the crew. Well, you can imagine our surprise to learn that Mike actually *was* the son of President Ronald Reagan. What's more, the curly-whirly six were his Secret Service detail, alongside him 24/7. Mike – or Michael, as we came to know him, was also the new presenter of *Lingo*. You could have knocked us down with a moose!

The stag horn burst into life as the restroom door swung open. Out came two curly-whirlies, who looked around and then, quick as a flash, out came Mike surrounded by the other four. Over the next seven days, everywhere that Mike, Bob and I went within the British Columbia studio complex, we were accompanied by these six shooters, uniformly in dark suits, white shirts, black ties and never without their curly-whirly ear pieces, mandatory shades and permanently preoccupied expressions on their spray-tanned faces.

Bob and I noticed how the six of them looked everywhere and in every direction, but never at Bob or myself. We fantasised that they were actually there to look after 'the float'. As production manager in the days before PayPal or even international credit cards, Bob carried large wads of cash around with him.

The immediate problem I foresaw was that, back home, the independent broadcast television regulator demanded that any quiz or gameshow format providing an opportunity for monetary gain must also have a reasonable element of competitive skill. *Lingo* had been a hit in the USA because it paid out fortunes. Its contestants required little or no knowledge or even intelligence, just plain old-fashioned luck. Being a nosey Brit, I wondered why the show was recorded in Canada for transmission over the border. With pride, the producer said: 'The Canadian dollar isn't worth as much as the American dollar. The American audience assume we are paying in American dollars. The prizes look and sound bigger and apart from the pronunciation of the letter Z there is little or no difference in language.' I felt really suburban not knowing this. He went on: 'You will also notice that for contestant applications the address to write to on the end-roller caption is Burbank, not British Columbia. This also feeds the illusion.' Embarrassed, I looked round at the 'dirty half dozen' and I swear one of them winked at me.

Upon my return to Britain and good old-fashioned hidden corruption, I produced and directed the *Lingo* pilot in the Thames Studios in Teddington. I handed my post-production notes over to the boss man and then moved on, awaiting a decision as to whether this mindless piece of wallpaper television would be promoted into a series. It was... but without me! It would be quite improper of me to say how delighted I was when it bombed.

The *Lingo* experience, though, had marked a moment of massive change and I do miss the curly-whirlies.

ONE thing I have always been quite sure of is this: just when you least expect it, something random will occur, something that would have been impossible to predict or plan for. It's a philosophy I hope this book thoroughly endorses. I'd get a feeling change was coming but no idea when or what it would involve. The next was even more dramatic than the Rockies but, it must be said, far less fun.

With hardly any exceptions, I had been very fortunate to find myself producing and/or directing shows with many of the UK's most talented people who, coincidentally, were often some of its nicest people too. Yes! At times, they could be demanding and a bit of a challenge, but I tended to find that the bigger the star, the more demanding and challenging they were with themselves first and foremost, any demands put on others following after.

There's a straightforward reason for this, as we saw at the start of this book in America with John Wayne etc. Most if not all stars right across the world become stars as a result of many years of grafting, rehearsing, learning, making mistakes, being humiliated, failing and succeeding. They know their craft and parameters ... when to stay within the confines of their bread and butter skills and when to venture into uncharted waters. Most, if not all of them, had a hidden case of imposter syndrome I strongly related to as well. A sufferer of it myself, I knew the only way to hide it was work, work and work until I got whatever it was that I thought I couldn't achieve achieved.

As a producer, I took these lessons from many talented mentors and, as a result, had built-in respect for the successful in anything. I have always been, and will always be, a great fan of skill in any form. I'm not a great fan of bullshit, unless it is delivered with skill. Most bullshit isn't. It's just forced through with the help of rank, pecking-order or pay-grade.

As we've progressed through my memoirs, you will undoubtedly have become familiar with a few of my favourite maxims, such as 'assumption is the mother of all fuck-ups.' That being the case, this next change came as quite an awakening.

About to work with a new star, I had assumed that he too would be as dedicated to his performance and image as the others I had encountered. Not so. It turned out I wasn't either equipped, trained or anywhere near ready for what was to come.

Here was a man with zero respect for anyone, someone who used his celebrity merely as an excuse to party. Due to his status within the public eye, sketches had been painstakingly written for him and then cast with supporting actors of great note and experience (all of whom had no idea of the 'amateur hour' ructions to come). Valuable rehearsal time was wasted waiting for him to arrive and/or sober up.

Of course, once the audience were sat in the studio, all this star had to do was pull a face or pretend to forget his lines ('pretend' being a very generous word here) to generate peels of laughter. This 'hilarity' would confirm to him, his agent and the chap who had contracted him in the first place that the show was a success. Sadly, everyone else connected with the show was having a miserable time. The entire cast and crew knew that had the script been treated with some degree of respect from its so-called star then the show would have been ten times funnier and possibly a delight to work on.

I sense you begging me to identify the culprit, which I am not willing to do by name. Let's just say that if I did so I might end up in not one 'nick', but two! This was one of those very rare occasions when change had proved to be a backward step. All the others had in some way presented me with a new and exciting challenge, and an opportunity to play with new equipment and fresh talent.

The biggest changes occurred outside the day to day UK system while making big specials in such as Belgium, Monte Carlo and, in 1996, India. In the United Kingdom, television had always seemed slow to recognise change, be it cultural, behavioural, class, social or doctrinal, so my India experiences and also in Japan served to show me how narrow-minded and bigoted UK broadcasters were. Every time I faced such realities I was forced to re-evaluate everything I'd grown up believing to be truth. On many occasions, in the privacy of a hotel room, I would weep at the propaganda the victorious imperialists fed me during my childhood and after World War Two.

And in fact I experienced similar again ahead of that 1972 trip to Tokyo described in chapter three, when our musical director Bob Sharples got it in the neck for a change, instead of giving us pains in ours. Shortly before departure, I received a very snotty letter from my father, who told me in no uncertain terms I was to have nothing whatsoever to do with the Japanese. At the time, I was a mere 31 years old and the last occasion my dad had written me a letter had been to congratulate me on passing my eleven-plus!

Anyway, the TV industry has always been quick to embrace and invest in technological change, mainly due to its initial (tax deductible) capital outlay, plus tax benefits of ongoing depreciation and built-in obsolescence. Acceleration in state-of-the-art technical improvements has also resulted in a reduction in permanent staffing.

As a freelance director (have pencil – will travel), I moved around the various ITV regional stations and became well versed in both producing and directing programmes using a variety of studios, crews, technical facilities and attitudes toward making programmes.

This period of my life, which lasted a good five years, taught me to embrace change as a non-negotiable fact, and simply to regard each region as a brand new set of rules that would, by necessity, have to be adopted and overcome as soon as was practically possible. It was during this time that I realised that if I was to succeed in these regions I would have to make the programme 'their way', no matter who or how many people attempted flattery by saying how much they were looking forward to working with a network director.

I also remembered a lesson that stayed with me, i.e. if confronted by a new director, the crew (as a group and individuals), spends the first hour at least trying to discover just how big a dickhead you are. Very rarely did any of us visiting freelancers ever let it be known to the new studio staff that we were doing the exact same thing to them. However, this mental jousting was, on more occasions than not, the start of a lifelong mutual respect among many technicians of a type I still enjoy. This mutual respect also had the bonus of providing a sense of goodwill that was always recognised and never abused.

It must be difficult for viewers nowadays who have only known the British television broadcasters as ITV, BBC, Channel 4 and Sky to even begin to imagine that, at one time, every geographical region in the UK had its very own quirky – and jealously idiosyncratic – independent television company. There were seventeen of them in total. Similarly, the BBC too had many regional television studios.

Such was the nature of their independence that each of these companies prided themselves on their very own methodology, studio discipline, schedules and technical proficiency. Of course, each insisted that their facilities, staffing, equipment and creative talent were the best in the land... and why not? It was this sense of pride that created a tremendously healthy competitive spirit for ITV, as those companies combined were generically known.

The genre of programme I specialised in, light entertainment, was always a source of joviality, especially in the drama, news and documentary departments. They sometimes called us the 'Red Nose and Funny Walks Department', or 'Department serving the Hard of Thinking.' In Tokyo, the light entertainment department went by the name 'Ongaku no Kabegami Bumon', which we shortened to the OKB. It was only as we left that I asked our translator and all-round guru of all things Japanese, Jo Miyasaki, what it meant. He smiled for only the second time of our visit: 'Musical wallpaper'.

As I hope is clear by now, I am far from averse to change. For me, it has been a driving force, a way of life, an essential element for as long as I can remember. Genuine change, that is. Change that occurs due to new equipment or technology, or a new style or trend or code of practice – or in attitudes. What I don't like is change for the sake of change, or when it's introduced as a selfish whim by someone in a position to impose it on we lesser mortals for their own personal benefit. Yes, that does tend to get right up my nose. And there always seemed to be a lot of that about. Thankfully it's relatively easy to spot.

Not so easy to spot is the change that catches most of us out, the stuff that creeps up on you so slowly that it's only when you stop and look back that you notice there has been any change at all. The awful thing about creeping change is that, almost without exception, it is infinitely more dramatic than any sudden obvious shift.

In my youth, one of the most widely used criticisms of a person who wasn't quite up to the job was to describe them as putting 'style before substance'. The actual quote, like all good quotes, got paraphrased to suit a situation, circumstance or job... hence phrases like 'all talk and no walk', 'all mouth and no trousers', 'no bubble and all squeak' (or as often mis-quoted, 'all bubble and no squeak'). 'Style before substance' was a short snappy way of describing a person who chose to camouflage their inadequate contribution or lack of know how by looking the part and/or talking the talk.

It has to be said that when I first became aware of this criticism I was very young and couldn't really understand why anyone would bother looking for a positive when the negative had so blatantly been apparent. Either a person could do the job or couldn't. I'd learned that if they didn't do what they were paid for doing (on a regular basis) then they were fired. Being the only child of a marriage where the father was consumed with practicalities – 'piss or get off the pot', as he used to say – had educated me in such a way that I'd grown up to believe that progression within anything was only achievable via the simple route of 'learning – perfecting – doing'. It wasn't until I was rescued by the television industry that I realised just about everything my father had taught me belonged in another dimension.

Oh, for sure, the formula 'learning – perfecting – doing' still applied, but not quite as simplistically as J.R.D. had insisted.

Dad was always referred to as J.R.D., whenever a member of our small family spotted him being overly nerdy. At work in the Shirley Institute for Cotton Research in Manchester, he was called either Mr Mayoh or J.R.D., which stood for his Christian name followed by a long list of forenames borrowed from the maiden names of our female ancestry, in dad's case John Raynor Deeley Mayoh. I was meanwhile lumbered with Royston Raynor Deeley Sherrington Mayoh, truncated by mum to plain Roy Mayoh, which upset the

Mayohs, but really pleased the Sherringtons. I had walked into a world where it was essential to be skilled. But in this brand new Canadian-inspired 'independent television' service, skill on its own wasn't quite enough... there had to be some 'flamboyance' attached.

It appeared to little old down-to-earth me that such floridity was unattainable, especially as it needed to be of a less predictable or stereotyped variety. It had to be unique and original, unmistakably branding that gifted person as a genuine 'one-off'.

In television, unlike in 'real life', these one-offs weren't a rare breed. They were everywhere you looked within the confines of the studio. It didn't matter what job these people did, or how old they were, or what sex they were ... each and every one had a totally definable individual quality. The logic of the accepted workplace – and I suspect page-one in any personnel (or as it's now called, Human Resources) handbook – would undoubtedly state that to put together any two, let alone fifty-two, of these beautiful oddballs would be a surefire recipe for a disaster of epic proportions.

My first realisation of this fundamental difference between my dad's colleagues in the cotton and man-made fibre ring-spinning world and my brand new work colleagues at ITV arose via the way a team was created. In my dad's world, teams were invariably made up of like-minded people who would have been drawn together for the long-haul, with a pecking order that would have been almost permanently set in stone. That pecking order was defined by external factors such as qualifications, longevity and experience. The team leader was, quite naturally, the one with the most experience and knowledge and always, irritatingly, older.

This is what I had grown up to believe was the irrefutable truth about the shape of a man's working life. In J.R.D.'s world, at that time, it very much was. This new world of independent television seemed to make a point of upturning everything I'd been taught about that.

Suddenly there were no rules, just the tightest code of unwritten practices.

There was no fixed pecking order, but an ever-changing leader supervising a team of individuals with no fixed responsibility. There was no permanent seniority, as this too shifted with every change of circumstance. All I could see within the boundaries of this huge and constantly evolving space (otherwise known as a studio) was a major re-write of all the rules every time it took on a new use and look.

It was easy for me to understand that an empty studio (with an intentional total lack of natural light) could change its character with the application of new scenery, furniture and several coats of paint. It was, however, much harder to look at the same bunch of people and watch a palpable change in their pecking order, behavioural pattern and aura of responsibility.

I saw this sea change occur for just about every programme and, after a while, began to note that the teams were noticeably different between the various genres, be it drama, documentary, current affairs, religion, situation comedy or light entertainment. But change there was and to try to explain this to my father just compounded his solid, unmovable assumption that the place I had chosen to work in was nothing more than an irresponsible playground built by idiots and populated by social outcasts, homosexuals and people the BBC had rejected. In short, my father was not a fan of ITV. He was convinced, like a remarkably large section of the population, that it was a flash in the pan and would not last.

To us new converts, it was another story. ITV was the future and in our turn we looked upon the BBC as a relic of the past. In fact, we insisted on referring to the Beeb as the British Broadcorping Castration. For me, this new studio space, created from that old Didsbury picturehouse in a leafy suburb of Manchester, was magical. Sad to relate, as I write this book the building has long since been pulled down to make room for a block of anonymous housing units.

No inch of the place has left my mind, however, where visions of its every nook and cranny remain as sharply in focus as they were some sixty years ago. It represented – still does – one of the most profound changes I was quickly able to embrace, simply because of the sheer excitement of it all. And thanks to the memory of those early days I can now embrace and accept how new changes will be just as exciting for today's newcomers as they were then for me.

During my attempts to re-establish myself in the UK television scene following my fall from grace at Tyne Tees, a remarkable lady was able to suggest me as a director for a very popular show on ITV. So began another brand new experience. Well, two actually, as the lady in question was Sarah, my beloved wife since 1998.

It was a Granada production, and my time as one of its many directors provided more memorable moments of delight coupled with a level of unprofessionalism and corporate stupidity than any other series in my career. Because of the nature of the presenters, it proved to be a decent consistent ratings success. Yet its popularity could and should have been even bigger and better were it not for the behind the scenes activities and constant interference of its two big television names.

Each day of the week had a specifically designated producer and pair of researchers, which meant the series had five experienced producers and ten-to-fifteen researchers, two programme directors and a couple of supervising series editors. So during the week before their show each team would tidy up from their previous transmission, take a deep breath and prepare a full script for the following week. The production office was abuzz with energy, laughter and bursting with enthusiasm.

This script would be sub-edited before being thoroughly vetted by the editor of the programme. Once signed off, it would be given to one of the directors to turn into a technical studio reality.

These scripts were always excellent. They were constructed with balance and the running order was designed to schedule those items with people arriving at the studio after we had gone on air. The running orders were also created to cover any movement in the studio (for example, re-positioning to another item) by inserting pre-recorded items or short films, which were made with great enthusiasm and care by the team of researchers in the week before transmission.

Every producer of every programme took deserved pride in the construction of their detailed running-order. They were never thrown together, but tailored and adjusted many times before the script and running order went into 'blue' (i.e. printed on light blue paper, making it definitive following many drafts and amendments), which meant that this version of the script was final.

So, is this an 'anti-presenters' piece? Well no, certainly not. It's an observation about the mechanics of making a daily programme (viewers of the US drama *The Morning Show* will have spotted this anomaly already).

The public loved this particular duo, but they never had to work with them or see any of those well thought-through programme segments rejected in favour of a quiet life on a busy studio floor. There may well be a member of the old crew who disagrees with all the above, but I haven't met one yet.

In remembering this period, I always try to tell myself: 'OK, so it was awful and at times seemed like a mammoth waste of time and effort, but think of the laughs, cohesion of the crews and creativity.'

ONE of the many, sometimes sickening, contrivances a TV light entertainment director had to employ was ego boosting.

Some of the newer TV personalities and wannabes arrived at the studio with a perception of their talent not shared by others. Some thought they were 'God's gift' while others suffered from imposter syndrome. That latter group, with less than a favourable opinion of their true selves, were relatively easy to deal with. I'd been there myself. All it took was a simple mixture of reassurance, patience and affirmation. Mike Yarwood, Les Dawson, and Little and Large were good examples of new performers who genuinely didn't have a clue how talented they were and how popular they were going to be in the future.

In the 'God's gift' group I could name quite a few who started off with an inflated opinion of their own talent and, after a relatively short period of time, burnt out.

There is no point in naming these as you will never have heard of them. You may be a relative or friend of one of these people who never made it, but still remember their early days on shows I was responsible for. If you are, I suspect you will recognise that there was no point in my trying to shout into a deaf ear! A few 'God's gifts' did make it through to the big time.

I shall probably go to my grave wondering how such people could sustain such lousy press, leave a trail of disenchanted production workers in their wake and turn in so many mediocre performances yet still be regarded as 'A' list.

By now, dear reader, it ought to have become obvious that climate change in the TV industry, as elsewhere, was ongoing and inevitable. Some of the changes I've chosen to feature were destined to alter or destroy methodology that seemed permanently set in stone, some to embrace new technology, some to reflect a new way of thinking in society. There were many occasions where a corporate change seemed unnecessary or unproductive, but it was always obvious that it had to be embraced and regarded as personal motivation towards future employment, which was not and still isn't easy to accomplish.

Back in the day there was a very tiny department called personnel which dealt with the welfare of employees. However there has been a marked change from personnel officer to aforementioned human resources. This has brought a more academic approach towards staff employment. Specialist departmental heads are now presented with applicants who have been chosen, mainly, by 'HR'.

So, on evaluating change in the television industry over the past sixty years, here are what I regard as irreversible HR-driven ones:-

- Quirkiness and individuality now signs of irresponsibility.

- Practical skill without personality generally disregarded.

- Practical skill with personality acceptable, as long as the practical skill is dominant.

- Qualification is 'all', practical skill is meaningless unless qualification can quantify it.

- Qualification accompanied by personality far outweighs practical skills.

Gone, it seems, is the celebration of craftsmanship, although there does appear to have been a resurgence of interest in programmes dedicated to practical skill for the viewers, such as the BBC's *The Great British Bake Off*, *The Great British Sewing Bee* and *The Repair Shop*, Channel 4's *Handmade: Britain's Best Woodworker*, and others dealing with pottery, jewellery and blacksmithery. All of them programmes that are helped along by the foreground presence of comedic personalities placed there to interpret and enhance their talented expert craftsmen and women co-stars, who it is assumed would otherwise lack televisually acceptable charisma.

In my opinion, these comedic characters get in the way of a better understanding of the contestants' differing levels of skill. However, the inclusion of comedic hosts has become mandatory, almost as if TV executives feel that the viewer is too stupid or lazy to form an opinion on his, her or their own, without the help of someone taking the mickey. And that, it could be said, is a perfect example of change for change's sake.

SYNERGY: Karun Prabhakaran, Siddhartha Basu and Anita Kaul Basu (Rosa), pictured in 1996. This was Royston's first encounter with India's TV industry and created a friendship still treasured to this day.

8.
A Life of S.I.N.

WRITING my memoirs has been a thoroughly enjoyable experience. However, in doing so, I've often been forced to stop, back pedal and ponder something automatically typed without thinking it through.

Self-doubt is part of everyone's life. I can certainly think of many occasions over the years when this demon has almost rendered me immobile. The production of this book has actually made me realise how essential a part it has played in my decision-making. This mild form of imposter syndrome has proved to be a regulator, navigator and, primarily, a friend.

As with most young people, anything able to help anaesthetise insecurity temporarily was welcome. The most commonplace ones being alcohol, drugs and music. In my case, there were also a couple of books I found compelling. They were:-

The Power of Your Subconscious Mind, by Dr Joseph Murphy.
In the Centre of Immensities, by Sir Bernard Lovell

It has done me good to look back and note that luckily – and I stress, luckily – alcohol and drugs never became an issue in my case.

My post-retirement experiences as a bit-part actor also brought self-doubt back into sharp focus. But this new and exciting activity delivered it in a completely unexpected package – stage fright!

To explain how and why, I have to return to my roots as a TV producer/director. As television was a novelty then, viewers tended to study the screen keenly, becoming familiar with the various jobs described and acknowledged during the end credits.

These viewers naturally assumed that the people on the list must be highly-skilled. So when members of the public came to be part of a live audience themselves, they were every bit as interested in the mass of technicians milling around the studio floor as they were in the star cast who actually appeared in what they had come to see.

While making live broadcasts in front of such audiences, it was always the responsibility of the producer to address them before the show began, warm them up if you like. This took the shape of a formal welcome to both show and studio, a brief explanation of what they were about to witness and hopefully enjoy, plus a light-hearted but essential legal obligation of pointing out the emergency exits. A person of authority was therefore required, rather than a performer. These were television's early days, however, so it was a procedure that had yet to develop into the art-form it is now.

When I became a trainee director, I knew that people perceived me as being full of confidence. That was an illusion! In reality I had a very real fear of speaking in public. I was terrified at the thought of fronting an audience, especially knowing how tensed up I'd be right before doing my 'proper job' of directing cameras from the control gallery which, in that era, were mainly live to air.

I was always delighted (and relieved) that it was my mentor (and producer) Milo Lewis who did the audience welcome. However, because Milo was a great teacher who knew about my stage fright, one day he forewarned me that I'd be required to deliver a future warm-up myself, before a specific show on a particular date. He made it very plain that – as with everything else in showbusiness – successful performances are achieved through practice, practice and a bit more practice as well, writing me a script with the instruction: 'Learn this until you are sick and tired of it!'

In every resting moment, Milo would make me recite this script. We could be sitting in a bar or driving to some function when he'd say: 'Ladies and Gentlemen, please welcome on stage the director of today's show, Mr Roy Mayoh...' and then point at me to start.

He never tired of telling me that the purpose of this intense personal and private rehearsal was to ensure that when, eventually, I was confronted with the daunting task of talking to five hundred strangers my reluctant brain would run on automatic and deliver the excellence they were surely expecting.

The script took the form of a monologue I could plough through, pausing at pre-rehearsed spots to take a breath. However, if anyone interrupted my flow the entire thing disappeared from my memory in a flash. So the two of us went over it and over it and over it until I found it monotonous and incredibly boring. The jokes didn't seem funny anymore, I got really sick and tired of reading and saying them and so, of course, was soon able to recite it in my sleep (which I'm sure I often did). This first script of Milo's was subsequently used on hundreds of occasions and went something like this:-

Roy

'Good evening, ladies and gentlemen. My name is Roy Mayoh and I'm the director of tonight's show!

It's my privilege to welcome you all to ABC Television and into this, our extraordinary Studio, here in sunny Didsbury.

Some of the programmes you will have seen that were made in this studio are

Armchair Theatre - The Clitheroe Kid - The David Nixon Show - Comedy Bandbox and Pathfinders In Space.

The career of well-known escape artist The Great Ernesto started - right here... And just over there... his career ended!

Roy (cont)

We are very proud of our studios and especially now that well-known stars who have appeared here pop in from time to time just to see us!

They sneak in at the back over there, hoping they won't be noticed ... But no such luck tonight Henry...

Ladies and gentlemen, give a great big Manchester welcome to the one and only 'our 'enry' ... Mr Henry Cooper!

APPLAUSE

I'm so so sorry, Madam!

I have a note here telling me to welcome some special groups in tonight's audience, so please stand up....

The Over 90s Kung Fu club.

APPLAUSE

We have a couple celebrating a wedding anniversary tonight. They have stuck together for 50 years, so a big welcome, wherever you are, to Mr and Mrs Bostick!

We also have a Mr and Mrs Delsey who I understand are a pair of tearaways!

Yes, you are right, it really is a mixed bag ... and you'll be meeting her later on!

At this point I must tell all you members of the audience that during tonight's show the cameras will be pointing at you!

Roy (cont)

So if you are sitting with anyone you shouldn't be... now's the time to move!

(allow stooges to run out of the audience)

So, if you see a camera looking at you please don't wave! Oh, people do you know ... you would be surprised (chooses a lady)

For instance, you would never do that would you? (Reply) Of course not. May I ask your name? (Reply) And where are you from? (Reply)

So 'Gladys' here would never wave, but just say she did.... There would be a couple of dozen people in Bolton saying 'Ooh, look there's Gladys on the telly!' which would be lovely for you, wouldn't it?

Trouble is that there would be another 16 million people saying: 'Who's that silly old cow waving...'?

Now the real reason I'm talking to you is to make you aware of a few safety notices! For instance, if you look above your heads, you see some microphones. Okay? If any of them should fall, please catch them... as they are very expensive.

In the event of a fire! The emergency exits are marked here, here and here ... there is no life jacket under your seat, simply because this is not an aeroplane.

Should you be asked to evacuate the studio, please use the exits I have just shown or follow Don, our floor manager, as he knows a much quicker way out.

Roy (cont)

Thanks, Don!

I understand that it's only a few minutes
before we are due to be going on the air, so
I have to hurry back to the control room
because, apart from anything else, there's
something worth watching on the telly!

Have a fantastic night; now, please meet
the star of tonight's show… (insert name)

APPLAUSE

So there you are. The first warm-up I ever attempted. It seems so
simple now, but I ask you to believe that at a time when I had never
spoken in public before, it felt like learning the complete works of
Shakespeare. Nevertheless, learn it I did, and sixty-plus years later
I still remember it as if it were yesterday (and you know what a bad
day yesterday was).

I doubt whether I would get away with the old cow joke in this
day and age, but at the time it was one of the guaranteed laughs of
the routine. This was because I spent the entire warm-up mentally
weighing up the front row, looking for the right person, a lady who
would find being called a cow amusing! She would also, typically,
look like a regular at one of the many pubs or clubs that offered live
entertainment and 'iffy' comedians back then.

There were at least a dozen such venues within a couple of miles
of the Didsbury studio, so we were never short of a good responsive
audience, or suitable cow-ladies! I didn't realise how lucky we were
with our audiences in Manchester until I produced a show at our
London studios in Middlesex.

At Teddington, audiences had to be bussed in from far and wide.
As a result they were generally from a quite different demographic
to those in the north west. They were less an audience, more a jury,
so the warm-up was both essential and a challenge. Making them

laugh was like pushing soot uphill. There was never an opportunity to perform the old cow joke south of Watford!

One result of this was that it was soon decided a budget should be allocated to pay for a professional comedian to do this essential rotuine. But having found a couple and contracted them we soon had a quite different problem.

How could we ensure that these professional artists would not be funnier than the star of the show? Imagine a situation where the big name on the bill is eventually introduced and the audience is disappointed. This was a real possibility because warm-up artists had a fairly free range when it came to choice of jokes, whereas the TV star could only perform material that was vetted and approved by the Independent Broadcasting Authority censorship procedures (although the official IBA wordage would not say 'censorship', but use words like 'regulatory control'.)

Very few warm-ups could walk this fine line between doing the difficult job of heating an audience up from zero degrees Celsius while not alienating a perhaps household name who was lumbered with the demands of officialdom. In the case of a particularly good audience, laughter and applause created before the show got going would in the early days be recorded on a separate audio tape and used to sweeten another programme that didn't receive the laughs and applause its producer thought it deserved.

And of course these were audiences of only five hundred. In later years, the age of the arena dawned when venues with audiences of 15,000-plus became a reality. Warm-ups would still be required to do the same job, but in an entirely different way. Some even went on to become comedy stars in their own right.

That said, although most of the shows I produced and directed involved playing to an audience, one of the most enjoyable was a wonderful programme that made a point of not having one!

This was *The Kenny Everett Video Show*, later renamed *The Kenny Everett Video Cassette*, made by Thames for ITV in Teddington, and which ran from July 1978 to May 1981. Although this series was a product of its time, writers Barry Cryer and Ray Cameron, plus its star Kenny Everett, created a timeless comedy classic that I'm quite sure will be enjoyed for many years in the future. Well, I say it had no audience. One of the most striking things about the series was that all the reaction to the comedy came randomly from the crew.

You could be forgiven for assuming that the word 'crew' means a formidable bunch of people spread around ample studio space involving multi-cameras, lighting, sound, scenes, props, make-up, floor managers and production team. Not in this instance. *The Kenny Everett Video Show* was recorded in the smallest studio at Thames – Studio 3 – and involved a very small, in fact, minute team.

Kenny first found fame as a pirate radio and Radio Luxembourg DJ in the mid-1960s, before going on to become one of the first to join the BBC's newly-created Radio 1 in 1967, thereafter having both a successful and somewhat controversial time of it at the Beeb. With us, on a typical recording day he'd adapt some of his many trademark voices and comical characters for television – and usually the most outrageous. Among his most popular were punk Sid Snot, French hairdresser Marcel Wave, the Vicar, General Bomb-the-Bastards, the 'half-suited' Angry Man and the Baby in the Pram.

There were plenty more too, each of them a product of Kenny's incredible imagination and characterised by some odd behavioural trait that could easily be recognised and laughed at. Kenny was in no way judgemental, but did like to hold a mirror up to stupidity and bigotry. He, Barry and Ray would come up with out-of-context one liners that typified or exposed particular attitudes, honing in on their essential ridiculousness and potential for hilarity.

Some sketches worked and some didn't, but that didn't matter to any of us because, due to advances in technology, we were now able to commit a whole string of jokes to videotape. Many weeks later the jokes that made the cut would be stitched together among all the other funny bits, anarchic dance numbers (plus the odd musical performance from a band or singer now and then) in the edit suite. That which hadn't worked was ignored and never spoken of again.

The visual devices used to move between one item and another were always technically innovative too. This sort of creative freedom delighted me as I was able to produce a final mosaic of unconnected moments in the delivery of a finished programme.

As in all edit situations, differences in sound needed to be ironed out. This would usually be done by adding a burst of pre-recorded studio ambience or audience reaction. But, as mentioned earlier, this series had no audience, so the only way to get around this was by adding pre-recorded laughter from the crew.

Pre-recording specially performed crew 'laffs' was unthinkable, so instead we compiled a library of sniggers, snorts, laughs, coughs and ambient atmosphere from the actual recordings and skilfully sewed them into the edit. Most viewers assumed that as the crew could be heard laughing and reacting to Kenny, the soundtrack had deliberately not been cleaned up and what they heard was therefore genuine. I apologise if this paragraph has burst anyone's bubble!

In my capacity as director, working on the studio floor was a joy. However, wearing my producer frock in the office block was most days a political nightmare. The 1970s were a time when conservative media activist and Christian decency campaigner Mary Whitehouse was very nearly at her peak. She kept herself very busy gunning at anything and anybody in broadcasting who was not in tune with her puerile sensitivities and it wasn't long before *The Kenny Everett Video Show* fell within her sights.

Given how Thames TV was the broadcaster of both *The Kenny Everett Video Show* and *The Benny Hill Show*, Mrs Whitehouse must have thought all her Christmases had come at once. She had a field-day droning on about how inappropriate the dance routines of Hot Gossip were in Kenny's programme and the adolescent barrage of double-entendres as peddled by Benny Hill. She never succeeded in finding anything illegal or improper in either of these extremely popular and successful shows, mind you, but really did try.

Choreographer, stage director and former dancer Arlene Phillips was responsible for Hot Gossip, whose innovative dance routines were brilliant and a million miles from anything seen on TV before. And because her dancers wore a variety of cheeky costumes sourced from Ann Summers sex shops they gave the impression of being far naughtier than they actually were.

Anyway, the press helped our ratings by publicising these dance routines as verging on the improper when, in truth, they were far from it, mostly using purposeful and brilliant illusions created by Arlene and her troupe. An opportunity any hot-blooded TV director would jump at committing to video, I certainly had a ball with it.

The production process was magical for a while – and it is worth describing as it is a technique which no longer exists, called Editech. As the name implies it was an editing technique, but with a massive difference. Usually, editing is done after the fact (post-production). Editech, however, was carried out as part of – and at the time of – production, not afterwards. It worked like this. A videotape was prepared with only the soundtrack recorded on it and then, during the making of Hot Gossip's dance routines, I would play that pre-prepared video soundtrack while simultaneously adding visuals. Sounds straightforward enough? It absolutely was not.

Arlene choreographed her dancers in tiny sections, each added as a separate entity (sometimes a section could be as fast as twenty-four frames, or one second... so a three-minute routine could have well over a hundred sections in it). This Editech process allowed for each detailed section to be appropriately and thoroughly rehearsed by the dancers. It also allowed the director (me) to treat each section differently (camera mount ... low/high angles ... lens/filter choice ... location ... and movement). It also meant that each area could be lit perfectly. A three-minute number could, and did, take all day from 8.00am to 6.00pm, including an hour's break for lunch.

On one occasion, we were shooting a Hot Gossip routine at the Thames water pumping station in Kew. The soundtrack was 'Muscle Bound' by Spandau Ballet and to dress the set, and add a little extra something, we'd booked a dozen or so actual musclemen who were duly stripped to their Speedos, bodies oiled like a Sunday roast! All they had to do was flex away in the background of shots featuring one or more of Arlene's dancers. It all worked exceptionally well. In fact, we were ahead of our projected schedule so decided to break for an extended lunch in a nearby public house.

By this time Hot Gossip had become quite famous due to the constant controversy created by the papers and Mary Whitehouse. So it was no surprise that members of the public flocked around as we entered the pub. The dancers were used to it and quite enjoyed being celebrities. However, on this occasion it was our anonymous musclemen who captured the attention. Hot Gossip were ignored.

We were all fascinated by the attention our extras were attracting. None of us knew we had a secret star in our midst. In their attempt to supply us with the most muscular specimens they could find, it transpired that our casting department had unwittingly booked us a well-known porn star – and this particular chap had a film playing in a back room here that very week. What had seemed like a very ordinary pub on the outside, was actually a well-known watering hole for male enthusiasts of a certain variety of adult entertainment.

Back at the pumping station we resumed our recording, which required a few more re-takes than usual owing to unplanned smiles and wardrobe malfunctions! The dance number can still be seen on YouTube, where you will instantly notice that one of the musclemen appears to have had his head removed. Well now you know why.

Each of those eight dance numbers took a full day to record and were a delight from start to finish. Working with a professional choreographer like Arlene is always a very pleasing aspect of the job for any entertainment director. The best possible shot for each move is the absolute priority. I'm lucky to have worked with the best.

However, the other half of me (the producer) didn't get the same sense of satisfaction or excitement. Each day my departmental head, Philip Jones, would pore over the latest draft script, for instance. In many ways this was a pointless exercise because our day was mainly made up of comedy material invented on the spur of the moment by Kenny Everett, Barry Cryer or Ray Cameron.

Once we had established with the IBA that all comedic matters were being dealt with properly, the only time I had to pull the plug on this brilliant writing team was for a series of sketches about the Snot family. Their language and subject matter was hysterical, but the scripts were better suited to the *The Young Ones* than our show.

The problem was our slot time. We went on air a good two hours before the 9.00pm watershed. The upsetting thing was that the script itself may have sneaked through on a nod and a wink, but when a superb bunch of guest stars and actors got hold of it and developed their own graphic persona, double entendre fast became single!

As amusing as it undoubtedly was, I had no option but to cancel the entire planned Snot family sketches from the series. For a day or two I was as popular as a union shop steward at a 1922 Committee meeting. It was far better to cancel this set of sketches before they were made and included in the finished programmes. Sid Snot's family were already a *cause célèbre*, any more public fuss might see the whole show be seen as untransmittable, possibly resulting in the *The Kenny Everett Video Cassette*, as it was by now known, being cancelled in its entirety. Sid as a solo routine remained one of Kenny's best loved characters.

The content was not the main problem preventing me from fully enjoying the gloriously innocent silliness of this comedy genius, though. As the producer/director responsible for the budget, Light Entertainment managers were constantly on my back about expenditure.

The preceding three series had been brilliantly produced and directed by David Mallet but, for whatever reason, he had gone over budget by some considerable amount. It was made blatantly clear to me that my brief, as incoming producer/director, was to produce this fourth series by incorporating that overspend. This meant I had less money to play with, every penny spent having to be adequately justified. So when asked to approve a receipt for £80 for a trouser belt, I refused as I felt this was an abuse of our restricted funds. My objection found its way back to the purchaser, who turned out to be Kenny Everett himself. He was none too pleased with me.

It was always easy for me to differentiate between my two roles, but most folk, Kenny included, found it impossible to separate the two. Naturally my apparent parsimony angered our zany front man, which didn't help our relationship. This was such a pity as I did so admire his extraordinarily innovative talent. That aside, I've always been proud that *The Kenny Everett Video Cassette* was nominated for a BAFTA, so I must have been doing something right.

VARIOUSLY, throughout this book, I've described myself as lucky, but one supreme example I have left until now to document was the result of a chance meeting during a moment of potential depression in a very foreign land.

In the early 1990s I had been asked by Stephen Leahy, managing director of one of the first TV format companies in the world, Action Time, founded in 1979, to help research and write a report for Carlton Television. The brief, simply put, was to consider '...the feasibility of television production in India, now that the Indian economy is opening up, enabling the entry of private broadcasters.'

Up to then, India only had one television channel, Doordarshan, a public service broadcaster founded by the Government in 1959. By 1991, India's population was approximately 889million, so it was easy to see why a major British TV company would want to expand into this new territory. Stephen put together a team from within Action Time to write a joint comprehensive report. It included Andrew Pemberton, at that time an executive in their overseas sales department; Jane Martin, a freelance production manager well versed in programme budgets; and myself, regularly employed by Action Time as a freelance producer/director. In its offices, our team quickly became known as 'The RAJ' (Royston Andrew and Jane).

In 1995, we left for New Delhi with open minds about what we might find. Well, we were in for a shock. Many shocks! There were so many aspects we hadn't considered, but three major ones were:-

1. The Hindi Government had only just allowed other TV stations to broadcast in India, wanting to protect their population from western influences. Up to this point it had succeeded, but with the emergence of satellite broadcasting it was becoming a classic case of 'King Canuteism'.
2. Indian people preferred film to television. Their Bollywood industry provided the populous with all the entertainment it needed (drama, romance, intrigue, popular music, new dance trends, classical music, classical dance, screen idols). Bollywood movies could be projected (via battery operated projectors) on massive make-do screens in a field to serve a whole village. TVs were small and required electricity.
3. The British weren't exactly welcomed with open arms. The

reasons for this I now totally understand but, at that time, was completely unaware of.

We arrived in the country on October 24 during a total solar eclipse which, as any Hindu will attest, indicates the beginning of a new bright and auspicious future. To us it was just a very odd experience going from blazing sunshine to night-time and back again to unbearable heat – all in the space of an hour.

We checked into The Marriott, a six star air-conditioned hotel in the heart of New Delhi, then each went our separate ways in search of research material for the joint-report. I thought I might try the Doordarshan studios to gain a proper perspective on the situation, but entry proved to be totally impossible without written permission from a dozen or so government departments. I was told this could take up to six months – life was too short!

My tour around addresses publicising television technicians did not produce any technicians who could actually make programmes or had anything to do with TV production, but did lead to hundreds of contacts for repair shops. I drew a blank everywhere I went.

At the end of a particularly tiring day I thought a shower, change of clothes and dinner was called for. I'd lost track of Andrew and Jane but wasn't concerned as I knew we would re-connect soon enough, most likely being the only British TV people within a hundred miles. The evening came and went. It was time to go to sleep, but my head was buzzing with the disappointing lack of progress. So, eventually, I thought a nightcap might be a good idea.

I got in the lift and went up to the sixth floor, which I knew had a rooftop bar. It was completely empty apart from a barman. I gravitated towards his inviting smile and took a seat, ordering an 'industrial' gin and tonic. He didn't understand the term, so instead of two large G&Ts in one glass, I sat nursing a very small drink until I became aware of someone else, now occupying a barstool six places up from me who the barman now moved towards. This newcomer ordered a large Chivas Regal, which if you don't know is a blended Scotch whisky. Soon the two of us were sat staring into our drinks until, after what seemed to be an age but was probably no longer than ten minutes, I broke the uneasy silence. 'I couldn't help noticing,' I began, 'a large Chivas Regal ... which must mean you are celebrating something or are about to go out onto the terrace and jump off!'

The stranger shrugged his shoulders and said: 'Jumping off the terrace sounds like a good idea.' Immediately concerned, I asked if there was anything I could do? His expression changed, replaced by a beautiful, if sad, smile. 'Thats very kind of you,' he said, 'but you wouldn't understand.' 'Try me,' I offered.

This chap began to explain how he had just lost an important contract involving television programming. I couldn't help snorting a stifled laugh, but realised my apparent mirth wasn't going down too well. I apologised and explained that I was a television producer of thirty years experience who had been walking around New Delhi all day looking for someone who knew something, anything, about the making of television programmes when, suddenly, out of the blue, here I am meeting one who is about to jump off a roof!

This made him laugh too. We introduced ourselves. This was my first meeting with incredibly talented Karun Prabhakaran, a man who would remain a close friend for many years.

Karun's problem had been with Doordarshan and the strange way they did business with producers. It was called the 'bartering system' and was brand new to me. It worked like this. A person with an idea or format would present it to a Doordarshan executive. If said executive liked the concept enough to commission it he would issue an approval notice, which that person would then walk out of the executive's office clutching it tightly. Another executive in the same building would then take both the idea/format and approval notice and, after studying them, declare a figure in rupees. If that figure was mutually agreeable, then this concept creator would write a cheque for that amount – in favour of Doordarshan! And receive yet another piece of paper, this time a receipt of payment.

Not understanding this system, it all sounded very dodgy to me. I couldn't get my head around an originator paying to have his own idea broadcast. But Karun further explained the system, marking the beginning of my education into the totally curious world of

Indian logic. Having paid the executive (I was still trying to absorb that), the person would then take their three pieces of paper (idea + approval + receipt) over the road to an advertising agency, the situation now being that they had in effect bought a time-slot within the Doordarshan schedules, a slot that also allowed for a number of commercial breaks. It was now up to that person to sell this air-space to whichever ad agency thought the programme idea/format would appeal to the demographic they were trying to target.

Karun further explained that the incoming funds from airtime sales were far more than the initial amount usually paid to Doordarshan. This 'new money' would pay for the production, staffing and specialised equipment necessary to make the programme and also provide a healthy profit for the production company.

Phew! A new dawn had broken on a fascinating world. I couldn't wait to tell Andrew and Jane about my discovery.

Karun explained that he had been through this procedure six weeks ago after gaining a commission for twenty-six programmes, before going through the appropriate financial dealings following the commission based on twenty-six shows. However this very night, just hours before our pivotal sixth floor meeting in the bar of the Marriott Hotel, Doordarshan had called Karun to inform him that those twenty-six programmes had been reduced to six! He had already employed staff, computers, office space, copiers, furniture, desks plus all the paraphernalia needed for a series that would last half a year. What was he going to do with it all now he had a far shorter run, especially as he was committed to payment on it all?

Karun was never nearer to being kissed by a complete stranger and a British one at that. I could not believe my luck! The following day (I didn't sleep much that night), I visited Karun's office in a basement somewhere in the suburbs. After meeting his colleagues headed by Siddhartha and Rosa Basu (collectively known as Big Synergy), it was clear that here was the prospect of a solid working relationship that could form a bespoke production team more than able to start the work of making UK product for an Indian audience.

Was it possible that Action Time could branch out into India and enjoy similar success as it had in the UK – only time would tell. The serendipitous meeting with Karun had given me a welcome and totally credible source for making a start on my immediate priority, which was to write my section of the report about the feasibility of TV production in India from a producer/director viewpoint.

I decided to break my section up into those headings which were specifically about production, virtually all of them sourced from Karun and his vast array of contacts. My headings were:-

- The number and technical efficiency of potentially available freelance crews.
- The source and costs of design/construction companies and graphic artists.
- The source and costs of available skilled production staff.
- The identity and number of skilled stage/prop crews available.
- The location, cost, size and suitability of available studios.
- The identity of skilled and available support staff such as make-up and wardrobe.
- The identity of casting directors and theatrical agents to source on-screen talent.
- The source and identity of writers able to adapt to TV.

My work virtually done, after a few days in my air conditioned hotel suite on a 'high-tech' one-megabyte Apple Mac word processor, I was able to pass my report to Andrew (one hard, one floppy copy). Andrew had taken on the job of rewriting all three sections into one coherent document written and formatted in the administrative language foreign to both Jane and myself. Job done, report finished, we returned to the UK.

Some weeks later, I was contacted by Synergy who had been approached by a brand new channel in India, Home TV, to supply entertainment programming. Which is how I found myself going back with three Action Time formats stuffed in my briefcase, two of which being *Every Second Counts* and an untitled film-clip show, the latter having a vast resource of international home-bloopers acquired by Action Time via our successful BBC series, *Caught In*

The Act, presented by the actor and comedian Shane Richie, which I had directed. The third Action Time format was retitled *Jaane Kya Tune Kahi* very soon after I presented it to Siddhartha Basu and Karan Thapar (programme controller of Home TV). Even now, none of us can remember its original English name. It must have been quite an obscure programme.

Every Second Counts became *Aao Guess Karan* and the host in India was an incredibly talented young lady called Divya Seth. *Jaane Kya Tune Kahi* was presented by the husband and wife team of Vandana and Desikan Ranganathan. Both of these productions were made in the wonderfully atmospheric Eagle Studios at Noida, a city in India's northern state of Uttar Pradesh.

The clip show based on *Caught In The Act* was of no interest to Karan, but it was of great interest to another producer I met in India based in Bombay. Fahad Samar ran his own production company, Bombay Talkie. When Bombay later became Mumbai, Fahad threatened to rename his company Mumbai Mumble, but never did.

So Action Time now had a clip show in India called *Duniya Gol Hai*, hosted by the most charming Mona Ambegaonkar, in addition to two game shows, *Aao Guess Karan* and *Jaane Kya Tune Kahi*, in New Delhi. The idea had always been to adapt popular UK formats owned or licensed by Action Time to suit the Indian market.

Eagle Studios was based some seventeen miles from New Delhi. Siddhartha and Karun had been working with the manager of the studio, Anil Malhotra, and made numerous successful series there for Doordarshan in the past. So they had already earned a great deal of respect from both within the industry and viewing public. It was a fascinating place, home to 'Star Films' during the 1940s – some suggested it was the site of the birth of Bollywood. An old-fashioned film studio with an earth floor and outside canteen, its atmosphere seemed to demand activity, a quite magical place just perfect for our purposes. The only downside was that prior to my meeting with Karun, this studio had been used by a British producer/director who had conducted himself very badly. This Brit had suffered from the old imperialistic tenet of superiority and had treated the staff employed there in a most unsatisfactory manner.

Karun, Siddhartha and his wife Rosa were totally up front about this awkward situation and made it clear that my predecessor had been an appalling bully. They pointed out that the staff were quite right to be sceptical about my presence and made it very clear that it was up to me to put them right by passing yet another audition, and proving that not all Brits were imperialistic scoundrels.

I could sense the reluctance of studio staff to agree to 'more of the same', especially as Doordarshan had tolerated him for such a long and miserable period. Having said a final goodbye and good riddance, here they were threatened with yet another unknown Brit as a potential pain in the neck. Of course, the first thing they wanted to know was whether or not I was similar to, if not worse than, my predecessor. After all, they could see and hear I was a Brit, but just how typical a Brit was I going to be?

I don't recall consciously doing anything specific to establish myself as acceptable, but I'm convinced that my open association and reciprocated friendship with Siddhartha, Rosa, Karun and Perry Mehta played a major part in undoing the harm done by my British predecessor. Once accepted, I enjoyed every single second of my long time in Noida and was soon working very closely with the Synergy team, a bunch of individuals who just happened to be Hindu, Muslim, Sikh, Christian, Roman Catholic, Jain and Buddhist – and yet there was not even the slightest hint of disharmony.

There were so many differences to enjoy aboutn life in India. I can almost hear you thinking '...but what about the homeless, the poor, the vulnerable and sick..?' and, yes, this too was forefront in my mind the moment I landed in the middle of a total eclipse of the sun. They worried me as I travelled by taxi from the airport to the Marriott, when we sped past huge shanty towns and people sleeping or going about their daily chores in the central reservation of the dual carriageway. I say 'speeding' and 'whistled past', but neither were possible in the ubiquitous Ambassador taxi (loosely based on the old British Morris Oxford). The other memorable part of these journeys was that Indian taxis must be among the most uncomfortable modes of transport known to humanity.

I once asked Karun why people chose to sleep in the most dangerous part of the road. He had a one-word answer: 'flies'. He explained that humans had learned this trick by watching their beloved sacred cows populating one section that was devoid of the things due to the draft caused by traffic moving in both directions.

Every time we stopped I was targeted by outstretched hands and a gesture with forefinger, thumb and mouth that could only mean hunger. This long car-journey was not a good introduction. Once I realised I could do nothing truly meaningful about such realities something very odd happened. Looking past the hands and gestures I became aware of the unbelievably beautiful smiles and eyes of these homeless folk. This was a revelation to me and the more I considered it the more profound it would come to seem.

When I got out of the taxi at the Marriott, I was paying the driver when a bunch of Americans assumed ownership of the cab. The taxi driver simply shook his head. It was a while before I realised that this exclusively Indian head movement could mean yes, no or I don't know. The movement (neither exclusively male or female) involved making a perfect figure of eight in the air and was used when replying to almost anyone about anything. I'd figured out that the gesture was simply an acknowledgement of a question and did not attempt to suggest either a positive or a negative response. It could be very confusing especially when what appeared to be a 'no' seemed to be accompanied by the word 'yes' and vice-versa! I tried to learn this idiosyncratic mannerism but never got it right, much to the amusement of my new friends.

I have to admit that on more than one occasion I experienced an internal shudder of shame, pondering the horrors the British imposed on these gracious people both before and during Partition in 1947. Every day these discoveries and observations made my Indian experience one of the most profound of my entire life. I am eternally grateful that I was disabused of so much irrational bigotry towards such a gentle and captivating people. What made this even more important for me was that I could share this overwhelming experience with my future wife, Sarah! Such exciting discoveries meant we could swap notes and enjoy the magic of India together.

As I write this chapter, India is commemorating seventy-five years of Independence from British colonial rule. During these celebrations there is a renewed awareness of the brutality and injustice. But even after all that time I am both embarrassed and astounded at the levels of stupidity and bigotry that remain.

FOR me, showbusiness has always generated an instant image of magic, glamour and gorgeous people. But I was always aware that it hid a minefield of prejudice and misuse, particularly when as a new producer I was introduced to the arduous task of casting.

When casting any show, it's impossible to ignore the reality that you are subconsciously employing an army of personal stereotypes before deciding on who we think might be the right actor for the part, images automatically and inexorably formed by our individual life experiences, background, upbringing, education and wisdom.

Before the modern-day emergence of 'woke' it was felt that one way of creating a tolerant society was to mock the stupidity of bigotry and expose it whenever possible. Its original meaning was to be awake to social injustice, particularly around race. However its meaning was soon hijacked and used all over social media and the news as an insult. The word had become weaponised.

'Woke' was now used to describe something people didn't like when they couldn't explain what it was and why they didn't like it.

Long before 'woke', comedians, writers, producers and casting directors would utilise a readily available and well-established checklist of typecast actors – or stereotypes – to depict specific sorts of characters. TV drama became predictable. It was even possible to identify 'the baddy' during their first appearance in any play or series because of its choice of a stereotypical 'baddy' actor.

Not many years ago, Liz Carr could never have been considered to play the role of Clarissa in *Silent Witness*. Her character in the show does not refer or pay lip service to disability, why would she? So from a casting standpoint this sea-change in attitudes meant that any female actor could have been cast in this role. Things looked rather different as my career took off, many years before 'woke' in the 1970s, but even then I was aware of the dangers of stereotyping. In that decade, a succession of programmes utilised stereotypes. Here are four of the most conspicuous examples:-

1. *The Black and White Minstrel Show* (created by George Inns and George Mitchell, 1958-1978)
2. *Till Death Us Do Part* (writer Johnny Speight, 1965-1975)
3. *Love Thy Neighbour* (writer Vince Powell, 1972-1976)
4. *Mind Your Language* (writer Vince Powell, 1977-1986)

Scottish musician George Mitchell enjoyed great fame and wealth over the twenty-year run of *The Black and White Minstrel Show* on the BBC. The television variety show he devised was to spawn stage shows too and record albums. In 1961, it swept the board against international competition at the European Broadcasting Union's Television Light Entertainment Festival in Montreux, winning not only the Golden Rose, but also the Silver Rose and the Press award for best show. Officially, then, *The Black and White Minstrel Show* was the best light entertainment programme in the world, in its heyday regarded as wholesome early evening family viewing. The idea that this 'innocent' show could be anywhere near offensive was unthinkable! And yet, looking back, how could it not be?

Nothing on British TV could be more guilty of the misuse of stereotypes or more insensitive towards the black community. Yet neither the BBC – or any regulatory body – was able to recognise it as anything other than a fun piece of light entertainment... over two long and financially profitable decades.

Johnny Speight wrote *Till Death Us Do Part* and Warren Mitchell played its lead character, Alf Garnett. Speight was ever keen to tell people that he created Alf to expose such small-minded stupidity, his creation's prejudice and bigotry embodied in a proud working-class misogynist who held – and very vocally shared – extreme right wing opinions on everything. Actor Mitchell, meanwhile, was as far removed from his alter-ego as is humanly possible, to the extent he refused to do interviews about the character for fear of destroying the illusion he had given 'life and breath' to.

For all the enlightened intentions of its makers, there were many people who nevertheless agreed with the bigotry coming out of Alf Garnett's mouth, often cited as a big reason for its success. The show was even threatened by Mary Whitehouse in her relentless campaign for cleaner television. There remains a wealth of information about the perception and eventual demise of *Till Death Us Do Part,* but again, for a long period of time, it was at the very top of the ratings.

In *Love Thy Neighbour,* the comedy was drawn from a friendly conflict between next door neighbours. One family was white, the other black. The dialogue, particularly from white neighbour Eddie Booth (played by Jack Smethurst) was openly and racially offensive, however writer Vince Powell was always keen to maintain a balance between insults from 'white to black' and 'black to white'.

The fact that the programme was a comedic rebuffal of racial intolerance, in which racist Eddie always came off second best, didn't occur until the popular press forced the regulatory bodies to refuse it more air time. Powell, like Speight, always maintained that his exposure of bigotry concerning skin colour did more to remove that evil than promote it. Did it? The jury is still out.

I once informed my head of department that I wanted to book Bernard Manning on *The Kenny Everett Video Cassette.* Bernard was an old school club-style comedian widely regarded (quite wrongly in my view) as the UK's leading racist comedian. I was threatened with my job until Kenny himself said he'd walk-off if we didn't book the man from Manchester's Embassy Club for the show.

The sketch, which aired in the fourth show of the fourth series in May 1981, saw Kenny leaping around the studio floor trying to kill Bernard, who was doing a near-the-knuckle stand-up routine that was nevertheless fully compliant with IBA restrictions. It ended with Kenny picking up the stage (on which Bernard was doing said act) with a forklift truck and driving it out of the studio and into the car park. To this day, it is still regarded as a classic Kenny sketch.

One memorable near miss with the authorities came early on in my career. On 15 January 1967 to be precise, while I was directing *The Eamonn Andrews Show* (live from London). A 45-minute late-night chat and music programme, the programme was transmitted late on Sunday evenings, in its day the prime talk show on British TV. By then, Eamonn had risen in the broadcasting ranks to being Britain's most acceptable and trustworthy television personality.

During morning rehearsals, my producer Malcolm Morris told me that a representative from the ITA (Independent Television Authority) had noticed that our show – set to go out that evening – contained a brand new song by The Rolling Stones entitled *Let's Spend the Night Together*, flip side to *Ruby Tuesday*, and he was 'very concerned about the sexual connotations of the song'. Malcolm informed me that he was on his way to a meeting with the Stones to ask if they could perform another, less controversial ditty. 'Best of luck with that, Mal', I said, before Malcolm disappeared into the bowels of Teddington studios and I got on with camera rehearsals.

A few days later the trade papers carried a photo of me telling a very serious Mick Jagger that he was unable to perform the very song the Stones agreed to appear on the show to promote... 'Let's Spend the Night Together'. In fact the picture, a clipping of which can be found in this very book, looked as if I was telling him off. I was doing no such thing (anyone who has ever met me knows that my face, in repose, can look very similar to the smacked arse of a very angry farmer). Mick was telling me that the band, in response to this intervention, had altered the line in the song from 'let's spend the night together' to 'let's spend some time together'. So, while the ITA had won, and producer Malcolm had won, so too had Mick and the Rolling Stones, without doubt a win, win, win situation. After a few uneasy moments of negotiation, the suggested compromise had been agreed to – 'some time' evidently being less offensive than 'the night'. However, there had been no mention of the rest of the lyrics to which, if you are not familiar with them, you really should listen to. They quite beautifully describe the gentle art of cunnilingus and the results of a more than satisfactory climax.

During my training as a director with ABC TV, it was made very clear to me that once my training was finished the company had no obligation to employ me again.

In the 1960s, this was a worrying reality and a fact I'd given no heed to, being far too busy learning the complexities of the highly complicated and technical processes involved in turning a programme from a notion into reality.

When my time on *The Eamonn Andrews Show* came to a close, it was a most pleasant surprise to discover that ABC now regarded me as a 'fully trained' programme director. Without my realising it, my mentors had reported that I was now ready to be employed as a fully-fledged mover and shaker entitled to proper money!

Since there was no programme on offer, however, and no sign of one being offered, I decided to take a holiday in Greece. So for a few weeks I lay in the sun without realising I was no longer earning. It was only upon my return to the UK, when I discovered I'd nowhere to display my magnificent tan, that the reality hit home.

In fairness, I had been warned about this at the start of my training, so the only person to blame for sudden unemployment was me. Malcolm Morris being my last producer, I thought I'd ask him what his next programme was and whether he was looking for a director. To my horror I discovered he was no longer resident in his Teddington office and no one seemed to know where he'd gone.

So I decided to seek the services of an agent, knowing there were a few who specialised in finding programme director placements. I did a trawl up and down Dean Street in the heart of Soho, where most of the London agents had offices. After a couple of big agents had virtually laughed me out of the building I found myself in The Swan With Two Necks, a pub famously frequented by media types, even then a peculiar bunch of people I knew I could relate to.

It wasn't long before I found a few friends who introduced me to David Wilkinson. He worked for the Noel Gay organisation and, after a few glorious pints, he became my first agent. That afternoon I also learned that Malcolm had just been appointed programme controller at Tyne Tees in Newcastle upon Tyne, Northumberland, nearly three hundred miles north. This discovery led me straight to a red phone box on the corner of Dean Street and Bateman Street, fully prepared with a handful of thru'penny bits from the bar.

It was a most successful call. Malcolm was eager to use me as a director. I was even able to tell him my agent would call him to talk money. I remember how impressed he was that I was now officially represented and it was on that day, while I was talking to said agent David about my forthcoming life as a freelance, that he taught me the value of living A LIFE OF S.I.N., more about which in a moment.

Until then, I'd spent the best part of two years flying between the London studios in Teddington and Manchester studios in Didsbury. So moving lock, stock and Helix Oxford Maths Set (with storage tin) to Newcastle upon Tyne and a gorgeous flat overlooking the sea in Percy Gardens, Tynemouth, was a massive culture shock. My latent imposter syndrome momentarily reared its ugly head, but the Geordie accents and sheer positivity of the studio crews almost immediately battered it back into obscurity.

I had as yet fully to appreciate the significance, but this was a brilliant way to start my new career as a genuinely freelance TV producer/director. As Malcolm was a brand new controller, both he and I were on a massive learning curve from day one. And it was apparent, from the first series I was commissioned to take on, that he had made his very first mistake by not understanding the pride of regionality enjoyed by every single viewer in England's north east.

Before the arrival of an ITV service, the BBC had done little to acknowledge the existence of any region north of Watford. This new service had given regionality a new lease of life. And in the tradition of Lord Reith's famous quote, it ensured that ITV were 'informing, educating and entertaining' viewers specific to their own region.

Tyne Tees had gone on the air in January 1959, a perfect example of the success of this new local approach. It began its life under the managing directorship of Anthony Jelly but had prominent board members George and Alfred Black, who knew how to put bums on seats from their many successes in theatre land (which, of course, involved the entire country, not just London). Their influence was instrumental in the formulation of many programmes specifically written and cast for the north east, principal among them the *One O'Clock Show*, a lunchtime chat, comedy and variety show directed by David Croft and Philip Jones and produced by Bill Lyon-Shaw. On launch, it was an immediate success and continued to define the identity of Tyne Tees. When it finished in 1964, most of its core cast had become stars in their own right so were no longer free to appear each and every day. These names included Anita Harris, Jack Haig, Len Marten, Donald Peers, David McBeth, Bill Maynard, Barbara Law, Chris Langford and Austin Steele (who later switched from comedy to being an MP – not such a big switch, I hear you say).

So between then and Malcolm's arrival as programme controller in 1968, the station had been without a flagship. Simultaneously, the general mood of the country was beginning to move away from regionality – which, I fear, had been taken for granted for far too long – and the same regional pride of place was fast disappearing from decision-making in most regional TV studios too, with a few notable exceptions like Granada.

Having arrived fresh-faced from London to work as a freelance director for my friend, I was unaware of the massive mistake he was about to make in asking me to create a brand new television series with his hero, Montague Modlyn. Monty was a regular contributor to Jack de Manio's early morning BBC radio programme *Today*.

Journalist Monty was pure East End of London. As a reporter, he famously asked Ugandan dictator Idi Amin how many people he had murdered. Amin's reply, 'You are a cheeky man', became the basis for Monty's personal strapline, 'Pardon my cheek'! A chunky little man, he always had a touch of Alfred Hitchcock about him. Malcolm was convinced the north easterners would take to his no-nonsense, straightforward, gloss-less style of interviewing.

Sadly, Malcolm was wrong. The show did not enjoy the success it might have enjoyed had it been produced in London. My maiden voyage into the hearts of the Tyne Tees crews was in urgent need of a Grace Darling!

Malcolm and I chewed over the failure of *The Monty Modlyn Show* and thought we'd try again with another of his radio heroes, the Scottish disc jockey Stuart Henry. This time I agreed. Stuart was the antithesis of Monty. A quiet, charming and engaging man, he gave the impression that he cared about the region.

I met Stuart in the coffee bar of The Langham Hotel, opposite the BBC in London. It was during this first meeting that the title of the show struck me like a bolt of lightning. I wanted to call it 'The Stuart Henry Speakeasy' and he loved the idea, in fact stood up and kissed me on the forehead! From that moment on, this glorious wee scotsman and I saw eye-to-eye. By the time my train got back to Newcastle I'd already developed a good basic working idea for the opening titles, set design and format to hand over to the graphics, design and casting departments.

In order to connect the show to viewers I wanted our first star guest to be Washington-born Alan Price. That's Washington in the north east, of course, not the USA. At the time, though, he was an enormously popular figure right across the world, having gone solo following his success with Eric Burdon, Chas Chandler and the rest of legendary rock band The Animals, sons of the north east all.

On BBC radio at that time there was a top-rated music show called *Country Meets Folk* and, while I was in London setting up *The Speakeasy,* Malcolm was visited in Newcastle by one of its creators, Jim Lloyd. Jim had formulated an idea featuring the extremely strong folk music scene in the north east. He called this brand new programme *Walk Right In* (you'll never guess its title tune). He also suggested its host should be London-born musician and songwriter Wally Whyton, who at that time was well known to the entire country for his contribution to the short-lived skiffle era, cut off in its prime by the sensational emergence of The Beatles.

Walk Right In was an excellent programme for any director to get their teeth into. When I first read Jim's proposal I saw that the acoustic musical content would be non-stop and segued between bands. Each band would also provide additional backing to the others. The idea of non-stop live music made me think of my days as assistant cameraman on the Jack Good fast-moving non-stop production of *Boy Meets Girls*. To choreograph camera movements with each camera attached to the wall by a heavy one-inch cable took some planning. However, done properly, the result was not just a thing of beauty, but an achievement to be enjoyed by the entire studio crew.

When we finally got to make a pilot for *Walk Right In*, though, we hadn't realised that our entire audience – from various folk clubs in and around the Newcastle area – would not just sit passively enjoying the music, but join in with full-throated choruses. Quickly, we re-designed the audience seating to be 270°, wrapped around a multi-level staging area that could easily accommodate four bands. So, with Wally centre stage, we had a perfect singalong folk and skiffle show with an occasional bit of country (Hawaiian guitars were banned, because *Walk Right In* was strictly acoustic).

Suddenly Malcolm Morris had three programmes in his new entertainment department, all originating from Tyne Tees studios, City Road, Newcastle upon Tyne. And all of them served the region. Malcolm also managed to get them transmitted in a number of other regions too, which qualified them as being mini-networked, unheard of in ITV's early days. I had the pleasure of both producing and directing the *Speakeasy* and Monty Modlyn, while working with Jim as he produced *Walk Right In*, a most satisfying situation.

And during this remarkably creative period, I took a night off to sit in a pub in the Fish Quay, North Shields, and watch a man land on the moon. Could life get any better? It didn't seem possible.

Such is the magic of youth.

ANYWAY, it's almost time for closedown, so here's an *Epilogue* – the meaning of S.I.N. as promised a couple or three pages back.

As a freelancer, each job I was asked to work on needed to be contracted separately. For instance, producing and directing a job attracted a better fee than just directing it. My new agent David Wilkinson had this well in hand, for which he earned a commission. And it was during these early days that the maxim S.I.N. became such an important motivator in my life. It still is!

S.I.N. Let me break it down: Sparkle – Invoice – Next.

It was a maxim that served me well throughout my entire career. Along the way, I may even have passed it on to others who suddenly found themselves described as 'freelance'.

The 'sparkle' bit refers to the quality of, and attitude towards, my work. The 'invoice' was a reminder that each and every show was totally different and therefore attracted a separate fee. This included confusing personal additions and deductions such as the relatively new tax, VAT, which needed to be calculated, documented and paid to HM Customs and Excise quarterly. The most crucial part of the acronym, though, was 'next', meaning to start the search for the next source of income without delay – i.e. now.

The reality of being freelance was that it was vital to do three jobs at the same time:-

- Tidying up the paperwork and writing 'thank you' notes for the previous employment.
- Giving 100 per cent to the current job in hand.
- Searching for the next job.

It was always the case that if any one of those three essential tasks was put off to a later date, stressful consequences were guaranteed.

The maxim S.I.N. was then – and still is – a life-saving mantra subconsciously chanted at times of potential confusion to ensure survival in relative peace. It has in fact become the story of my life.

So remember: Sparkle – Invoice – Next.

In television, as in life, it is a splendid code to live by.

Acknowledgements

BEHIND any autobiography or memoir there will be far too many people to mention by name for the part played in accompanying the author on various points of his or her journey.

Fact is, though, that we all of us get to where we are going in life not only through our own drive, luck and imagination, but also via the influence and support of countless and often nameless others. That certainly hit home as I completed *Revelations of a TV Director*.

Put simply, I would like to thank everyone within these pages for their help and befriending me along the way – and no doubt a fair few whose names haven't got into print, but doubtless should have.

I would however like to acknowledge the support and expertise of these people in particular: Sarah Mayoh; Freddie Davies; Gerry Mitchell; Brian Tesler CBE; Philip Jones OBE; the staff of ABC TV in Didsbury; Andrea Wonfor; Stephen Leahy; Rocky Oldham; Hugh David; Andy Ward; Gunnar Bemert; Frank Van Hoorn; Jan Vanderstraeten and his company The Idea Whisperer, and Tony Hannan, my editor at Scratching Shed Publishing.

Plus you, of course, the television viewer – and reader!

Index

Index

Index

Investigate our other titles and
stay up to date with all our latest releases at
www.scratchingshedpublishing.co.uk